A YEAR-LONG BIBLE STUDY

EXPERIENCING
the HEART *of*
JESUS

FOR 52 WEEKS

REVISED & UPDATED

MAX LUCADO

HarperChristian
Resources

Experiencing the Heart of Jesus for 52 Weeks
© 2003, 2024 by Max Lucado

Requests for information should be sent to customercare@harpercollins.com.

ISBN 978-0-310-16170-7 (softcover)
ISBN 978-0-310-16171-4 (ebook)

First Printing March 2024 / Printed in the United States of America

CONTENTS

UNIT 6: EXPERIENCING THE LOVE OF JESUS

UNIT 7: EXPERIENCING THE POWER OF JESUS

UNIT 8: EXPERIENCING THE FORGIVENESS OF JESUS

UNIT 9: EXPERIENCING THE PRAYER OF JESUS

UNIT 10:   EXPERIENCING THE HOPE OF JESUS

UNIT 11:   EXPERIENCING THE CALLING OF JESUS

INTRODUCTION

When I was young, we used to take our family vacations in Colorado. We'd drive from Texas to Colorado every summer. It was what my dad loved to do. It was a long drive, though. We'd drive through West Texas, up through New Mexico, and then into eastern Colorado. The land along that whole route is relatively flat, but then about fifty miles east of Denver, you begin spotting the Rocky Mountains. They just dominate the whole landscape.

You know, we could have stopped right there, fifty miles from the Rockies, and said, "Well, we've finished our vacation. We've seen the Rockies." We could have turned around and gone back home. Then when people would say, "Where'd you go on your vacation?" we could say, "Well, we went to the Rockies."

Well, yeah. I guess you could say we saw the Rockies. But who would do that? Who wants to view the Rockies from a distance?

We want to get into the Rocky Mountains. We want to smell the mountain air. We want to smell the evergreen and the pine trees. We want to hear the running brook and put a hand into the ice-cold water. We want to hook a speckled trout. That's the difference between seeing the Rockies and experiencing the Rockies.

Experiencing the Heart of Jesus for 52 Weeks is intended to take you from the flatlands—from seeing Christ at a distance—to the experience of being surrounded by Christ. Each week begins with a short reading to help you experience Jesus' encouragement, encounter his love, join in his friendship, and bask in his presence. This is followed by a brief summary of the reading in "The Heart of the Matter," a space for writing out the memory verse, a concluding section titled "The Heart of Jesus," and then two passages of Scripture to read and seven daily Bible study questions to work through during the week.

The psalmist declared, "You make known to me the path of life; you will fill me with joy in your presence" (Psalm 16:11). There is great joy to be found in spending time in God's presence! So lean into this study and commit to engaging with him each day of this coming year. As you do, I pray that you will experience the heart of Jesus and his love for you.

EXPERIENCING THE
CARE OF JESUS

When I see a flock of sheep, I see exactly that—a flock. A rabble of wool. A herd of hooves. I don't see a sheep. I see sheep. All alike. None different. That's what I see.

But not so with the shepherd. To him, every sheep is different. Every face is special. Every face has a story. And every sheep has a name. The one with the sad eyes? That's Droopy. The fellow with one ear up and the other down? That's Oscar. The small one with the black patch on his leg? He's an orphan with no brothers. He's called Joseph.

The shepherd knows his sheep and calls them by name.

When we see a crowd, we see exactly that—a crowd. Filling a stadium or flooding a mall. We see people, not persons, but people. A herd of humans. A flock of faces.

But not so with the Shepherd. To him every face is different. Every face is a story. Every face is a child. And every child has a name. The one with the sad eyes? That's Sally. The old fellow with one eyebrow up and the other down? Harry's his name. And the young one with the limp? He's an orphan with no brothers. He's called Joey.

The Shepherd knows his sheep. He knows each one by name. The Shepherd knows you. He knows your name. And he will never forget it. He has said, "I have written your name on my hand" (Isaiah 49:16 NCV).

Quite a thought, isn't it? Your name on God's hand. Your name on God's lips.

Maybe you've seen your name in some special places. On an award or diploma or walnut door. Or maybe you've heard your name from some important people—a coach, a celebrity, a teacher. But to think that your name is on God's hand and on God's lips . . . my, could it be?

Or perhaps you've never seen your name honored. You can't remember when you heard it spoken with kindness. If so, it may be more difficult for you to believe that God knows your name. But he does. Written on his hand. Spoken by his mouth. Whispered by his lips. Your name. And not only the name you now have, but the name he has in store for you. A new name he will give you . . . but wait, I'm getting ahead of myself. I'll tell you about your new name in the last lesson that we'll share in this unit. This is just the introduction.

You've been on my mind as I've been writing. I've thought of you often. I honestly have. Over the years, I've gotten to know some of you folks well. I've read your letters, shaken your hands, and watched your eyes. I think I know you.

You're busy. Time passes before your tasks are finished. And if you get a chance to read, it's a slim chance indeed.

You're anxious. Bad news outpaces the good. Problems outnumber solutions. And you are concerned. What future do your children have on this earth? What future do you have?

You're cautious. You don't trust as easily as you once did. Politicians lied. The system failed. The minister compromised. Your spouse cheated. It's not easy to trust. It's not that you don't want to. It's just that you want to be careful.

There is one other thing. You've made some mistakes. I met one of you at a bookstore in Michigan. A businessman, you seldom came out of your office at all, and never to meet an author. But then you did. You were regretting the many hours at work and the few hours at home and wanted to talk.

And the single mom in Chicago. One kid was tugging, the other crying, but juggling them both, you made your point. "I made mistakes," you explained, "but I really want to try again."

And there was that night in Fresno. The musician sang, I spoke, and you came. You almost didn't. You almost stayed home. Just that day, you'd found the note from your wife. She was leaving you. But you came anyway. Hoping I'd have something for the pain. Hoping I'd have an answer. Where is God at a time like this?

And so as I wrote, I thought about you. All of you. You aren't malicious. You aren't evil. You aren't hardhearted (hardheaded occasionally, but not hard-hearted). You really want to do what is right. But sometimes life turns south. Occasionally you need a reminder.

Not a sermon. A reminder. A reminder that God knows your name.[1]

— PRAYER —

Dear Father, my heart is filled with anticipation for the week ahead. I want to feel the gentle touch of Jesus. I want to understand his concern for me. I want to know that he will catch me if I stumble. I want him to soothe my aching heart. I am ready, Father. Let me experience the care of Jesus. Amen.

— MEMORY VERSE —

But if any person loves God, that person is known by God.

1 CORINTHIANS 8:3 NCV

Week 1: THE GOD YOU CAN TRUST

Here is a big question: What is God doing when you are in a bind? When the lifeboat springs a leak? When the rip cord snaps? When the last penny is gone before the last bill is paid? When the last hope left on the last train? What is God doing?

I know what we are doing. Nibbling on nails like corn on the cob. Pacing floors. Taking pills. I know what we do. But what does God do? Big question. Real big. If God is sleeping, we're duck soup. If he is laughing, we're lost. If he is crossing his arms and shaking his head, then saw off the limb, honey, it's time to crash. What is God doing?

I decided to research that question. And being the astute researcher that I am, I discovered some ancient writings that may answer this question. Few people are aware—in fact, no one is aware—that newspaper journalists roamed the lands of the Old Testament era. Yes, it is true that in the days of Noah, Abraham, and Moses, reporters were fast on the scene recording the drama of their days.

And now, for the first time, their articles are to be shared. So, I proudly share with you heretofore undiscovered conversations with a man who can answer the question: *What does God do when we are in a bind?* This interview is between the Holy Land Press (HLP) and Moses.

HLP: Tell us about your conflict with the Egyptians.

MOSES: Oh, the Egyptians—big people. Strong fighters. Mean as snakes.

HLP: But you got away.

MOSES: Not before they got washed away.

HLP: You're talking about the Red Sea conflict.

MOSES: You're right. That was scary.

HLP: Tell us what happened.

MOSES: Well, the Red Sea was on one side, and the Egyptians were on the other.

HLP: So you attacked?

MOSES: Are you kidding? No, my people were too afraid. They wanted to go back to Egypt.

HLP: So you told everyone to retreat?

MOSES: No, we didn't have anywhere to go. I told the people to stand still.

HLP: You mean, with the enemy coming, you told them not to move?

MOSES: Yep. I told the people, "Stand still and you will see the Lord save you."

HLP: Why would you want the people to stand still?

MOSES: To get out of God's way. If you don't know what to do, just sit tight until he does his thing.

HLP: That's an odd strategy, don't you think?

MOSES: It is if you are big enough for the battle. But when the battle is bigger than you are and you want God to take over, it's all you can do.

HLP: Okay, so then you escaped . . .

MOSES: We were delivered.

HLP: What's the difference?

MOSES: There is a big difference. When you escape, you do it. When you are delivered, someone else does it and you just follow.

So, what do you think? What does God do when we are in a bind? That question can be answered with one word: *fight.* He fights for us. He steps into the ring, points us to our corner, and takes over. "You only need to remain calm; the LORD will fight for you" (Exodus 14:14 NCV).

His job is to fight. Our job is to trust. Just trust. Not direct. Or question. Or try to yank the steering wheel out of his hands. Our job is to pray and wait. We wait for God to catch us.

Much like I would catch my daughter Sara. I can remember standing six steps from the bed's edge, my arms extended, hands open. On the bed, Sara—all four years of her—crouches, poised like a playful kitten. She's going to jump. "Back more, Daddy," she stands and dares. I dramatically comply, confessing admiration for her courage. With each step she laughs and claps and motions for more.

When I'm on the other side of the canyon, she stops me. I extend my arms. Once again she crouches, then springs. Superman without a cape. Skydiver without a chute. In that airborne instant, her only hope is her father. If he proves weak, she'll fall. If he proves cruel, she'll crash. If he proves forgetful, she'll tumble to the floor. But such fear she does not know, for her father she does know. She trusts him.

Four years under the same roof have convinced her that he is reliable. He is not superhuman, but he is strong. He is not holy, but he is good. He's not brilliant, but he doesn't have to be to remember to catch his child when she jumps.

And so she flies. And so she soars. And so he catches her, and the two rejoice at the wedding of her trust and his faithfulness.

How do I know this is true, that his care is enough? Nice prose, but give me the facts. How do I know these aren't just fanciful hopes?

Part of the answer can be found in Sara's little leaps of faith. Her older sister, Andrea, was in the room watching, and I asked Sara if she would jump to Andrea. Sara refused. I tried to convince her. She wouldn't budge. "Why not?" I asked.

"I only jump to big arms."

If we think the arms are weak, we won't jump. For that reason, the Father flexes his muscles. "God's power is very great for us who believe," Paul taught. "That power is the same as the great strength God used to raise Christ from the dead" (Ephesians 1:19–20 NCV).

Next time you wonder if God can catch you, read those verses. The very arms that defeated death are the arms awaiting you.

Next time you wonder if God can forgive you, read those verses. The very hands that were nailed to the cross are open for you.

And the next time you wonder if you will survive the jump, think of Sara and me. If a flesh-and-bone-headed dad like me can catch his child, don't you think your eternal Father can catch you?

THE HEART OF THE MATTER

- If you're not sure what to do, allow God to take the lead.
- God's job is to fight for you. Your job is to trust in him.
- The very arms that defeated death are the arms awaiting you.
- You can trust that God will catch you when you leap to him.

MEMORY VERSE

Take a few moments to review your Bible memory verse for this unit, and then write out the words of 1 Corinthians 8:3 by heart in the space below.

The Heart of Jesus

Jesus was a teller of parables on this earth, and his stories reached into the very hearts of his listeners. Can you find yourself in the parable of the lost sheep? Are you one of the ninety-nine, safe in the fold of faith? Or are you the wanderer, the stray, the outsider?

This one lonely straggler, stumbling in the darkness with jumbled emotions and mounting fears. With wistful eyes and tearstained cheeks, you walk aimlessly. Uncertain of your path, you wish for the Shepherd's guiding staff.

Limping, you long for the Shepherd's gentle touch.

Then your ears turn at the sound of a voice, calling your name.

Relief floods your weary heart as the Shepherd lifts you onto his shoulders. Tears of gratitude fill your eyes as he tends to your bumps and bruises. The Scripture says that we all, like sheep, have gone astray.

But Jesus calls to us, cares for us, and carries us home.

WEEKLY BIBLE STUDY

READ: 2 CORINTHIANS 1:1–11 AND EXODUS 14:1–14

1. *Does God care?* We are not the first to ask that question. What trials did Paul face that could have caused him to question God's care (see 2 Corinthians 1:8–9)?

2. How did Paul choose to respond to these trials? How would you describe the extent of his trust in God's care based on his words (see verses 9–11)?

3. What did Paul say that he experienced during his trials? What did he say had "abounded" in his life because of everything that he had gone through (see verses 3–7)?

4. God revealed his care for the Israelites by freeing them from bondage in Egypt. But what did he tell Moses would happen when they arrived at the Red Sea (see Exodus 14:1–4)?

5. What questions did the people have about God's care when they saw the Egyptian army approaching them as they camped by the Red Sea (see verses 10–12)?

6. What strategy did Moses give the people for how they would survive (see verses 13–14)? How do you think you would have reacted if you were in the Israelites' place?

7. Our approach to life says a lot about how much we believe God cares for us. Do you believe that God's arms are "big enough" to catch you when you take a leap of faith?

Week 2: GOD'S PROVISION

You, me, and Dorothy of *The Wizard of Oz*—we have a lot in common.

We all know what it's like to find ourselves in a distant land surrounded by strange people. Though our chosen path isn't paved with yellow bricks, we still hope it will lead us home. The witches of the East want more than our ruby slippers. And Dorothy is not the first person to find herself surrounded by brainless, heartless, and spineless people.

We can relate to Dorothy. But when Dorothy gets to the Emerald City, the comparison is uncanny. For what the Wizard said to her, some think God says to us.

You remember the plot. Each of the chief characters comes to the Wizard with a need. Dorothy seeks a way home. The Scarecrow wants wisdom. The Tin Man desires a heart. The Lion needs courage. The Wizard of Oz, they've heard, could grant all four. So they come. Trembling and reverent, they come. They shiver in his presence and gasp at his power. And with all the courage they can muster, they present their requests.

His response? He will help after they demonstrate their worthiness. He will help as soon as they overcome the source of evil. Bring me the witch's broom, he says, and I will help you.

So they do. They scale the castle walls, make wax of the witch, and, in the process, they make some startling discoveries. They discover they can overcome evil. They discover that, with a little luck, a quick mind can handle the best the worst has to give. And they discover they can do it all without the Wizard.

The movie ends with Dorothy discovering that her worst nightmare was, in reality, just a bad dream. That her somewhere-over-the-rainbow home was right where she'd always been. And that it's nice to have friends in high places, but in the end, it's up to you to find your own way home.

The moral of *The Wizard of Oz*? Everything you need, you've already got. The power you desire is really a power you already have. Just look deep enough, long enough, and there's nothing you can't do.

I'm an offspring of sturdy stock. A product of a rugged, blue-collar culture that honored decency, loyalty, hard work, and Bible verses like "God helps those who help themselves." (No, it's not actually in the Bible.) "God started it and now we must finish it" was our motto. He's done his part; now we do ours. It's a fifty-fifty proposition. A do-it-yourself curriculum that majors in our part and minors in God's part.

"Blessed are the busy," this theology proclaims, "for they are the true Christians."

No need for the supernatural. No place for the extraordinary. No room for the transcendent. Prayer becomes a token. (The real strength is within you, not "up there.") Communion becomes a ritual. (The true hero is you, not him.) And the Holy Spirit? Well, the Holy Spirit becomes anything from a sweet disposition to a positive mental attitude.

It's a wind-up the-world-and-walk-away view of God. And the philosophy works . . . as long as *you* work. Your faith is strong as long as you are strong. Your position is secure as long as you are secure. Your life is good as long as you are good.

But, alas, therein lies the problem. As the Teacher said, "No one is good" (Matthew 19:17 NKJV). Nor is anyone always strong; nor is anyone always secure. Do-it-yourself Christianity is not much encouragement to the done in and worn out. Self-sanctification holds little hope for the addict. "Try a little harder" is little encouragement for the abused.

Jesus promises us the Holy Spirit so he can care for us at every level of our need. Don't know what to do? He will guide us. Need an answer for life's questions? He will bring Scripture to mind. Suddenly speechless in a witnessing opportunity? He will give the right words to say.

At some point we need more than good advice; we need help. Somewhere on this journey home we realize that a fifty-fifty proposition is too little. We need more—more than a pudgy wizard who thanks us for coming but tells us the trip was unnecessary.

We need help. Help from the inside out. The kind of help Jesus promised. "I will ask the Father, and he will give you another advocate to help you and be with you forever—the Spirit of truth. The world cannot accept him, because it neither sees him nor knows him. But you know him, for he lives with you and will be *in* you" (John 14:16–17, emphasis added).

Note the dwelling place of God—"in you." Not near us. Not above us. Not around us. But in us. In the part of us we don't even know. In the heart no one else has seen. In the hidden recesses of our being dwells, not an angel, not a philosophy, not a genie, but God.

Imagine that.

When my daughter Jenna was six years old, I came upon her standing in front of a full-length mirror. She was looking down her throat. I asked her what she was doing, and she answered, "I'm looking to see if God is in my heart." I chuckled and turned, and then I overheard her ask him, "Are you in there?" When no answer came, she grew impatient and spoke on his behalf. With a voice deepened as much as a six-year-old can, she said, "Yes."

She's asking the right question. "Are you in there?" Could it be what they say is true? It wasn't enough for you to appear in a bush or dwell in the temple? It wasn't enough for you to become human flesh and walk on the earth? It wasn't enough to leave your Word and the promise of your return? You had to go further? You had to take up residence in us?

"Do you not know," Paul penned, "that your bodies are temples of the Holy Spirit?" (1 Corinthians 6:19). Perhaps you didn't. Perhaps you didn't know God would go that far to make sure you got home. If not, thanks for letting me remind you.

The Wizard says look inside yourself and find self. God says look inside yourself and find God. The first will get you to Kansas. The latter will get you to heaven.

Take your pick.

THE HEART OF THE MATTER

- The world tries to tell you that everything you need, you already have.
- But a try-harder-and-do-it-yourself faith will just leave you exhausted.
- Jesus promises real help to you in the form of the Holy Spirit.
- The Bible says that the Holy Spirit's dwelling place is *within* you.

MEMORY VERSE

Your memory verse for this unit is 1 Corinthians 8:3. Take a few moments to review this verse, and then write it out from memory in the space below.

The Heart of Jesus

He was a leper—avoided, outcast, untouchable. A rough cloak and hood masked his withered body. A scrap of cloth covered his ghastly face. Coming into a town, he would swing a clumsy bell and announce, "Unclean, unclean." All around him, people would look the other way, edge in another direction, pretend not to see, and turn their backs in hasty retreat. Though disease ate away at his body, his soul was ravaged by loneliness. No one ever looked him in the eyes. No one ever reached out to him. He felt utterly alone. But he was on a mission.

Word had reached him of a healer in the area—a man who could make a leper clean again. He found Jesus, approached him, and kneeled before him. "If you are willing, you can make me clean," he said with pleading eyes (Matthew 8:2). Jesus did not recoil. He did not step back. He didn't turn away or ignore the man's plea. Jesus was moved with compassion. He reached out to the kneeling man and touched him. "I am willing," he said (verse 3). And with a word and a touch, the leper was healed. He is a man who can testify that Jesus cares—even for the avoided, the outcasts, and the untouchables.

WEEKLY BIBLE STUDY

READ: 2 PETER 1:3–9 AND EZEKIEL 36:24–27

1. God never intended for you to go it alone in your faith or try to lead a godly lifestyle through your own efforts. What does he instead offer to you (see 2 Peter 1:3–4)?

2. Peter says that God empowers us so that we can "participate in the divine nature." What does it look like for you to participate in God's divine nature?

3. What does Peter say that followers of Jesus should "make every effort" to do? What benefits does a person receive who has the qualities that he lists (see verses 5–8)?

4. What promise did God make to the Israelites who had been taken into bondage and captivity because of their idolatry (see Ezekiel 36:24)?

5. God said that he would "sprinkle clean water" on them. What was the Lord saying that he would do for them through this act (see verse 25)?

6. What else does God say that he will provide for those who truly seek to follow after him? What is the significance of God putting his Spirit within us (see verses 26–27)?

7. Jesus promises you the Holy Spirit so he can care for you at every level of your need. How have you seen the Holy Spirit at work in your life this week?

Week 3: GOD'S GIFT TO THE WORLD

Late-night news is a poor sedative. Last night, it was for me. All I wanted was the allergen count and the basketball scores. But to get them, I had to endure the usual monologue of global misery. And last night, the world seemed worse than usual.

Watching the news doesn't usually disturb me so. I'm not a gloom-and-doom sort of fellow. I feel I'm as good as the next guy in taking human tragedy with a spoon of faith. But last night . . . well, the world just seemed dark.

Perhaps it was the two youngsters shot in a drive-by shooting. Perhaps it was the reassuring announcement that thousands of highway bridges in America are near collapse. The national debt is deeper. Our taxes are higher. The pollen count is up. "And that's the world tonight!" the well-dressed man announces. I wonder why he's smiling.

On the way to bed, I step into the rooms of my three sleeping daughters. At the bedside of each, I pause and ponder the plight of their future. "What in the world awaits you?" I whisper as I brush back hair and straighten blankets.

Their greatest concerns today are math tests, presents, and birthday parties. Would that their world always be so innocent. It won't be. Forests shadow every trail and cliffs edge every turn. Every life has its share of fear. My children are no exception. Nor are yours. And as appealing as a desert island or a monastery might be, seclusion is simply not the answer for facing a scary tomorrow.

Then what is? Does someone have a hand on the throttle of this train? Or has the engineer bailed out just as we come in sight of dead-man's curve?

One of the themes running through the entire Bible can be summarized in two words: "fear not." Angels spoke it as a greeting. God commanded it from his people. Jesus used it to comfort his fearful disciples. No matter how out of control things appear, we are not to be afraid. He is in control. He will take care of us.

I may have found part of the answer in, of all places, the first chapter of the New Testament. I've often thought it strange that Matthew began his book with a genealogy. Certainly not good journalism. A list of who-sired-whom wouldn't get past most editors.

But then again, Matthew wasn't a journalist, and the Holy Spirit wasn't trying to get our attention. He was making a point. God had promised that he would give a Messiah through the bloodline of Abraham (see Genesis 12:3), and he did.

"Having doubts about the future?" Matthew asks. "Just take a look at the past." And with that, he opens the cedar chest of Jesus' lineage and begins pulling out the dirty laundry. You and I would have kept some of the stories in the closet. Jesus' lineage is anything but a roll call at the Institute for Halos and Harps.

It begins with Abraham, the father of the nation, who more than once lied like Pinocchio just to save his neck (see Genesis 12:10–20). Abraham's grandson Jacob was slicker than a Las Vegas card shark. He cheated his brother, lied to his father, got swindled, and then swindled his uncle (see Genesis 27; 29). Jacob's son Judah was so blinded by testosterone that he engaged the services of a streetwalker, not knowing she was his daughter-in-law! When he learned her identity, he threatened to have her burned to death for solicitation (see Genesis 38).

Special mention is made of Solomon's mother, Bathsheba, who bathed in questionable places, and Solomon's father, David, who watched her bathe (see 2 Samuel 11:2–3).

Rahab was a harlot (see Joshua 2:1). Ruth was a foreigner (see Ruth 1:4). Manasseh made the list, even though he forced his children to walk through fire (see 2 Kings 21:6). His son Amon is on the list, even though he rejected God (see 2 Kings 21:22).

Seems that almost half the kings were crooks, half were embezzlers, and all but a handful worshiped an idol or two for good measure. And so reads the list of Jesus' not-so-great grandparents. It appears the only common bond between this lot was a promise. A promise from heaven that God would use them to send his Son.

The promise held true—even during the darkest periods. When it seemed like God might have to scrap his plan—the promise held true. When it seemed like things were going from bad to worse—the promise held true.

Why did God use these people? Didn't have to. Could have just laid the Savior on a doorstep. Would have been simpler that way. And why does God tell us their stories? Why does God give us an entire testament of blunders and stumbles of his people? Simple. He knew what you and I saw on the news last night. He knew you would fret. He knew I would worry. And he wants us to know that when the world goes wild, he stays calm.

Want proof? Read the last name on the list. In spite of all the crooked halos and tasteless gambols of his people, the last name on the list is the first one promised—Jesus. "Joseph was the husband of Mary, and Mary was the mother of Jesus. Jesus is called the Christ" (Matthew 1:16 NCV). Period. No more names are listed. No more are needed. As if God is announcing to a doubting world, "See, I did it, just like I said I would. The plan succeeded."

The promise of the Messiah threads its way through forty-two generations of rough-cut stones, forming a necklace fit for the King who came. Just as promised.

And the promise remains. "The one who stands firm to the end will be saved," Joseph's child assures (Matthew 24:13). "In this world you will have trouble. But take heart! I have overcome the world" (John 16:33). The Engineer has not abandoned the train. Nuclear war is no threat to God. Yo-yo economies don't intimidate the heavens. Immoral leaders have never derailed the plan. God keeps his promise.

See for yourself. In the manger. He's there. See for yourself. In the tomb. He's gone.

THE HEART OF THE MATTER

- The pages of the Bible are filled with God's admonition to "fear not."
- No matter how out of control things appear, you don't have to fear.
- God has kept all of his promises to his people.
- Nothing and no one can thwart God's promise to save you.

MEMORY VERSE

Your memory verse for this unit is 1 Corinthians 8:3. Take a few moments to review this verse, and then write it out from memory in the space below.

The Heart of Jesus

Crowds milled in front of the house, but the low roof of the stable in the back had presented a solution. Four men, with a determined set to their jaws, were easing a man strapped to a pallet up onto the roof. "Are you sure about this?" The man gave a quick gasp as his pallet was hefted from shoulders up to waiting hands. "It's the only way. Don't worry."

Up the slant of the low roof, over the low wall, onto the flat rooftop. "Now what?" one man growled as he nudged the packed flooring with his toe in frustration. The muddy clay cracked and chipped beneath his sandal. He brightened. "Where is the Master from here? Which room is he in?" Leaning over the sides and listening carefully, they chose their spot and began to dig. The paralyzed man groaned inwardly. How would Jesus look at him when his friends were causing such a commotion? They were acting like vandals! Surely the Teacher would turn them away. Doubt and fear mingled with desperate hope as his friends tied ropes to his pallet and began to lower him into the room below.

The faces of the four friends were pleased—triumphant. They had found a way in. Would Jesus still be there? Would he be angry? What would he do? The pallet gently bumped the floor, and the room that had echoed with surprised exclamations and hushed whispers a moment ago fell quiet. The paralyzed man looked from one face to another fearfully. But then one man stepped forward. He was not angry. He was not shocked. His eyes were filled with kindness—caring. Jesus reached out his hand and helped the man on the pallet . . . to his feet.

WEEKLY BIBLE STUDY

READ: PSALM 27:1–5 AND ISAIAH 41:8–10

1. One of the themes running throughout the Bible is that God is in control and we have no need to fear. How did David reveal that he understood this truth (see Psalm 27:1)?

2. David was often surrounded by enemies who wanted to take his life. In spite of this, what confidence was he able to express in God's care (see verses 2–3)?

3. David had his eyes set on something greater than just the trials and tribulations that confronted him each day. On what was his gaze set (see verses 4–5)?

4. The prophet Isaiah also encouraged God's people to not be afraid. What reminder did he give to the Israelites about their status before God (see Isaiah 41:8)?

5. Isaiah reminded God's people that the Lord had chosen them and called them together "from the ends of the earth" (see verse 9). How might this have encouraged them?

6. The Israelites were to remember that they did not need to fear or be dismayed because they belonged to the Lord. What other promise are they given (see verse 10)?

7. How do the passages that you've studied this week help you to not fear in spite of the situations you are facing? What reassurances do they provide to you?

Week 4: THE GIFT OF UNHAPPINESS

There dwells inside you, deep within, a tiny whip-poor-will. Listen. You will hear him sing. His aria mourns the dusk. His solo signals the dawn.

It is the song of the whip-poor-will.

He will not be silent until the sun is seen.

We forget he is there, so easy is he to ignore. Other animals of the heart are larger, noisier, more demanding, more imposing.

But none is so constant.

Other creatures of the soul are more quickly fed. More simply satisfied. We feed the lion who growls for power. We stroke the tiger who demands affection. We bridle the stallion who bucks control.

But what do we do with the whip-poor-will who yearns for eternity?

For that is his song. That is his task. Out of the gray he sings a golden song. Perched in time he chirps a timeless verse. Peering through pain's shroud, he sees a painless place. Of that place he sings.

And though we try to ignore him, we cannot. He is us, and his song is ours. Our heart song won't be silenced until we see the dawn.

"God has planted eternity in the hearts of men" (Ecclesiastes 3:11 TLB), says the wise man. But it doesn't take a wise person to know that people long for more than earth. When we see pain, we yearn. When we see hunger, we question why. Senseless deaths. Endless tears. Needless loss. Where do they come from? Where will they lead?

Isn't there more to life than death? Will we never be satisfied this side of heaven?

The human search for satisfaction winds its way through history. Every man and woman has longed for it. Some seek it in relationships, some in possessions, still others in wealth. But as the ancient church father Augustine once declared, "The only ultimate disaster that can befall us, I have come to realize, is to feel ourselves to be home on earth. As long as we are aliens, we cannot forget our true homeland."[2]

Unhappiness on earth cultivates a hunger for heaven. By gracing us with a deep dissatisfaction, God holds our attention. The only tragedy, then, is to be satisfied prematurely. To settle for earth. To be content in a strange land. We are not happy here because we are not at home here. We are not happy here because we are not supposed to be happy here. We are like "foreigners and exiles" in this world (1 Peter 2:11).

Take a fish and place him on the beach.[3] Watch his gills gasp and scales dry. Is he happy? No! How do you make him happy? Do you cover him with a mountain of cash? Do you get him a beach chair and sunglasses? Do you bring him a martini? Do you wardrobe him in double-breasted fins and people-skinned shoes? Of course not!

Then how do you make him happy? You put him back in his element. You put him back in the water. The fish will never be happy on the beach simply because he was not made for the beach. And you will never be happy on earth simply because you were not made for earth. Oh, you will have your moments of joy. You will catch glimpses of light. You will know moments or even days of peace. But they simply do not compare with the happiness that lies ahead.

"Thou hast made us for thyself and our hearts are restless until they rest in thee."[4]

Strangely enough, even when we do happen upon earthly pleasures, the happiness is usually temporary at best. Soon we are on the lookout again, our eyes peeled for the next perk in our existence.

Sometimes we doubt Jesus cares for us because we confuse our desires with our needs. When our desires go unmet, despite having all we really need, we are disappointed. Disappointed with what we perceive as a lapse in care. "If God really cared for me, he would . . ." And we fill in the blank.

Only when we find him will we be satisfied. Moses can tell you.

He had as much of God as any man in the Bible. God spoke to him in a bush. God guided him with fire. God amazed Moses with the plagues. And when God grew angry with the Israelites and withdrew from them, he stayed close to Moses. He spoke to Moses "as one speaks to a friend" (Exodus 33:11). Moses knew God like no other man. But that wasn't enough. Moses yearned for more. Moses longed to see God. He even dared to ask, "Now show me your glory" (verse 18).

Isn't that why we long for heaven? We may speak about a place where there are no tears, no death, no fear, no night. But those are just the benefits of heaven. The beauty of heaven is seeing God. Heaven is God's ultimate expression of a continuum of care. He provides the promise of heaven one day to get us through the stuff of earth. Yet at the same time, he also promises to provide what we need most—a vision of himself.

And our hearts will only be at peace when we see him. "Because I have lived right, I will see your face. When I wake up, I will see your likeness and be satisfied" (Psalm 17:15 NCV).

Satisfied? That is one thing we are not. We are not satisfied. We push back from the Thanksgiving table and pat our round bellies. "I'm satisfied," we declare. But look at us a few hours later, back in the kitchen picking the meat from the bone.

We wake up after a good night's rest and hop out of bed. We couldn't go back to sleep if someone paid us. We are satisfied—for a while. But look at us a dozen or so hours later, crawling back in the sheets.

We take the vacation of a lifetime. For years we planned. For years we saved. And off we go. We satiate ourselves with sun, fun, and good food. But we are not even on the way home before we dread the end of the trip and begin planning another.

We are not satisfied. Why? Because there is nothing on earth that can satisfy our deepest longing.

We long to see God. The leaves of life are rustling with the rumor that we will—and we won't be satisfied until we do.

THE HEART OF THE MATTER

- The human search for satisfaction winds its way through history.
- Unhappiness on earth cultivates a hunger for heaven.
- You can never find true satisfaction in the things of this world.
- Nothing on earth can satisfy your deepest longing—to see God.

MEMORY VERSE

Your memory verse for this unit is 1 Corinthians 8:3. Take a few moments to review this verse, and then write it out from memory in the space below.

The Heart of Jesus

Jesus knows us intimately. He welcomes us to tell him our troubles. He has offered to carry our burdens for us. His caring touches our deepest places, giving us comfort, assurance, and peace. This same Jesus has gone ahead and is preparing a place for us (see John 14:2). He is the architect of our heavenly home—its builder and interior decorator, too. He who knows our secret woes also knows our heart's desires. He knows our favorite color, our favorite flower, our favorite views. Jesus knows what will delight us. He knows how to surprise us. He knows what we've always longed for. And in his infinite care for us, he prepares the perfect place for us. Jesus can't wait to show us our new home, made with heavenly TLC.

WEEKLY BIBLE STUDY

READ: ECCLESIASTES 5:10–15 AND EXODUS 33:12–23

1. People today try to seek satisfaction in life by acquiring money and worldly possessions. What does Solomon say about such pursuits (see Ecclesiastes 5:10–11)?

2. How does Solomon contrast the "sleep" of the laborer to that of the rich person? Why does the pursuit of more and more goods lead only to greater anxiety (see verse 12)?

3. What are some of the "grievous evils" that Solomon says he has seen? What reminder does he give to all who chase after wealth (see verses 13–15)?

4. Moses knew God like no other person on earth did. Yet Moses yearned for more. What request did he initially make of the Lord in this regard (see Exodus 33:12–13)?

5. What request did Moses then make to the Lord? What reasons did he provide for making these particular requests (see verses 15–16)?

6. Moses made one last request—to see the glory of God's presence. How did God respond to this request? What did he instruct Moses to do (see verses 18–23)?

7. What are some ways you've tried to find satisfaction in life through worldly means? What are some ways you've sought *God* to satisfy the longings of your soul?

Week 5: WHEN GOD WHISPERS YOUR NAME

"I could have gone to college on a golf scholarship," a fellow told me just last week on the fourth tee box. "Had an offer right out of school. But I joined a rock-and-roll band. Ended up never going. Now I'm stuck fixing garage doors."

"Now I'm stuck." Epitaph of a derailed dream.

Pick up a high-school yearbook and read the "What I want to do" sentence under each picture. You'll get dizzy breathing the thin air of mountaintop visions. Yet take the yearbook to a twentieth-year reunion and read the next chapter. Some dreams have come true, but many have not. Why? Because something happens to us along the way.

Convictions to change the world downgrade to commitments to pay the bills. Rather than make a difference, we make a salary. Rather than look forward, we look back. Rather than look outward, we look inward. And we don't like what we see.

If anyone had reason to doubt that God cared for his broken dreams, it was Moses. You remember his story. Adopted nobility. An Israelite reared in an Egyptian palace. A privileged upbringing. But his most influential teacher had no degree. His mother was a Jewess hired to be his nanny. "Moses," you can almost hear her whisper, "God has put you here on purpose. Someday you will set your people free. Never forget, Moses. Never forget."

Moses didn't. The flame of justice grew hotter until it blazed. Moses saw an Egyptian beating a Hebrew slave, and something inside him snapped. He lashed out and killed the Egyptian guard. The next day, Moses saw the Hebrew. You'd think the slave would say thanks. He didn't. Rather than express gratitude, he expressed anger. "Are you thinking of killing me as you killed the Egyptian?" he asked (Exodus 2:14).

Moses knew he was in trouble. He fled Egypt and hid in the wilderness. He went from dining with the heads of state to counting heads of sheep. And so it happened that a bright, promising Hebrew began herding sheep in the hills. From the Ivy League to the cotton patch. From the Oval Office to a taxicab. From swinging a golf club to digging a ditch.

Moses thought the move was permanent. There is no indication he ever intended to go back to Egypt. In fact, there is every indication he wanted to stay with his sheep. Standing barefoot before the bush, he confessed, "Who am I that I should go to Pharaoh and bring the Israelites out of Egypt?" (Exodus 3:11).

Why Moses? Or, more specifically, why eighty-year-old Moses?

The forty-year-old version was more appealing. The Moses we saw in Egypt was brash and confident. But the Moses we find four decades later is reluctant and weather-beaten. Had you or I looked at Moses back in Egypt, we would have said, "This man is ready for battle." Educated in the finest system in the world. Trained by the ablest soldiers. Instant access to the inner circle of the Pharaoh. Moses spoke their language and knew their habits. He was the perfect man for the job.

Moses at forty we like. But Moses at eighty? No way. Too old. Too tired. Smells like a shepherd. Speaks like a foreigner. What impact would he have on Pharaoh? He's the wrong man for the job. And Moses would have agreed. "Tried that once before," he would say. "Those people don't want to be helped. Just leave me here to tend my sheep. They're easier to lead."

Moses wouldn't have gone. You wouldn't have sent him. I wouldn't have sent him. But God did. God said Moses was ready. And to convince him, God spoke through a bush. (Had to do something dramatic to get Moses' attention.) "School's out," God told him. "Now it's time to get to work." Poor Moses. He didn't even know he was enrolled.

God puts us back in service to remind us that he cares for us. When we make mistakes, he does not banish us to a spiritual junkyard. No, he salvages our mistakes because he cares for us. He removes the rust and grime, buffs out the scratches, and hammers out the dents in our frame until we are in working condition again.

The voice from the bush is the voice that whispers to us. It reminds us that God is not finished with us yet. Oh, we may think he is. We may think we've peaked. We may think he's got someone else to do the job. But if so, think again.

"God began doing a good work in you, and I am sure he will continue it until it is finished when Jesus Christ comes again" (Philippians 1:6 NCV). Did you see what God is doing? A good work in you. Did you see when he will be finished? When Jesus comes again. May I spell out the message? *God ain't finished with you yet.* Your Father wants you to know that.

"This is what the LORD says . . . 'I have summoned you by name; you are mine'" (Isaiah 43:1). I can't say that I've given a lot of thought to my given name. But there is one name that catches my interest. A name only God knows. A name only God gives. A unique, one-of-a-kind, once-to-be-given name. You may not have known it, but God has a new name for you. When you get home, he won't call you Alice or Bob or Juan or Geraldo. The name you've always heard won't be the one he uses. When God says he will make all things new, he means it.

You will have a new home, a new body, a new life, and—you guessed it—a new name. "To the one who is victorious, I will give some of the hidden manna. I will also give that person a white stone with a new name written on it" (Revelation 2:17).

Isn't it incredible to think that God has saved a name just for you? One you don't even know? We've always assumed the name we got is the name we will keep. Not so. Imagine what that implies. Apparently, your future is so promising it warrants a new title. The road ahead is so bright a fresh name is needed. Your eternity is so special no common name will do.

So God has one reserved just for you. There is more to your life than you ever thought. There is more to your story than what you have read. There is more to your song than what you have sung. A good author saves the best for last. A great composer keeps his finest for the finish. And God, the author of life and composer of hope, has done the same for you.

The best is yet to be.

And so I urge you, don't give up. And so I plead, finish the journey. And so I exhort, be there. Be there when God whispers your name.

THE HEART OF THE MATTER

- God wants you to look forward instead of looking back.
- God won't be finished with you until Jesus comes again.
- God has a one-of-a-kind name for you that only he knows.
- God urges you to run the race and finish the journey.

MEMORY VERSE

This is it . . . one last review of your memory verse. Write out the words of 1 Corinthians 8:3 from memory in the space below. Reflect on what these words mean to you.

The Heart of Jesus

Much is made of Peter's humorous outburst when Jesus washed his disciples' feet at the Last Supper. Peter first insisted that Jesus should not stoop to scrub his toes, then begged him to wash his head and hands, too (see John 13:3–9)! But Peter wasn't the only one whose sandals were removed and whose feet were doused. Jesus gave this care to each one of the twelve, one at a time. He looked into the eyes of Thomas. He soothed the tired feet of Matthew. He poured the water over Judas's feet. Andrew felt the Lord's hands massage his soles. Bartholomew's feet were toweled by his Teacher. James met his Master's eyes over the basin. John returned Jesus' smile as the water splashed. One by one. Jesus tends to his people individually. He personally sees to our needs. We all receive Jesus' touch. We all experience his care.

WEEKLY BIBLE STUDY

READ: EXODUS 3:1–15 AND PHILIPPIANS 1:3–6

1. Moses had every reason to doubt that God still had plans for his life. What was his situation when God called out to him from the burning bush (see Exodus 3:1–3)?

2. God instructed Moses to remove his sandals because he was standing on "holy ground." What mission did God then say that he had for Moses (see verses 4–10)?

3. What was Moses' response when he learned that God wanted to use him to free the Israelites? What does this say about his confidence that God *could* use him (see verse 11)?

4. How did God reassure Moses that he would be with him in this task? What is the significance of God revealing his divine name to Moses (see verses 12–15)?

5. God has not finished writing your story. He still has great plans and purposes for your life. How does Paul affirm this truth (see Philippians 1:3–6)?

6. The believers in Philippi were doing the "good work" of partnering with Paul to share the gospel. What "good work" do you sense God is calling you to do?

7. How do the passages you've studied this week help you to know that God can use you in spite of your past or your mistakes? What encouragement does this provide?

EXPERIENCING THE
PEACE OF JESUS

Maybe you can relate to the morning I just had.

It's Sunday. Sundays are always busy days for me. Sundays are always early days for me. Today promised to be no exception. With a full slate of activities planned, I got up early and drove to church. There was not much traffic at 6:00 AM. I had the roads to myself.

The orange of dawn had yet to break the nighttime spell on the summer's black sky. The twilight sparkled. Cool air wafted. I parked outside my church office and took a minute to enjoy the quietude. I set down my books, picked up my coffee, and leaned against the car.

It was calm. But calm has a way of becoming chaos.

With a briefcase in one hand and a coffee cup in the other, I walked and whistled across the parking lot to the office door. To enter my office, I had to get past the sleeping dog of the modern century: the alarm system. I set down my briefcase and unlocked the door. I picked up my briefcase and walked in. The code box on the wall was flashing a red light.

I'm not too electronically inclined, but I do know what a red light on an alarm system means: "Punch in the code, buddy, or get ready for the music." I punched in the code. Nothing happened. I punched in the code again. The little red light kept blinking. I kept pushing, the clock kept ticking, and the light kept flashing.

The siren pounced on me like a mountain lion. I thought we were under nuclear attack. Floodlights flash flooded the hallway. Red strobes turned. I kept pushing buttons, and the alarm kept blaring. You'd have thought it was a breakout at Alcatraz.

My situation was desperate. I raced down the hall to my office, pulled open the lap drawer of my desk, and found the phone number of the alarm company. The next twenty minutes were loud, demanding, confusing, and aggravating. I was speaking to technicians I couldn't see about equipment I didn't understand trying to understand words I couldn't hear.

Ever happened to you? When was the last time your life went from calm to chaos in half a minute? ("How many examples would you like?" you ask.) When was the last time you found yourself pushing buttons that didn't respond, struggling with instructions you couldn't hear, or operating a system you didn't understand?

If you've ever had your spouse call and say, "Just got a letter from the IRS. They are going to audit . . ."

If your boss has ever begun a conversation with these words: "You're a good worker, but with all this talk about a recession, we have to cut back . . ."

If your teenager has ever walked in and asked, "Does our car insurance cover the other guy's car . . . ?"

Then you know that life can go from calm to chaos in a matter of moments. No warnings. No announcements. No preparation. Little red lights blink, and you start pushing buttons. Sometimes you silence the alarm; sometimes it rips the air like a demon. The result can be peace or panic. The result can be calm or chaos.

It all depends on one factor: *Do you know the code?*

For me, this morning became chaos. Had I been prepared . . . had I known the code . . . had I known what to do when the warning flashed . . . calm would have triumphed.

The next pages in this unit will usher you into a day in Jesus' life when the calm could have become chaos. It has all the elements of anxiety: bad news and a death threat, followed by swarming demands, interruptions, inept disciples, and a blazing temptation to follow the crowd. In twenty-four pressure-packed hours, Jesus was carried from the summit of celebration to the valley of frustration.

It was the second most stressful day of his life. As soon as one alarm was disarmed, another began blinking. The rulers threatened. The crowds pressed. The followers doubted. The people demanded. When you see what he endured that day, you will wonder how he kept his cool. Somehow, though, he did. Although the people pressed and the problems monsooned, Jesus didn't blow up or bail out. In fact, he did just the opposite. He served people, thanked God, and made coolheaded decisions.

I want to help you see how he did it—to share a few "internal codes" that you desperately need. Equip yourself with these internal codes, punch them in when the red lights of your world start to flash, and you will be amazed at how quickly the alarms will be disarmed.[5]

— PRAYER —

Dear Father, I need to hear your voice above the chaos in my life. Sometimes I am faced with hard decisions, and sometimes I am plagued with doubts. Teach me to trust you. I want to experience the peace of Jesus. Help me see his peaceful attitudes, decisions, and demeanor. Help me mirror him in my own life. Amen.

— MEMORY VERSE —

"Peace I leave with you; my peace I give you. I do not give to you as the world gives. Do not let your hearts be troubled and do not be afraid."

JOHN 14:27

Week 6: JESUS UNDER PRESSURE

If you've ever had a day in which you've been blitzkrieged by demands . . . if you've ever ridden the roller coaster of sorrow and celebration . . . if you've ever wondered if God in heaven can relate to you on earth, then take heart. Jesus knows how you feel.

In the Gospels, we read of a time when Jesus began the morning by hearing about the death of John the Baptist: his cousin, his forerunner, his coworker, his friend (see Matthew 14:1–13). The man who came closer to understanding Jesus than any other was dead.

Imagine losing the one person who knows you better than anyone else, and you will feel what Jesus was feeling. Reflect on the horror of being told that your dearest friend has just been murdered, and you will relate to Jesus' sorrow. Consider your reaction if you were told that your best friend had just been decapitated by a people-pleasing, incestuous monarch, and you'll see how the day began for Christ. His world was beginning to turn upside down.

The emissaries brought more than news of sorrow, however; they brought a warning: "The same Herod who took John's head is interested in yours." Listen to how Luke presents the monarch's madness: "Herod said, 'I beheaded John. Who, then, is this I hear such things about?' *And he tried to see him*" (Luke 9:9, emphasis added). Something tells me that Herod wanted more than a social visit.

So, with John's life taken and his own life threatened, Jesus chose to get away for a while. But before he could get away, his disciples arrived. Mark states that the "apostles gathered around Jesus and reported to him all they had done and taught" (Mark 6:30). They returned exuberant. Jesus had commissioned them to proclaim the gospel and authenticate it with miracles. "They went out and preached that people should repent. They drove out many demons and anointed many sick people with oil and healed them" (verses 12–13).

In a matter of moments, Jesus' heart went from the pace of a funeral dirge to the triumphant march of a ticker-tape parade.

Look who followed the disciples to locate Jesus. About five thousand men plus women and children (see Matthew 14:21)! Rivers of people cascaded out of the hills and villages. Some scholars estimate the crowd was as high as twenty-five thousand.[6] They swarmed around Jesus, each with one desire: to meet the Man who had empowered the disciples.

What had been a calm morning now buzzed with activity. "So many people were coming and going that they did not even have a chance to eat" (Mark 6:31).

I've had people demand my attention. I know what it's like to have a half-dozen kids wanting different things at the same time. I know the feeling of receiving one call with other people waiting impatiently on other lines. I even know what it's like to be encircled by a dozen or so people, each making a separate request. But twenty-five thousand? That's larger than many cities! No wonder the disciples couldn't eat. I'm surprised they could breathe!

The morning had been a jungle trail of the unexpected. First, Jesus grieved over the death of a dear friend and relative. Then his life was threatened by Herod. Next he celebrated the triumphant return of his followers. Then he was nearly suffocated by a brouhaha of humanity. Bereavement . . . jeopardy . . . jubilation . . . bedlam.

Are you beginning to see why I call this the second most stressful day in the life of Christ? And it's far from over. Jesus decided to take the disciples to a quiet place where they could rest and reflect. He shouted a command over the noise of the crowd: "Come with me by yourselves to a quiet place and get some rest" (Mark 6:31). The thirteen fought their way to the beach and climbed into a boat.

Who would question Jesus' desire to get away from the people? He just needed a few hours alone. Just a respite. Just a retreat. Time to pray. Time to ponder. Time to weep. A time without crowds or demands. A campfire wreathed with friends. An evening with those he loved. The people could wait until tomorrow.

The people, however, had other ideas. "The crowds learned about it and followed him" (Luke 9:11). It's a six-mile walk around the northeastern corner of the Sea of Galilee, so the crowd took a hike. When Jesus got to Bethsaida, his desired retreat had become a roaring arena. "Surprise!"

Add to the list of sorrow, peril, excitement, and bedlam the word *interruption*. Jesus' plans were interrupted. What he had in mind for his day and what the people had in mind for his day were two different agendas. What Jesus sought and what Jesus got were not the same.

Sound familiar? Remember when you sought a night's rest and got a colicky baby? Remember when you sought to catch up at the office and got even further behind? Remember when you sought to use your Saturday for leisure but ended up fixing your neighbor's sink?

Take comfort, friend. It happened to Jesus, too. In fact, this would be a good time to pause and digest this important truth: *Jesus knows how you feel*. Ponder this and use it the next time your world goes from calm to chaos. His pulse has raced. His eyes have grown weary. His heart has grown heavy. He has had to climb out of bed with a sore throat. He has been kept awake late and has gotten up early. He knows how you feel.

You may have trouble believing that. You probably believe that Jesus knows what it means to endure heavy-duty tragedies. You are no doubt convinced that Jesus is acquainted with sorrow and has wrestled with fear. Most people accept that. But can God relate to the hassles and headaches of my life? Of your life?

For some reason, that is harder to believe. Perhaps that is why portions of this day are recorded in all the Gospel accounts. No other event, other than the crucifixion, is told by all four Gospel writers. Not Jesus' baptism. Not his temptation. Not even his birth. But all four writers chronicle this day. It's as if Matthew, Mark, Luke, and John knew that you would wonder if God understands. And they proclaim their response in four-part harmony: *Jesus knows how you feel*.

THE HEART OF THE MATTER

- Jesus knows how it feels to endure through stress-filled days.
- Jesus faced many interruptions and demands on his time.
- Jesus can relate to the hassles and headaches of your life.
- Jesus can help you get through your angst-ridden days.

MEMORY VERSE

Take a few moments to review your Bible memory verse for this unit, and then write out the words of John 14:27 by heart in the space below.

The Heart of Jesus

"I can't believe he is sleeping through this," muttered a disciple through clenched teeth. Straining at the oars as another swell lifted them high, the twelve clung to the sides for dear life. Water had washed over the sides, nearly swamping them. The fishermen—Peter and Andrew, James and John—were used to rough seas, but Matthew the tax collector was looking pretty green. The storm had come up suddenly, and they had been engulfed by its fury with almost no warning. Eyes narrowed against the wind and spray, feet spread to balance himself on the pitching deck, Peter finally called out the order. "Wake him." The disciple nearest Jesus crept forward and shook his shoulder, panic tingeing his voice. "Teacher, don't you care if we drown?" (Mark 4:38). Then Jesus stood up and addressed the storm, "Quiet! Be still!" (verse 39). The suddenness of the calm sent a few disciples sprawling. The wind they had been leaning into was simply . . . gone! Exchanging wondering glances for a moment, they turned their eyes as one to their Teacher. He had quieted the storm. He had given them peace.

WEEKLY BIBLE STUDY

READ: MATTHEW 14:1–14 AND HEBREWS 4:14–16

1. Jesus understands what it means to feel sorrow at the death of a close friend. What was the situation that led to John the Baptist being imprisoned (see Matthew 14:1–5)?

2. King Herod eventually made a foolish promise to Herodias that resulted in John's death. How did Jesus respond when he heard of this news (see verses 6–13)?

3. What Jesus had in mind for his day and what the people had in mind for his day were two different agendas. In spite of this, how did he react to the crowds (see verse 14)?

4. The author of Hebrews elaborates on this idea that Jesus knows *exactly* how you feel. What does he say about Jesus' ability to empathize with you (see Hebrews 4:14–15)?

5. In the Old Testament, one of the roles of the high priest was to intercede between God and humans. How does Jesus perform this same function for you?

6. Jesus' actions as your *great* high priest means that you can approach the throne of God with confidence. What will you receive when you do this (see verse 16)?

7. What is a situation you are facing right now where you need to know that God understands what you are going through? How will you take that to him today?

Week 7: HEARING JESUS' VOICE

You've heard them. They tell you to swap your integrity for a new sale. To barter your convictions for an easy deal. To exchange your devotion for a quick thrill. They whisper. They woo. They taunt. They tantalize. They flirt. They flatter. The voices of the crowd.

Our lives are Wall Streets of chaos, stock markets loud with demands. Grown men and women barking in a frenzied effort to get all they can before time runs out. "Buy. Sell. Trade. Swap. But whatever you do, do it fast—and loud."

Even the voices that Jesus heard promised something. "After the people saw the sign Jesus performed, they began to say, 'Surely this is the Prophet who is to come into the world'" (John 6:14). To the casual observer, these are the voices of victory. To the untrained ear, these are the sounds of triumph. What could be better?

Five thousand men plus women and children were proclaiming Christ to be the prophet. Thousands of voices were swelling into a roar of revival, an ovation of adulation. The people had everything they needed for a revolution. They had an enemy: Herod. They had a martyr: John the Baptist. They had leadership: the disciples. They had ample supplies: Jesus the bread maker. And they had a king: Jesus of Nazareth. Why wait? The time had come.

"King Jesus!" someone proclaimed. And the crowd chimed in.

Don't think for a minute that Christ didn't hear their chant. A chorus promising power intoxicates. No cross needed. No sacrifice required. An army of disciples at his fingertips. Power to change the world without having to die doing it.

Yes, Jesus heard the voices. He heard the lurings. But he also heard someone else. And when Jesus heard him, he sought him. "Jesus, knowing that they intended to come and make him king by force, withdrew again to a mountain by himself" (John 6:15). Jesus preferred to be alone with the true God rather than in a crowd with the wrong people.

Logic didn't tell him to dismiss the crowds. Conventional wisdom didn't tell him to turn his back on a willing army. No, it wasn't a voice from without that Jesus heard. It was a voice from within.

The mark of a sheep is its ability to hear the shepherd's voice. "The sheep listen to the voice of the shepherd. He calls his own sheep by name and leads them out" (John 10:3 NCV). The mark of a disciple is his or her ability to hear the Master's voice. "Here I am! I stand at the door and knock. If anyone hears my voice and opens the door, I will come in and eat with that person, and they with me" (Revelation 3:20).

The world rams at your door; Jesus taps at your door. The voices scream for your allegiance; Jesus softly and tenderly requests it. The world promises flashy pleasure; Jesus promises a quiet dinner . . . with God. "I will come in and eat." Which voice do you hear?

Let me state something important. There is never a time during which Jesus is not speaking. Never. There is never a place in which Jesus is not present. Never. There is never a room so dark . . . a lounge so sensual . . . an office so sophisticated . . . that the ever-present, ever-pursuing, relentlessly tender Friend is not there, tapping gently on the doors of our hearts—waiting to be invited in.

Few hear his voice. Fewer still open the door. But never interpret our numbness as his absence. For amid the fleeting promises of pleasure is the timeless promise of his presence. "Surely I am with you always, to the very end of the age" (Matthew 28:20). "Never will I leave you; never will I forsake you" (Hebrews 13:5). There is no chorus so loud that the voice of God cannot be heard . . . if we will but listen.

There is another side to the voices that rob our peace—those that attempt to confuse good with better, and better with best. When it comes to having peace in our decision-making process, we need to study the example of Jesus.

There is only so much sand in the hourglass. Who gets it? You know what I'm talking about, don't you?

"The PTA needs a new treasurer. With your background and experience and talent and wisdom and love for kids and degree in accounting, *you* are the perfect one for the job!"

"The company is looking for a bright, young salesperson who is willing to demonstrate dedication to the organization by taking on some extra projects . . . and working some late hours."

"I apologize that I have to ask you again, but you are such a good Sunday school teacher. If you could only take one more quarter . . ."

It's tug-of-war, and you are the rope. On one side are the requests for your time and energy. They call. They compliment. They are valid and good. Great opportunities to do good things. If they were evil, it'd be easy to say no. But they aren't, so it's easy to rationalize.

On the other side are the loved ones in your world. They don't write you letters. They don't ask you to consult your calendar. They don't offer to pay your expenses. They don't use terms like "appointment," "engagement," or "do lunch." They don't want you for what you can do for them; they want you for who you are.

A world of insight is hidden in four words in Matthew 14:22: "He dismissed the crowd." This wasn't just any crowd that Jesus dismissed. These weren't casually curious. These weren't coincidental bystanders. This was a multitude with a mission. They had heard the disciples. They had left their homes. They had followed Jesus around the sea. They had heard him teach and had seen him heal. They had eaten the bread. And they were ready to make him king.

Surely, Jesus would commandeer the crowd and focus their frenzy. Surely, he would seize the chance to convert the thousands. Surely, he would spend the night baptizing the willing followers. No one would turn down an opportunity to minister to thousands of people, right?

Jesus did.

"He dismissed the crowd." Why? Read verse 23: "After he had dismissed them, he went up on a mountainside by himself to pray." He said no to the important in order to say yes to the vital. He said no to a good opportunity in order to say yes to a better opportunity. It wasn't a selfish decision. It was a deliberate choice to honor priorities. If Jesus thought it necessary to say no to the demands of the crowds in order to pray, don't you think you and I should, too?

THE HEART OF THE MATTER

- The voices of the crowd are persuasive and clamor for attention.
- Jesus heard the voices but preferred to be alone with his Father.
- Sheep know the voice and call of their shepherd.
- Sometimes it is necessary to say *no* to the demands of the crowd.

MEMORY VERSE

Your memory verse for this unit is John 14:27. Take a few moments to review this verse, and then write it out from memory in the space below.

The Heart of Jesus

Martha's world had been turned upside down. How could this have happened? Her brother had seemed so . . . alive just a couple of weeks ago. The house was so quiet now. Empty. Lonely. And there was tension in the air because of the question she dared to ask out loud: *Why hadn't Jesus come?* He could have healed Lazarus. They had sent a messenger. They had asked for him to come. The message had been delivered. But still Jesus had not come. Why not?

When word arrived that Jesus was finally coming, Martha gathered herself up and trudged down the road to meet him. When he drew near, the accusations leapt from her lips. "If you had been here, my brother would not have died" (John 11:21). Jesus' words gave her a glimmer of hope: "Your brother will rise and live again" (verse 23 NCV).

Eyeing him cautiously, Martha retorted, "I know he will rise again . . . at the last day." Jesus replied, "I am the resurrection and the life. The one who believes in me will live. . . . Do you believe this?" (verses 24–26). With a trembling sigh and lift of her chin, Martha stated with confidence, "Yes, Lord" (verse 27). It was enough. Jesus had reminded her of her faith and renewed her assurance. Martha had experienced the peace of Jesus.

WEEKLY BIBLE STUDY

READ: JOHN 6:5-15 AND JOHN 10:1-5

1. Jesus often heard the "voices of the crowd" after performing a miracle. What was the problem that led to Jesus miraculously feeding the five thousand (see John 6:5–7)?

2. What question did Andrew pose to Jesus after he delivered the boy's lunch of five loaves and two fish? What was Jesus teaching the disciples in this moment (see verses 8–13)?

3. What did the people in the crowd say after they witnessed this miracle from Jesus? What did Jesus understand about their motives (see verses 14–15)?

4. The mark of a sheep is its ability to hear the shepherd's voice. What does Jesus say about his role as the Shepherd of his flock? What does he do (see John 10:1–3)?

5. What does Jesus say the sheep do when they hear his voice (see verse 4)? What does this say about the importance of being able to hear Jesus' voice?

6. What should the sheep do when they hear a stranger calling out to them (see verse 5)? What does this imply about rejecting the voices of the crowd?

7. What voices of the crowd are you tempted to follow today? How do the passages that you've studied this week encourage you to seek only Jesus' voice?

Week 8: DOUBTSTORMS

There is a window in your heart through which you can see God. Once upon a time that window was clear. Your view of God was crisp. You could see God as vividly as you could see a gentle valley or hillside. The glass was clean, the pane unbroken.

You knew God. You knew how he worked. You knew what he wanted you to do. No surprises. Nothing unexpected. You knew that God had a will, and you continually discovered what it was.

Then, suddenly, the window cracked. A pebble broke the window. A pebble of pain.

Perhaps the stone struck when you were a child and a parent left home—forever. Maybe the rock hit in adolescence when your heart was broken. Maybe you made it into adulthood before the window was cracked. But then the pebble came.

Was it a phone call? "We have your daughter at the station. You'd better come down."

Was it a letter on the kitchen table? "I've left. Don't try to reach me. Don't try to call me. It's over. I just don't love you anymore."

Was it a diagnosis from the doctor? "I'm afraid the news is not very good."

Whatever the pebble's form, the result was the same—a shattered window. The crash echoed down the halls of your heart. Cracks shot out from the point of impact, creating a spiderweb of fragmented pieces. Suddenly, God was not so easy to see. The view that had been so crisp had changed. You turned to see God, and his figure was distorted. It was hard to see him through the pain. It was hard to see him through the fragments of hurt.

The moment the pebble struck, the glass became a reference point for you. From then on, there was life before the pain and life after the pain. Before your pain, the view was clear; God seemed so near. After your pain, well, he was harder to see. He seemed a bit distant . . . harder to perceive. Your pain distorted the view—not eclipsed it, but distorted it.

Most of us know what it means to feel disappointed by God. A story told in Matthew's Gospel shows that Jesus' disciples could relate. Matthew is specific about the order of events. Jesus had just performed the miracle of feeding the five thousand. Then he sent the disciples into a boat, dismissed the crowd, and ascended a mountainside. The storm struck immediately after. The sun had scarcely set before typhoon-like winds began to roar.

Note that Jesus sent the disciples out into the storm *alone*. Even as he was ascending the mountainside, he could feel and hear the gale's force. Jesus was not ignorant of the storm. He was aware that a torrent was coming that would carpet-bomb the sea's surface. But he didn't turn around. The disciples were left to face the storm . . . alone.

The greatest storm that night was not in the sky; it was in the disciples' hearts. The greatest fear was not from seeing the storm-driven waves; it came from seeing the back of their leader as he left them to face the night with only questions as companions. *Surely Jesus will help us*, they thought. They had seen him still storms like this before. On this same sea, they had awakened him during a storm, and he had commanded the skies to be silent. They had seen him quiet the wind and soothe the waves. Surely he would come off the mountain.

But he didn't. The disciples' arms began to ache from rowing. Three hours. Four hours. Still no sign of Jesus. The winds raged. The boat bounced. Midnight arrived. By now, the disciples might have been on the sea for as long as six hours, fighting the storm and seeking the Master. So far, the storm was winning—and the Master nowhere to be found.

"Where is he?" cried one. "Has he forgotten us?" yelled another. "He feeds thousands of strangers and yet leaves us to die?" muttered a third.

There are snowstorms. There are hailstorms. There are rainstorms. And then there are doubtstorms: turbulent days when the enemy is too big, the task too great, the future too bleak, and the answers too few. "If God is so good, why do I sometimes feel so bad?" "If his message is so clear, why do I get so confused?" "If the Father is in control, why do good people have gut-wrenching problems?" Tough questions. Throw-in-the-towel questions.

Questions the disciples must have asked in the storm. All they could see were black skies as they bounced in the battered boat. Swirling clouds. Wind-driven whitecaps. Pessimism that buried the coastline. Gloom that swamped the bow.

Their question—*What hope do we have of surviving a stormy night?*

My question—*Where is God when his world is stormy?*

Peter, Andrew, James, and John had seen storms like this. They were fishermen; the sea was their life. They knew the havoc the gale-force winds could wreak. They had seen the splintered hulls float to shore. They had attended the funerals. They knew, better than anyone, that this night could be their last. "Why doesn't he come?" they sputtered.

Finally, he arrived. "Shortly before dawn [3:00 to 6:00 AM] Jesus went out to them, walking on the lake" (Matthew 14:25). Jesus came. He finally came! But between verse 24—being buffeted by waves—and verse 25—when Jesus appeared—a thousand questions were asked. Questions you have probably asked, too.

Perhaps you know the angst of being suspended between verses 24 and 25. Maybe you're riding a storm, searching the coastline for a light, a glimmer of hope. You know that Jesus knows what you are going through. You know that he's aware of your storm. But as hard as you look to find him, you can't see him.

Every so often a storm will come and I'll look up into the blackening sky and say, "God, a little light, please?" The light came for the disciples. A figure came walking on the water. It wasn't what they expected. Perhaps they were looking for angels to descend or heaven to open. Maybe they were listening for a divine proclamation to still the storm. We don't know. But one thing is for sure, they weren't looking for Jesus to come walking on the water.

"'It's a ghost,' they said, and cried out in fear" (verse 26). And since Jesus came in a way they didn't expect, they almost missed seeing the answer to their prayers.

The message? When you can't see him, trust him. The figure you see is not a ghost. The voice you hear is not the wind. Jesus is closer than you've ever dreamed.

THE HEART OF THE MATTER

- It can be hard to see God when you are in a painful situation.
- It can be hard to trust God when you don't sense his presence.
- When all you have are questions, still cling to your faith.
- You will find that Jesus is closer than you ever imagined.

MEMORY VERSE

Your memory verse for this unit is John 14:27. Take a few moments to review this verse, and then write it out from memory in the space below.

The Heart of Jesus

His life was torment. His days were spent raging among the tombs of the dead. Nights found him wandering through the mountains, keening and wailing through the cold nights. He was lonely, but never alone, this demon-possessed man. Those who pitied him could not tame him. Those who feared him could not bind him. His arms and legs bore the scars of rope and chain. Rocks had cut into his flesh. He ran about naked, hair and beard unkempt and matted. A prisoner who had abandoned hope. A slave to forces beyond his control. All he knew was madness and mayhem. Then Jesus stepped onto his shore, and everything changed. The hand that touched him was gentle. The voice that reached him spoke peace. Jesus did not fear him—he freed him! Word spread, and by the time the townspeople arrived on the scene, they barely recognized the man. He was clothed and in his right mind. He was released from his torment. Jesus had made him whole again. The man now knew the peace of Jesus (see Mark 5:1–20).

WEEKLY BIBLE STUDY

READ: MATTHEW 14:22–27 AND PROVERBS 3:5–8

1. Jesus' disciples knew what it meant to be disappointed by God. What happened after they followed Jesus' instructions to go across the lake (see Matthew 14:22–24)?

2. Put yourself in the place of the disciples. What questions would you have been asking your fellow crew members as the waves threatened to sink the boat?

3. Jesus finally arrived on the scene "shortly before dawn," walking on the surface of the water. How did the disciples react when they saw him (see verses 25–26)?

4. Jesus told his disciples to take courage and not be afraid (see verse 27). Why do you think he said this to them? What do you feel he was trying to teach them?

5. You won't always be able to see how God is working in a given situation in your life. But what is the promise if you choose to trust in him anyway (see Proverbs 3:5–6)?

6. What does it mean to be "wise in your own eyes" (verse 7)? What are some of the dangers in trusting your own wisdom instead of relying on the Lord's wisdom?

7. What situations are you facing that are causing you to doubt whether God will show up? How have the passages you've studied this week encouraged you that he will?

Week 9: FEAR THAT BECOMES FAITH

"Lord, if it's you . . . tell me to come to you on the water" (Matthew 14:28).

Fear propelled Peter out of the boat. All night he had wanted out. For nine hours he had tugged on sails, wrestled with oars, and searched every shadow on the horizon for hope. He was soaked to the soul and bone weary of the wind's banshee wail.

Look into Peter's eyes and you won't see a man of conviction. Search his face and you won't find a gutsy grimace. You will only find fear—a suffocating, heart-racing fear of a man who had no way out. But out of this fear would be born an act of faith, for faith is often the child of fear. "Peter got down out of the boat, walked on the water and came toward Jesus" (verse 29).

Biographies of bold disciples begin with chapters of honest terror. Fear of death. Fear of failure. Fear of loneliness. Fear of a wasted life. *Faith* begins when we see God on the mountain, and we are in the valley, and we know we're too weak to make the climb. We see what we need and see what we have—and what we have isn't enough to accomplish anything.

"But when he saw the wind, he was afraid and, beginning to sink, cried out, 'Lord, save me!'" (verse 30). Peter became aware of two facts: he was going down, and Jesus was staying up. He knew where he would rather be and cried out to Jesus for help. There is nothing wrong with this response. Faith that begins with fear will end up nearer the Father.

I went to West Texas some time back to speak at the funeral of a godly family friend. He had raised five children. One son, Paul, told a story about his earliest memory of his father. It was spring in West Texas— tornado season. Paul was only three or four years old at the time, but he remembered vividly the day a tornado hit their small town.

His father hustled the kids indoors and had them lie on the floor while he laid a mattress over them. But his father didn't climb under the protection. Paul remembered peeking out from under the mattress and seeing him standing by an open window, watching the funnel cloud twist and churn across the prairie.

When Paul saw his father, he knew where he wanted to be. He struggled out of his mother's arms, crawled out from under the mattress, and ran to wrap his arms around his dad's leg. "Something told me," Paul said, "that the safest place to stand in a storm was next to my father." Something told Peter the same thing.

The peace *of* God is one thing. Experiencing Jesus' presence in our lives has a calming effect. However, we cannot have the peace of God until, through Jesus, we have experienced peace *with* God. Faith comes first.

Peter's act of stepping onto a stormy sea was not a move of logic; it was a move of desperation. Peter grabbed the edge of the boat, threw out a leg, and followed it with the other. Several steps were taken. It was as if an invisible ridge of rocks ran beneath his feet. At the end of the ridge was the glowing face of a never-say-die friend.

We do the same, don't we? We come to Christ in an hour of deep need. We abandon the boat of good works. We realize, like Peter, that spanning the gap between us and Jesus is a feat too great for our feet. So we beg for help. Hear his voice. And step out in fear, hoping that our little faith will be enough.

Faith is not born at the negotiating table where we barter our gifts in exchange for God's goodness. Faith is not an award given to the most learned. It's not a prize given to the most disciplined. It's not a title bequeathed to the most religious. Faith is a desperate dive out of the sinking boat of human effort and a prayer that God will be there to pull us out.

Paul wrote about this kind of faith in the letter to the Ephesians: "For it is by grace you have been saved, through faith—and this is not from yourselves, it is the gift of God—not by works, so that no one can boast" (Ephesians 2:8–9). Paul is clear. The supreme force in salvation is God's grace. Not our works. Not our talents. Not our feelings. Not our strength.

Salvation is God's sudden, calming presence during the stormy seas of our lives. We hear his voice; we take the step.

We, like Paul, are aware of two things: we are great sinners and we need a great Savior.

We, like Peter, are aware of two facts: we are going down and God is standing up. So we scramble out. We leave behind the Titanic of self-righteousness and stand on the solid path of God's grace. And, surprisingly, we are able to walk on water. Death is disarmed. Failures are forgivable. Life has real purpose. And God is not only within sight; he is within reach.

With precious, wobbly steps, we draw closer to him. For a season of surprising strength, we stand on his promises. It doesn't make sense that we are able to do this. We don't claim to be worthy of such an incredible gift. When people ask how in the world we can keep our balance during such stormy times, we don't boast. We don't brag. We point unabashedly to the one who makes it possible. Our eyes are on him.

Some of us, unlike Peter, never look back. Others of us, like Peter, feel the wind and are afraid. Maybe we face the wind of pride: "I'm not such a bad sinner after all. Look at what I can do." Perhaps we face the wind of legalism: "I know that Jesus is doing part of this, but I have to do the rest." Most of us, though, face the wind of doubt: "I'm too bad for God to treat me this well. I don't deserve such a rescue."

And downward we plunge. Weighted down by mortality's mortar, we sink. Gulping and thrashing, we fall into a dark, wet world. We open our eyes and see only blackness. We try to breathe, but no air comes. We kick and fight our way back to the surface.

With our heads barely above the water, we have to make a decision. We know Peter's choice. "When he saw the wind, he . . . cried out, 'Lord, save me!' Immediately Jesus reached out his hand and caught him" (Matthew 14:30–31).

THE HEART OF THE MATTER

- Faith begins when you recognize that you need God's help.
- Even faith that begins with fear will bring you closer to Christ.
- You cannot have the peace *of* God until you have peace *with* God.
- Jesus is there to catch you when you cry out, "Lord, save me!"

MEMORY VERSE

Your memory verse for this unit is John 14:27. Take a few moments to review this verse, and then write it out from memory in the space below.

The Heart of Jesus

His heart was beating fast. His mouth had gone dry. He was nearly beside himself with impatience. The ever-present crowds were making it difficult to reach the Teacher, to get a word with him. Jairus's heart was wrenched, for his little daughter was dangerously ill. He had done all he could. Desperation had driven him from his child's side. Tears stung at his eyelids as he tried to swallow the lump rising in his throat.

At last it was his turn before Jesus, and he gasped out his request. When Jesus agreed to accompany him to his home, Jairus had to fight back a sob of relief. Then, when they were nearly there, a servant came to tell him it was too late. "Your daughter is dead" (Mark 5:35). The impact of those words left him numb. *Dead.* It was too late. She was gone.

But then the gentle voice of the Teacher was in Jairus's ear. "Don't be afraid; just believe" (verse 36). Jesus was guided past the mourners and musicians, into the tiny room where the girl lay so still. It was almost more than Jairus could bear. But Jesus' next words whisked away every doubt and replaced it with joy. "Little girl . . . get up!" (verse 41). She sat up. She blinked. She smiled. She reached out to her parents. In a home where there had been nothing but fear, desperation, and grief, there only remained joy and peace—perfect peace.

WEEKLY BIBLE STUDY

READ: MATTHEW 14:24–33 AND EPHESIANS 2:8–10

1. Peter had been fearing for his life for nine long hours when Jesus finally appeared. What act of incredible faith then came out of his fears (see Matthew 14:28–29)?

2. Peter stepped out of the boat, saw the wind and the waves, and quickly realized that he was going down. What did he do in that moment (see verse 30)?

3. Jesus answered Peter's desperate prayer by reaching out his hand and catching him (see verse 31). When has Jesus answered a desperate prayer like this for you?

4. When Peter and Jesus returned to the boat, the wind immediately died down and the disciples experienced God's peace. What did they do next (see verses 32–33)?

5. Faith is a desperate dive out of the sinking boat of human effort and a prayer that God will pull you out. What does Paul say about this kind of faith (see Ephesians 2:8–9)?

6. What does it mean that you are "God's handiwork"? What does God want you to do as a natural response to receiving his free gift of grace (see verse 10)?

7. Are you still trying to cling to the sinking boat of human effort when it comes to living for God? What area of your life do you sense God is calling you to release to him?

Week 10: THE JOURNEY'S END

I drove the family to Grandma's last night for Thanksgiving. Three hours into the six-hour trip, I realized I was in a theology lab. A day with a car full of kids will teach you a lot about God. Transporting a family from one city to another is akin to God transporting us from our home to his. Some of life's stormiest hours occur when the passenger and driver disagree on the destination.

A journey is a journey, whether the destination is to the Thanksgiving table or the heavenly one. Both demand patience, a good sense of direction, and a driver who knows that the feast at the end of the trip is worth the hassles in the midst of the trip. The fact that my pilgrims were all under the age of seven only enriched my learning experience.

As the minutes rolled into hours, I began to realize that what I was saying to my kids had a familiar ring. I had heard it before—from God. I was doing for a few hours what God has done for centuries: encouraging travelers who would rather rest than ride.

I shared the idea with my wife, Denalyn. We began to discover similarities between the two journeys. Here are a few we noted.

First, *in order to reach the destination, we have to say no to some requests.*

Can you imagine the outcome if a parent honored each request of each child during a trip? We'd inch our bloated bellies from one ice-cream store to the next. Our priority would be popcorn and our itinerary would read like a fast-food menu. "Go to the Cherry Malt and make a right. Head north until you find the Chili Cheeseburger. At the sixth toilet . . ."

Can you imagine the chaos if a parent indulged every indulgence? Can you imagine the chaos if God indulged each of ours? *No* is a necessary word to take on a trip. Destination has to reign over Dairy Deluxe Ice Cream Sundae.

Of course, some of us don't do "no" very well. We just don't like the sound of it. So final. So confounding. The requests my children made last night on the road to Grandma's weren't evil. They weren't unfair. They weren't rebellious. In fact, we had a couple of cones and Cokes. But most of the requests were unnecessary.

This brings us to a second point: *children have no concept of minutes or miles.*

"We'll be there in three hours," I said.

"How long is three hours?" Jenna asked. (How do you explain time to a child who can't tell time?)

"Well, it's about as long as three *Sesame Streets*," I ventured.

The children groaned in unison. "Three *Sesame Streets*?! That's forever!" And to them, it is. And to us, it seems that way, too.

He who "lives forever" (Isaiah 57:15) has placed himself at the head of a band of pilgrims who mutter, "How long, O Lord? How long?" (see Psalm 74:10; 89:46).

"How long must I endure this sickness?"

"How long must I endure this spouse?"

"How long must I endure this paycheck?"

Do you really want God to answer? He could, you know. He could answer in terms of the here and now with time increments we know. "Two more years on the illness." "The rest of your life in the marriage." "Ten more years for the bills."

But he seldom does that. He usually opts to measure the here and now against the there and then. And when you compare this life to that life, this life ain't long.

In light of God's Word, periods of unrest along the journey (that seem to stretch for miles to us) will seem like a mere matter of minutes in eternity.

Here's a final point to consider: *children can't envision the reward.*

For me, six hours on the road is a small price to pay for my mom's strawberry cake. I don't mind the drive because I know the reward. I have three decades of Thanksgivings under my belt, literally. As I drive, I can taste the turkey. Hear the dinner-table laughter. Smell the smoke from the fireplace.

I can endure the journey because I know the destiny.

My daughters have forgotten the destiny. After all, they are young. Children easily forget. Besides, the road is strange, and the dark night has come. They can't see where we're going. It's my job, as their father, to guide them. I try to help them see what they can't see.

It's not easy to get three girls under the age of seven to see a city they can't see. But it's necessary. It's not easy for us to see an eternal City we've never seen, either, especially when the road is bumpy . . . the hour is late . . . and companions are wanting to cancel the trip and take up residence in a motel. It's not easy to fix our eyes on what is unseen. But it's necessary.

The apostle Paul provides us with a way to stay motivated. He had a clear vision of the reward: "Therefore we do not lose heart. Though outwardly we are wasting away, yet inwardly we are being renewed day by day. For our light and momentary troubles are achieving for us an eternal glory that far outweighs them all. So we fix our eyes not on what is seen, but on what is unseen, since what is seen is temporary, but what is unseen is eternal" (2 Corinthians 4:16–18).

One line in this passage makes me smile: "our light and momentary troubles." Long and trying ordeals, perhaps. Arduous and deadly afflictions, okay. But small troubles? How could Paul describe endless trials like that? He tells us. He could see "an eternal glory that far outweighs them all."

For some of you, the journey has been long. In no way do I want to minimize the difficulties you have faced along the way. Some of you have shouldered burdens that few of us could ever carry. And you are tired. It's hard for you to see the City in the midst of the storms. The desire to pull over to the side of the road and get out entices you. You want to go on, but some days the road seems so long.

God never said that the journey would be easy, but he did say that the arrival would be worthwhile.

Remember this: God may not do what you want, but he will do what is right . . . and best. He is the Father of forward motion. Trust him. He will get you home. And the trials of the trip will be lost in the joys of the feast.

THE HEART OF THE MATTER

- God loves you too much to indulge your every whim and request.
- Compared to your life in eternity, this life on earth is fleeting.
- God instructs you to fix your eyes on what is "unseen."
- The journey is never easy, but the arrival is always worthwhile.

MEMORY VERSE

This is it . . . one last review of your memory verse. Write out the words of John 14:27 from memory in the space below. Reflect on what these words mean to you.

The Heart of Jesus

Jesus wanted to prepare his disciples for what lay ahead. He began early with the difficult task of saying goodbye. "I am going away," he said (John 14:28), but "do not let your hearts be troubled" (verse 27). The disciples had questions for him. They did not fully understand him. Though they knew him so well, Jesus seemed to be talking in riddles. "I will not leave you as orphans" (verse 18). "The Holy Spirit . . . will remind you of everything I have said" (verse 26).

But the last words he gave them must have rung clearly in their ears: "Peace I leave with you; my peace I give you. . . . Do not let your hearts be troubled and do not be afraid" (verse 27). Like a final bequest, Jesus promised that they would experience his peace, even when he returned to his Father. "I leave you my peace." Peace that passes understanding. *Perfect* peace.

WEEKLY BIBLE STUDY

READ: HEBREWS 12:1–3 AND 2 CORINTHIANS 4:16–18

1. It's not easy to fix your eyes on what is unseen. But it is necessary. What does the author of Hebrews advise you to "throw off" as you run the race of faith (see Hebrews 12:1)?

2. How are you as a follower of Jesus to run the race that God has "marked out" for you? What should be your focus as you do this (see verses 1–2)?

3. What do you think it means that Jesus is the "pioneer" of your faith? What does it mean to you that he is also the "perfecter" of your faith (see verse 2)?

4. Why did Jesus choose to endure the suffering and shame of the cross? How can remembering what Jesus has done help you to not lose heart (see verses 2–3)?

5. Paul also states that you should "not lose heart" as you run your race. What did Paul understand about the prize that awaited him (see 2 Corinthians 4:16)?

6. How does Paul describe the troubles that you will face in this world? What does he advise you to "fix" your eyes on to persevere in your faith (see verses 17–18)?

7. How have the passages you've studied this week helped you to experience the peace of Jesus? How have they helped you stay focused on Christ?

EXPERIENCING THE
GRACE OF JESUS

My only qualification for writing on grace is the clothing I wear. Let me explain.

For years, I owned an elegant suit complete with coat, trousers, and even a hat. I considered myself quite dapper in the outfit and was confident others agreed. The pants were cut from the cloth of my good works, sturdy fabric of deeds done, and projects completed. Some studies here, some sermons there. Many people complimented my trousers, and I confess, I tended to hitch them up in public so people would notice them.

The coat was equally impressive. It was woven together from my convictions. Each day I dressed myself in deep feelings of religious fervor. My emotions were quite strong. So strong, in fact, that I was often asked to model my cloak of zeal in public gatherings to inspire others. Of course, I was happy to comply. While there, I'd also display my hat, a feathered cap of knowledge. Formed with my own hands from the fabric of personal opinion, I wore it proudly.

Surely God is impressed with my garments, I often thought. Occasionally I strutted into his presence so he could compliment the self-tailored wear. He never spoke. *His silence must mean admiration,* I convinced myself.

But then my wardrobe began to suffer. The fabric of my trousers grew thin. My best works started coming unstitched. I began leaving more undone than done, and what little I did was nothing to boast about.

No problem, I thought. *I'll work harder.* But working harder *was* a problem. There was a hole in my coat of convictions. My resolve was threadbare. A cold wind cut into my chest. I reached up to pull my hat down firmly, and the brim ripped off in my hands.

Over a period of a few months, my wardrobe of self-righteousness completely unraveled. I went from tailored gentlemen's apparel to beggars' rags. Fearful that God might be angry at my tattered suit, I did my best to stitch it together and cover my mistakes. But the cloth was so worn. And the wind was so icy. I gave up.

I went back to God. (Where else could I go?) On a wintry Thursday afternoon, I stepped into his presence, not for applause, but for warmth. My prayer was feeble. "I feel naked."

"You are," he said. "And you have been for a long time."

What he did next I'll never forget. "I have something to give you," he said. He gently removed the remaining threads and then picked up a robe—the clothing of his own goodness. He wrapped it around my shoulders. His words to me were tender. "My son, you are now clothed with Christ" (see Galatians 3:27).

Though I'd sung the hymn "The Solid Rock" a thousand times, I finally understood it: "Dressed in his righteousness alone, faultless to stand before the throne."

I have a hunch you know what I'm talking about. You're wearing a handmade wardrobe yourself. You've sewn your garments, and you're sporting your religious deeds . . . and, already, you've noticed a tear in the fabric. Before you start stitching yourself together, I'd like to share some thoughts with you on the greatest discovery of my life: the grace of God.

My strategy in this unit is for us to spend some time walking the mountains of Paul's letter to the Romans. An epistle for the self-sufficient, Romans contrasts the plight of people who choose to dress in self-made garments with those who accept the robes of grace. Romans is the grandest treatise on grace ever written. You'll find the air fresh and the view clear.[7]

— PRAYER —

Dear Father, forgive me for trying to impress you with garments of my own making. You have shown me grace and clothed me with Christ. It is only through your grace that I have been saved. Guide my studies this week. Teach me about you. Let me experience the amazing grace of Jesus. Amen.

— MEMORY VERSES —

For by grace you have been saved through faith, and that not of yourselves; it is the gift of God, not of works, lest anyone should boast.

EPHESIANS 2:8–9 NKJV

Week 11: WE NEED GRACE

The first few chapters of Paul's letter to the Romans are not exactly upbeat. Paul gives us the bad news before he gives us the good news. He will eventually tell us that we are all equal candidates for grace, but not before he proves that we are all desperately sinful.

We have to see the mess we are in before we can appreciate the God we have. Before presenting the grace of God, we must understand the wrath of God. So, what are some of the reasons why God gets stirred up?

For one, God is angry at evil. Paul writes that God is "against all the godlessness and wickedness of people" (Romans 1:18). For many, this is a revelation. Some assume God is a harried high-school principal, too busy monitoring the planets to notice us. He's not.

Others assume he is a doting parent, blind to the evil of his children.

Wrong.

Still others insist he loves us so much he cannot be angry at our evil. They don't understand that love is *always* angry at evil.

Many people don't understand God's anger because they confuse the wrath of God with the wrath of man. The two have little in common. Human anger is typically self-driven and prone to explosions of temper and violent deeds. We get ticked off because we've been overlooked, neglected, or cheated. This is not the anger of God.

God doesn't get angry because he doesn't get his way. He gets angry because disobedience always results in self-destruction. What kind of father would sit by and watch his children hurt themselves? What kind of God would do the same?

Do we think he giggles at adultery or snickers at murder? Does he just shake his head and say, "Humans will be humans"? I don't think so. Mark it down and underline it in red. God is rightfully angry. God is a holy God. Our sins are an affront to his holiness. His eyes "are too pure to look on evil; [he] cannot tolerate wrongdoing" (Habakkuk 1:13).

God is angry at the evil that ruins his children.

Paul is also clear in the first few chapters of his letter about the stark reality of the human condition—the condition of everyone who has ever walked this earth. What separates us from God is sin. We aren't strong enough to remove it, and we aren't good enough to erase it. For all of our differences, there is one problem we all share. We are separated from God.

Paul describes three kinds of people in the world: the hedonist (see Romans 1:21–25); the judgmentalist (see 2:1–6); and the legalist (see 2:17–24). Let's look at each one.

The hedonist lives as if there is no creator at all. He says, "I may be bad, but so what? What I do is my business." The hedonist is more concerned about satisfying his pleasures than in knowing the Father. His life is so desperate for pleasure that he has no time or room for God.

The judgmentalist says, "Why deal with my mistakes when I can focus on the mistakes of others? I may be bad, but as long as I can find someone worse, I am safe." He fuels his goodness with the failures of others.

He is the self-appointed teacher's pet in elementary school. He tattles on the sloppy work of others, oblivious to the F on his own paper. He's the neighborhood watchdog, passing out citations for people to clean up their act, all the while never noticing the garbage that litters his own front lawn.

Then there is the legalist. Ah, here now is a person we can respect. Hardworking. Industrious. Zealous. Intense. He is a fellow who sees his sin and sets out to resolve it by himself. Surely he is worthy of our applause. Surely he is worthy of our emulation.

The legalist thinks: *If I do this, God will accept me.* The problem? We can never earn our salvation based on our own efforts. We can never do enough mission work, go through enough Bible studies, spend enough time in church—we can never do *enough* to save ourselves.

Every person on earth has blown it. The hedonists blow it because they are pleasure-centered and not God-centered. The judgmentalists blow it because they are high-minded and not God-minded. The legalists blow it because they are work-driven and not grace-driven.

Now, while these three types of individuals may appear different, they are very much alike. All are separated from the Father—and none of them are asking for help. The first indulges his passions; the second monitors his neighbor; the third measures his merits. Self-satisfaction. Self-justification. Self-salvation. The operative word is *self*. Self-sufficient. "They never give God the time of day" (Romans 3:18 MSG).

Paul's word to describe all three is *godlessness* (see 1:18). The word defines itself. A life minus God. Worse than a disdain for God, it is a disregard for God. A disdain at least acknowledges his presence. Godlessness doesn't. Whereas disdain will lead people to act with irreverence, disregard causes them to act as if God were not a factor at all in the journey.

So now that we've considered God's rightful wrath and our own condition, as well as humanity's universal problem, the question remains: *How does God respond to godless living?* Not flippantly. Again, we read, "The wrath of God is being revealed from heaven against all the godlessness and wickedness" (Romans 1:18). Paul's main point is not a light one. God is justly angered over the actions of his children.

We all stand "guilty as charged," rightly condemned before a holy God. We all deserve to be on a kind of spiritual death row. Hopeless. The good news of Jesus isn't good until we first wrestle with the unspeakably bad news of our lostness. We can't rush on to grace until we have felt the awful weight of human sin and its consequences.

We can summarize the first three and a half chapters of Romans with three words: *we have failed.* We have attempted to reach the moon but scarcely made it off the ground. We tried to swim the Atlantic but couldn't get beyond the reef. We have attempted to scale the Everest of salvation but have yet to leave the base camp, much less ascend the slope. The quest is simply too great. We don't need more supplies or muscle or technique; we need a helicopter.

"God has a way to *make people right with him*" (Romans 3:21 NCV, emphasis added). How vital that we embrace this truth. God's highest dream is not to make us rich—not to make us successful or popular or famous. God's dream is to make us right with him.

THE HEART OF THE MATTER

- God is angry at the evil that ruins his children.
- The human condition is *godlessness*—a disregard for God.
- We all stand rightly condemned before a holy God.
- God has made a way for you to be right with him.

MEMORY VERSES

Take a few moments to review your Bible memory verses for this unit, and then write out the words of Ephesians 2:8–9 by heart in the space below.

The Heart of Jesus

No one wants to spend a lot of time dwelling on sin and the wrath of God. But experiencing God's grace becomes all the more precious to us when we realize exactly what we have been rescued from. Remember the woman caught in adultery in John 8:1–11?

Caught in sin. Dragged before a holy judge. No defense for her actions. No hope.

According to the letter of the law, all she deserved was death. The men ringed about her were clamoring for the Teacher to give the word. Then she would be stoned. But Jesus did not call the wrath of the crowd down on her head. Instead, the woman who had been caught experienced the grace of Jesus.

He dismissed the accusers. His next words were a gift: "Neither do I condemn you" (verse 11). A new lease on life. Forgiveness. Grace.

WEEKLY BIBLE STUDY

READ: PSALM 78:23–39 AND ROMANS 1:18–25

1. God brought the Israelites out of slavery in Egypt and guided them toward a new promised land. How did he show his grace by providing for their needs (see Psalm 78:23–27)?

2. God provided for his people in abundance during their time in the wilderness. How did the people of Israel respond to this incredible act of grace (see verses 28–32)?

3. God is angry at the evil that ruins his children. How did he respond to the Israelites' sin? What pattern of behavior did the Israelites adopt toward God (see verses 33–37)?

4. God could have chosen to destroy the Israelites because of their repeated acts of rebellion against him. But what does the psalmist say that God did instead (see verses 38–39)?

5. Paul writes that God's wrath is poured out against godlessness and wickedness on earth. Why are people "without excuse" when it comes to their sin (see Romans 1:18–23)?

6. What did God do as a result of the sinful desires in people's hearts? What is "exchanged" when people decide to follow after sin instead of God (see verses 24–25)?

7. How do you respond to these passages about God's anger? Why is it necessary to first understand God's wrath toward sin in order to understand God's grace toward you?

Week 12: GOD TO THE RESCUE

I'm glad the letter wasn't sent from heaven. It came from my automobile insurance company . . . my *former* automobile insurance company. I didn't drop them; they dropped me. Not because I didn't pay my premiums; I was on time and caught up. Not because I failed to do the paperwork; every document was signed and delivered. I was dropped for making too many mistakes.

Which is odd. I bought the insurance to cover my mistakes. But then I got dropped for making mistakes. Hello. Did I miss something? Did I fail to see a footnote? Did I skip over some fine print in the contract? Did I overlook a paragraph that read, "We, the aforesaid company, will consider one Max Lucado insurable until he shows himself to be one who needs insurance, upon which time his coverage ceases"?

Isn't that like a doctor only treating healthy patients? Or a dentist hanging a sign in the window that says, "No cavities, please." Or a teacher penalizing a student for asking too many questions? What if the fire department said it would protect you until you had a fire?

Or what if, perish the thought, heaven had limitations to its coverage? What if you got a letter from the Pearly Gate Underwriting Division that read:

Dear Mrs. Smith,

I'm writing in response to this morning's request for forgiveness. I'm sorry to inform you that you have reached your quota of sins. Our records show that, since employing our services, you have erred seven times in the area of greed and your prayer life is substandard when compared to others of like age and circumstances.

Further review reveals that your understanding of doctrine is in the lower 20th percentile and you have excessive tendencies to gossip. Because of your sins, you are a high-risk candidate for heaven. You understand that grace has its limits. Jesus sends his regrets and kindest regards and hopes that you will find some other form of coverage.

Many fear receiving such a letter. Some worry they already have! If an insurance company can't cover my honest mistakes, can I expect God to cover my intentional rebellion?

Paul answers that question with what Anglican priest and theologian John Stott called "the most startling statement in Romans."[8] God "makes even evil people right in his sight" (Romans 4:5 NCV). What an incredible claim!

Think about it. It's one thing to make good people right, but those who are evil? We can expect God to justify the decent, but the dirty? Surely, coverage is provided for the driver with the clean record, but the speeder? The ticketed? The high-risk client? How in the world can justification come for the evil?

It can't. It can't come from the world. Humanity has inflated its balloon with its own hot air and not been able to leave the atmosphere. The conclusion is unavoidable: self-salvation simply does not work. Humans have no way to save themselves.

But Paul announces that *God has a way*. Where man fails, God excels. Salvation comes from heaven downward, not from earth upward. "A new day *from* heaven will dawn upon us" (Luke 1:78 NCV, emphasis added). "Every good action and every perfect gift is *from* God" (James 1:17 NCV, emphasis added). Please note: salvation is God-given, God-driven, God-empowered, and God-originated. The gift is not from humans to God. It is from God to humans.

At this point, we may be tempted to put conditions on grace. *We can be forgiven for certain sins, but not for others.* Or, *Yes, I can see where so-and-so might make it into heaven, but her?* Such attitudes fly in the face of God's infinite grace. Moreover, they ignore biblical truths that, apart from Christ, we are all equally guilty before a holy God. We *all* have sinned and fallen short of God's standard (see Romans 3:23). In heaven's economy, nobody is better off than anybody else. We all have a massive sin debt that only Jesus has the ability to pay.

Holiness demands that sin be punished. Mercy compels that the sinner be loved. How can God do both? Paul reveals the answer: "God [reconciled] the world to himself in Christ, not counting people's sins against them. . . . God made him who had no sin to be sin for us, so that in him we might become the righteousness of God" (2 Corinthians 5:19, 21). The perfect record of Jesus was given to you, and your imperfect record was given to Christ.

As a result, God's holiness is honored and his children are forgiven. By Jesus' perfect life, he fulfilled the commands of the law. By his death, he satisfied the demands of sin. Jesus suffered not *like* a sinner but *as* a sinner. Why else would he cry, "My God, My God, why have You forsaken Me?" (Matthew 27:46 NKJV). When God sent Jesus as a sacrifice or substitute for our sins, he put grace in motion. Simply put, the cost of our sins is infinitely more than we can pay. Grace must come to our rescue—in the person of Jesus Christ.

This may very well be the most difficult spiritual truth for us to embrace. For some reason, people accept Jesus as Lord before they accept him as Savior. It's easier to comprehend his power than his mercy. We'll celebrate the empty tomb long before we'll kneel at the cross.

Deep down, we often believe that what Jesus has done for us is too good to be true. All of us at times wonder if we're overextended our "credit line" with God. The vast majority of people simply state, "God may give grace to you, but not to me. You see, I've charted the waters of failure. I've pushed the envelope too many times. I'm not your typical sinner, I'm guilty of _____." And they fill in the blank.

But Paul states, "Since we have been made right with God by our faith, we have peace with God. This happened through our Lord Jesus Christ, who through our faith has brought us into that blessing of God's grace that we now enjoy. And we are happy because of the hope we have of sharing God's glory. We also have joy with our troubles, because we know that these troubles produce patience. And patience produces character, and character produces hope. And this hope will never disappoint us, because God has poured out his love to fill our hearts" (Romans 5:1–5 NCV).

The phrase "brought us into" in the Greek means "to usher into the presence of royalty." Christ meets us outside the throne room, takes us by the hand, and walks us into the presence of God. There we find grace, not condemnation; mercy, not punishment. Where we would never be granted an audience with the King, we are now welcomed into his presence.

THE HEART OF THE MATTER

- Apart from Christ, all are equally guilty before a holy God.
- Grace came to your rescue in the person of Jesus Christ.
- Grace means that your past is forgiven and forgotten.
- Jesus takes you by the hand and ushers you into God's presence.

MEMORY VERSES

Your verses to memorize for this unit are Ephesians 2:8–9. Take a few moments to review these verses, and then write them out from memory in the space below.

The Heart of Jesus

Levi was not a popular man. At least not among those of good society. Folks distrusted him, avoided him, cast suspicious glances his way. They were afraid of the power he held, and they hated him for it. Such was the life of a tax collector. Levi was not alone, though. He had his own circle of friends—thugs, prostitutes, outcasts, and others the Jews had branded as "sinners."

Then one day, Jesus popped in while Levi was at work and said, "Follow me" (Luke 5:27). For a moment, Levi wondered if he had heard correctly. Everyone knew Jesus was a righteous man. Not the sort to have anything to do with tax collectors. But the invitation had been extended, and he would follow. In return, Levi extended an invitation of his own.

"Levi held a great banquet for Jesus at his house, and a large crowd of tax collectors and others were eating with them" (verse 29). All good society was scandalized, but Jesus was unconcerned. He hadn't come for good society. He came so sinners could experience grace.

WEEKLY BIBLE STUDY

READ: 2 CORINTHIANS 5:16–21 AND ROMANS 3:21–26

1. Self-salvation does not work. Humans have no way to save themselves. *But God has a way.* What does Paul say that you have become because of Christ (see 2 Corinthians 5:17)?

2. Holiness demands that sin be punished. Mercy compels that the sinner be loved. How did God accomplish both by punishing sin yet loving the sinner (see verses 19, 21)?

3. God has reconciled you to himself through the sacrifice of Jesus. What mission has he now given to you? What role has he assigned to you (see verses 19–20)?

4. God has truly provided a way to make people right with him! What does Paul say is required on your part to receive this righteousness of God (see Romans 3:21–22)?

5. Paul states that there is "no difference between Jew and Gentile" when it comes to sin. Who does he say is eligible to receive God's redemption (see verses 22–24)?

6. What does it mean that "God presented Christ as a sacrifice of atonement" (verse 25)? What was God demonstrating by presenting Jesus as a sacrifice (see verse 26)?

7. Those who are reconciled with God are given the mission of helping others be reconciled with God. What are you actively doing to participate in this mission?

Week 13: THE ROYAL PAUPERS

One of the more incredible realizations that we can make about God's gift of grace is his timing. It wasn't after we changed that he loved us. It wasn't after we had been in church for ten years that he decided to love us. It wasn't after we had filled out all the applications, submitted three recommendations, and passed an extensive interview that he loved us. No, God loved us *while* we were still sinners. Incredible. He loved us without provocation. He treated us like royalty at a time when we were mere paupers.

My first ministry position was in Miami, Florida. In our congregation, we had more than our share of Southern ladies who loved to cook. I fit in well at the time because I was a single guy who loved to eat. The church was fond of having Sunday evening potluck dinners, and about once a quarter they *feasted*.

Some church dinners live up to the "potluck" name. The cooks empty the pot, and you try your luck with what you get. Not so with this church. Our potlucks were major events. Area grocery stores asked us to advise them in advance so they could stock their shelves. Cookbook sales went up. People never before seen in the pews could be found in the food line. For the women it was an unofficial cookoff, and for the men it was an unabashed pig-out.

My, it was good. Juicy ham bathed in pineapple, baked beans, pickled relish, pecan pie . . . (Oops, I just drooled on my computer keyboard.) Ever wondered why there are so many hefty preachers? You enter the ministry for meals like those.

As a bachelor, I counted on potluck dinners for my survival strategy. While others were planning what to cook, I was studying the storage techniques of camels. Knowing I should bring something, I would make it a point to raid my kitchen shelves on Sunday afternoon. The result was pitiful. One time, I took a half-empty jar of Planters Peanuts. Another time, I made a half-dozen jelly sandwiches. One of my better offerings was an unopened sack of chips. A more meager gift was a can of tomato soup, also unopened.

Wasn't much, but no one ever complained. In fact, the way those ladies acted, you would've thought that I brought the Thanksgiving turkey. They would take my jar of peanuts and set it on the long table with the rest of the food and hand me a plate. "Go ahead, Max, don't be bashful. Fill up your plate." And I would! Mashed potatoes and gravy. Roast beef. Fried chicken. I took a little bit of everything, except the peanuts.

I came like a pauper and ate like a king!

Though Paul never attended a potluck, he would have loved the symbolism. He would say that Christ does for us precisely what those women did for me. He welcomes us to his table by virtue of his love and our request. It is not our offerings that grant us a place at the feast; indeed, anything we bring appears puny at his table. Our admission of hunger is the only demand, for "blessed are those who hunger and thirst for righteousness" (Matthew 5:6).

Our hunger, then, is not a yearning to be avoided but rather a God-given desire to be heeded. Our weakness is not to be dismissed but to be confessed. This is at the heart of Paul's words when he writes, "At just the right time, when we were still powerless, Christ died for the ungodly. . . . While we were still sinners, Christ died for us" (Romans 5:6, 8).

The portrait that Paul paints of us is not pretty. We were "unable to help ourselves," "living against God," "sinners," and "God's enemies" (verses 6, 8, 10 NCV). Pitiful and pathetic, really. Yet we are the very people for whom Jesus died. We come to Christ as is—or we cannot come to him at all. He alone can change us into the people we were meant to be. We are wasting time when we try to "clean up our act" before we come to him.

Family therapist Paul Faulkner once told of a man who set out to adopt a troubled teenage girl. One would question the father's logic. The girl was destructive, disobedient, and dishonest. One day, she came home from school and ransacked the house looking for money. By the time he arrived, she was gone and the house was in shambles.

When the man's friends heard of her actions, they urged him not to finalize the adoption. "Let her go," they said. "After all, she's not really your daughter."

His response was simply, "Yes, I know. But I told her she was."[9]

God, too, has made a covenant to adopt his people. His covenant is not invalidated by our rebellion. It's one thing to love us when we are strong, obedient, and willing. But when we ransack his house and steal what is his? This is the test of love.

And God passes the test. "God demonstrates his own love for us in this: While we were still sinners, Christ died for us" (Romans 5:8).

The ladies at our church didn't see me and my peanuts and say, "Come back when you've learned to cook." The father didn't look at the wrecked house and say, "Come back when you've learned respect." And God didn't look at our frazzled lives and say, "I'll die for you when you deserve it."

Many of you know what it's like to carry a stigma. Each time your name is mentioned, your calamity soon follows.

"Have you heard from John lately? You know, the fellow who got divorced?"

"Sharon is in town. What a shame that she has to raise those kids alone."

"I saw Melissa today. I don't know why she can't keep a job."

Like a pesky sibling, our past follows us wherever we go. Isn't there anyone who sees us for who we are and not what we did? Yes. There is one who does. Our King. When God speaks of us, he doesn't mention our plight, pain, or problem. He calls us his children.

THE HEART OF THE MATTER

- God loved you even while you were still a sinner.
- You can never "clean up your act" before you come to God.
- Only Jesus can make you into the person you were meant to be.
- When God speaks of you, he calls you his child.

MEMORY VERSES

Your verses to memorize for this unit are Ephesians 2:8–9. Take a few moments to review these verses, and then write them out from memory in the space below.

The Heart of Jesus

She didn't belong in the home of that Pharisee. Simon was an upstanding Jew and his home the setting for a fine banquet. He was playing host to a virtual celebrity, and Simon wanted everything to go smoothly. But then *she* slipped into the house.

She interrupted the dinner conversation. She made heads turn. She caused whispers to relay around the room. This was "a woman in that town who lived a sinful life" (Luke 7:37). What was worse, this sinful woman began tearfully anointing the feet of his guest with perfume! How had she gotten in here? Simon was scandalized.

But Jesus was not scandalized. He wasn't shocked by her reputation. He wasn't put off by her emotional display—even after she began to kiss his feet and bathe them with her tears. Instead, Jesus reached out to this repentant sinner and said, "Your sins are forgiven" (verse 48). The woman left Simon's house with peace in her heart, having experienced the grace of Jesus.

WEEKLY BIBLE STUDY

READ: ROMANS 5:6–11 AND PSALM 103:9–14

1. One of the more incredible realizations that can be made about God's grace is his timing. What does Paul say about the timing of Jesus' death for you (see Romans 5:6)?

2. Paul writes that it's rare for someone to die for even a "good" person. So what does it say about God's love that he was willing to send Christ for sinners (see verses 7–8)?

3. God treated you like royalty at a time when you were a mere pauper. What does Paul say about your status now before him because of Jesus' sacrifice (see verses 9–11)?

4. It is human nature to slip up, make mistakes, and rebel against God. What does the psalmist write about how God treats you in spite of these tendencies (see Psalm 103:9–10)?

5. What does the psalmist write about the "height" of God's love for you? What does he say about the extent to which God has removed your sins (see verses 11–12)?

6. God is described throughout the Bible as a loving heavenly Father. How does the psalmist draw on this same image to describe God's compassion for you (see verses 13–14)?

7. How do the passages that you've read this week help you to understand your condition when Jesus rescued you? What do they tell you about God's grace toward you?

Week 14: HOW GRACE WORKS

Sometimes, I give away money at the end of a sermon. Not to pay the listeners (though some may feel they've earned it) but to make a point. I offer a dollar to anyone who will accept it. Free money. A gift. I invite anyone who wants the cash to come and take it.

The response is predictable. A pause. Some shuffling of feet. A wife elbows her husband, and he shakes his head. A teen starts to stand and then remembers her reputation. Finally, some courageous (or impoverished) soul says, "I'll take it!" The dollar is given, and the application begins. "Why didn't you take my offer?" I ask the rest.

Some say they were too embarrassed. The pain wasn't worth the gain. Others feared there was a catch. And then there are those whose wallets are fat. What's a buck to someone who has hundreds? Then the obvious follow-up question: "Why don't people accept Christ's free gift?" The answers are similar. Some are too embarrassed. To accept forgiveness is to admit sin, a step we are slow to take. Others fear a trick. Surely there is some fine print in the Bible. Others think, *Who needs forgiveness when you're as good as I am?*

Though grace is available to all, it is accepted by few. Many choose to sit and wait, while only a few choose to stand and trust. This leads us to a critical question from Paul: "How can we who died to sin go on living in it?" (Romans 6:2 NRSV). How can we who have been made right not live righteous lives? How can we who have been loved not love? How can we who have been blessed not bless? How can we who have been given grace not live graciously?

Paul seems stunned that an alternative would even exist! How could grace result in anything but gracious living? "Shall we go on sinning so that grace may increase? By no means!" (verses 1–2). We would scoff at such hypocrisy. We wouldn't tolerate it, and we wouldn't do it.

Or would we? Perhaps we don't sin *so* God can give grace, but do we ever sin *knowing* God will give grace? Do we ever compromise tonight, knowing we will confess tomorrow? But is that the intent of grace? Is God's goal to promote disobedience? Hardly. "Grace . . . teaches us not to live against God nor to do the evil things the world wants to do. Instead, that grace teaches us to live in the present age in a wise and right way and in a way that shows we serve God" (Titus 2:11–12 NCV). God's grace has released us from selfishness. Why return?

Think of it this way. Sin put us in prison. It locked us behind the bars of guilt, shame, deception, and fear. The only way we could be set free from that prison of sin was to serve its penalty. In this case, that penalty was death. We could not leave the prison unless there was a death—a death that occurred at Calvary. When Jesus died, we died to sin's claim on our lives.

Christ has taken our place and we are now set free. There is no need for us to remain in the cell. Ever heard of a discharged prisoner who wanted to stay? When the doors open, the prisoners leave. The thought of a person preferring jail over freedom doesn't compute. Once the penalty is paid, why live under bondage? We are discharged from the penitentiary of sin. So why, in heaven's name, would we ever want to set foot in that prison again?

Paul reminds us, "Our old life died with Christ on the cross so that our sinful selves would have no power over us and we would not be slaves to sin. Anyone who has died is made free from sin's control" (Romans 6:6–7 NCV). Paul is not saying that it is impossible for believers to sin. He is saying that it is stupid for believers to sin.

Not only has a price been paid, but a vow has been made. "Did you forget that all of us became part of Christ when we were baptized?" (Romans 6:3 NCV). Baptism was no casual, no ho-hum ritual. Baptism was, and is, "the pledge of a good conscience toward God" (1 Peter 3:21 CSB). What form of amnesia is this? Like a bride horrified to see her new husband flirting with women at the wedding reception, Paul asks, "Did you forget your vows?"

Indeed, baptism is a vow, a sacred vow of the believer to follow Christ. Just as a wedding celebrates the fusion of two hearts, baptism celebrates the union of sinner with Savior. We "became part of Christ when we were baptized" (Romans 6:3 NCV).

So who, in their right mind, would want to abandon these vows? Have we forgotten what life was like before our baptism? Have we forgotten the mess we were in before we were united with him?

Most of my life I've been a closet slob. I was slow to see the logic of neatness. Then I got married. Denalyn was so patient. She said she didn't mind my habits . . . if I didn't mind sleeping outside. Since I did, I began to change. By the time Denalyn's parents came to visit, I was a new man. I could go three days without throwing a sock behind the couch.

But then came the moment of truth. Denalyn went out of town for a week. Initially I reverted to the old man. I figured I'd be a slob for six days and clean on the seventh. But something strange happened—a curious discomfort. I couldn't relax with dirty dishes in the sink. When I saw an empty potato-chip sack on the floor I—hang on to your hat—bent over and picked it up! I actually put my bath towel back on the rack. What had happened to me?

I'd been exposed to a higher standard. Isn't that what has happened with us? Isn't that the heart of Paul's argument? How could we who have been freed from sin return to it?

Can a discharged prisoner return to confinement? Yes. But let him remember the gray walls and the long nights. Can a newlywed forget his vows? Yes. But let him remember his holy vow and his beautiful bride. Can a converted slob once again be messy? Yes. But let him consider the difference between the filth of yesterday and the purity of today.

Can one who has been given a free gift not share that gift with others? I suppose. But let him remember that all of life is a gift of grace. And let him remember that the call of grace is to live a gracious life. For that is how grace works.

THE HEART OF THE MATTER

- Grace is available to all yet accepted by few.
- God's grace has freed you from the prison of sin.
- Believers make a sacred vow to follow Christ.
- God gives you the desire to do what pleases him.

MEMORY VERSES

Your verses to memorize for this unit are Ephesians 2:8–9. Take a few moments to review these verses, and then write them out from memory in the space below.

The Heart of Jesus

The afternoon sun was getting lower in the sky. The workmen studied its slow descent with a sinking feeling. They had been sitting in the square all day, shifting their weight from foot to foot, scuffing their sandals in the dust, waiting. Unless someone came along soon with even the smallest request for work, they would have no money—and no food—to bring home.

When a prosperous farmer came into view, the spirits of the workers lifted. The man said that he would put the lot of them to work for the rest of the day. The workers figured that they wouldn't be able to earn much in these last few hours—a few shekels at best—but it was better than nothing. Gratefully, they joined the other workers in the fields.

At the day's end, they filed out of the fields past the owner with his money purse. It was then each man experienced an astonishing kindness. A *full day's* wage was placed in each hand. Even though they had arrived late and accomplished little, they experienced the fullness of grace (see Matthew 20:1–16).

WEEKLY BIBLE STUDY

READ: ROMANS 6:1–7 AND TITUS 2:11–15

1. Jesus offers an escape from the prison of sin. There is no need for his followers to remain in the cell. What questions does Paul ask his readers in light of this truth (see Romans 6:1–2)?

2. Baptism is a sacred vow of the believer to follow Christ. What does Paul remind his readers about the vow they took when they chose to follow Jesus (see verses 3–4)?

3. Paul states that believers have been united with Jesus in death. Given that the old self is crucified with Christ, how should that influence how you live (see verses 5–7)?

4. The intent of God's grace is never to promote disobedience. What does Paul say that God's grace teaches you to do and not to do (see Titus 2:11–12)?

5. What does Paul say is your hope as you continue to pursue godliness every day? Why is this important for believers to keep in mind as they go through their days (see verse 13)?

6. What does Paul remind his readers that Jesus' sacrifice has done for them? Why do you think he felt it necessary to stress this particular point (see verse 14)?

7. When it comes to God's grace, is there any area in your life where you are choosing to remain in the prison of sin? What step will you take this week to live in Jesus' freedom?

Week 15: SUFFICIENT GRACE

Imagine you are flying across the country in a chartered plane. All of a sudden, the engine bursts into flames, and the pilot rushes into in the cabin. "We're going to crash!" he yells. "We've got to bail out!" He hands out parachutes, gives a few pointers, and instructs everyone to stand in line as he throws open the door.

The first passenger steps up and shouts over the wind, "Is there any way that I could get a pink parachute?" The pilot shakes his head in disbelief. "Isn't it enough that I'm giving you a parachute at all?" The first passenger jumps.

The second steps to the door. "Please, Captain," he says, "I'm afraid of heights. Would you remove my fear?" The pilot again shakes his head. "No, I can't do that, but I can ensure that you will have a parachute for the fall."

Another pleads for a different strategy. "Couldn't you change the plans? Let's crash with the plane. We might survive." Exasperated, the pilot shouts, "You people don't understand! I've given you a parachute! That is enough!" Only one item was necessary for the jump, and he had provided it. The gift was adequate. But were the passengers content? No.

Too crazy to be possible? Maybe in a plane with pilots and parachutes, but not on earth with people and grace. God hears thousands of appeals per second. Some are legitimate. We, too, ask God to remove the fear or change the plans. Some of us ask for certainty and facts. We want to know all is going to work out the way we planned.

Some of us ask for the one thing we never get. We're not being demanding; we're just obeying the command to "present your requests to God" (Philippians 4:6). All we want is an open door or an answered prayer.

May I ask a very important question? *What if God says no?* What if the request is delayed or even denied? And when God does says no to you, how do you respond? If God says, "I've given you my grace, and that is enough," are you content?

Content . . . that's the word. A state of heart in which you would be at peace if God gave you nothing more than he already has. Test yourself with this question: What if God's only gift to you were his grace to save you? Would you be content? You beg him to save the life of your child. You plead with him to keep your business afloat. You implore him to remove the cancer from your body. What if his answer is "My grace is enough." Would you be content?

You see, from heaven's perspective, grace *is* enough. If God did nothing more than save us from hell, could we really complain? If God saved our souls and then left us to spend our lives leprosy-struck, would he be unjust? Having been given eternal life, dare we grumble at an aching body? Having been given heavenly riches, dare we bemoan earthly poverty?

Still, we wrestle with those times when God hears our appeals and replies, "My grace is sufficient for you." So did Paul. He knew the angst of unanswered prayer. At the top of his prayer list was an unidentified request that dominated his thoughts. He gave the appeal a code name: "a thorn in my flesh" (2 Corinthians 12:7). Perhaps the pain was too intimate to put on paper. Maybe the request was made so often he reverted to shorthand. Or it could be that by leaving the appeal generic, Paul's prayer could be our prayer. Don't we all have a thorn in the flesh?

Somewhere on life's path our flesh is pierced by a person or a problem. Our stride becomes a limp; our pace is slowed to a halt; we try to walk again only to wince at each effort. Finally, we plead with God for help. Such was the case with Paul. This was no casual request, no PS in a letter. It was the first plea of the first sentence. "Dear God, I need some help!"

Nor was this a superficial prickle. It was a "torment" to Paul (verse 7). Three different times he limped over to the side and pleaded with God to take it away. His request was clear, and so was God's response: "My grace is sufficient" (verse 9).

Experiencing Jesus is not a nirvana-like experience—oblivious or exempt from personal pain. In fact, pain is essential to experiencing the fullness of Jesus—his strength, his faithfulness, his comfort. The Bible teaches we are to share in the "fellowship of His sufferings" (Philippians 3:10 NKJV).

Pain was a central feature of Jesus' life—betrayal, heartache, suffering, and even death. It is one thing to go through pain alone. Jesus promises his fellowship—he's been down that road before. Those who have yet to go through the yaw and pitch of life have not tasted the sweet fellowship that results from experiencing these trying times with him.

Had God removed temptation, Paul might never have embraced God's grace. Only the hungry value a feast, and Paul was starving. The self-given title on his office door read, "Paul, Chief of Sinners." No pen ever articulated grace like Paul's. That may be because no person ever appreciated grace like Paul.

You wonder why God doesn't remove temptation from your life? If he did, you might lean on your strength instead of his grace. A few stumbles might be what you need to convince you: his grace is sufficient for your sin.

You wonder why God doesn't remove the enemies in your life? Perhaps because he wants you to love like he loves. Anyone can love a friend, but only a few can love an enemy. So what if you aren't everyone's hero? His grace is sufficient for your self-image.

You wonder why God doesn't heal you? He *has* healed you. If you are in Christ, you have a perfected soul and a perfected body. His plan is to give you the soul now and the body when you get home. He may choose to heal parts of your body before heaven. But if he doesn't, don't you still have reason for gratitude? His grace is sufficient for gratitude.

For all we don't know about thorns, we can be sure of this: God would prefer we have an occasional limp than a perpetual strut. And if it takes a thorn for him to make his point, he loves us enough not to pluck it out. He has every right to say no to us. We have every reason to say thanks to him. The parachute is strong and the landing will be safe. His grace is sufficient.

When we are hurting, it doesn't matter how much we know about doctrine or theology. What we really need to know is Jesus. To walk with him. Talk to him. Crawl into his lap and let him hold us for a while. Perhaps we'll never say, "Jesus is all I need" until he is all we have. At that moment, he will prove to be all we need and more.

THE HEART OF THE MATTER

- God will not always take away your troubles.
- From heaven's perspective, grace is enough.
- Pain is essential to experiencing the fullness of Jesus.
- The grace of God is truly all that you need.

MEMORY VERSES

This is it . . . one last review of your memory verses. Write out the words of Ephesians 2:8–9 from memory in the space below. Reflect on what these words mean to you.

The Heart of Jesus

Peter thought he was being generous. "Lord," he said to Jesus, "how many times shall I forgive my brother or sister who sins against me? Up to seven times?" (Matthew 18:21). The Jewish law stipulated that the wounded person forgive the offender three times. Peter was willing to double that amount and throw in one more for good measure. No doubt he thought that Jesus would be impressed. Jesus wasn't. "Seven! Hardly. Try seventy times seven" (verse 22 MSG). If we're pausing to multiply seventy times seven, we're missing the point. Keeping tabs on our mercy, Jesus is saying, is not being merciful. If we are calibrating the grace we extend to others, we're not being gracious. There should never be a point when our grace is exhausted.

WEEKLY BIBLE STUDY

READ: 2 CORINTHIANS 12:6–10 AND PSALM 34:15–22

1. Paul writes that his "boasting" was done with the intent of telling others what God had done for him. What does he say about these kinds of boasts (see 2 Corinthians 12:6)?

2. Paul had received "surpassingly great revelations" from God that could have caused him to become conceited. What does he say God gave him to prevent this (see verse 7)?

3. How did Paul respond when confronted with this issue in his life? What did the Lord reveal to Paul in response to his repeated requests (see verses 8–9)?

4. How did this "thorn in the flesh" that God did not take away affect Paul's "boasting" for Christ? What does Paul say is now his delight (see verses 9–10)?

5. When you are suffering, you want to know that God is aware of your trials and is with you. What does the psalmist write about God's attentiveness (see Psalm 34:15–18)?

6. What promise does God make to the righteous person who endures troubles? What does the psalmist say will happen to those who choose the path of wickedness (see verses 19–22)?

7. Think about some of the trials that you are enduring right now. Is it enough for you to know that God's grace is sufficient in that situation? Why or why not?

Unit 4

EXPERIENCING THE
FREEDOM OF JESUS

I fell asleep at the Louvre. The most famous museum in the world. The best-known building in Paris. Tourists are oohing and aahing, and that's me, nodding and snoring. Seated on a bench. Back to the wall. Chin to my chest. Conked out.

I should have been more like the fellow next to me. When I dozed off, he was transfixed on a seventeenth-century Dutch artist's rendering of a flower. When I awoke, the guy was still staring. I closed my eyes again. When I opened them, he hadn't moved.

I leaned toward him and tried to sound reflective. "Awesome, eh?" No response. "The shades are masterful." Still no reply. "Do you think it's a number painting?" He sighed and said nothing, but I knew what he was thinking. *Uncultured klutz.*

He's right. I was. But it wasn't my fault. I like seventeenth-century art as much as the next guy . . . well, maybe not that much. But at least I can usually stay awake.

But not that day. Why did I fall asleep at the Louvre? Blame it on the bags, baby; blame it on the bags. I was worn out from lugging the family luggage. I can't fault my wife and daughters. They learned it from me. I've never been one to travel light.

I've tried. Believe me, I've tried. But ever since I stuck three fingers in the air and took the Boy Scout pledge to be prepared, I've been determined to be exactly that—prepared.

Prepared for a bar mitzvah, baby dedication, or costume party. Prepared to parachute behind enemy lines or enter a cricket tournament. And if, perchance, the Dalai Lama might be on my flight and invite me to dine in Tibet, I carry snowshoes. One has to be prepared.

I don't know how to travel light.

Fact is, there's a lot about travel I don't know. I don't know how to interpret the restrictions of an airline supersaver seat—*half price if you leave on Wednesdays during duck-hunting season and return when the moon is full in a non-election year*. I don't know why they don't build the whole plane out of the same metal they use to build the little black box. I don't know how to escape the airplane toilet without sacrificing one of my extremities to the jaws of the folding door. And I don't know what to say to guys like the taxi driver in Rio who learned I was an American and asked me if I knew his cousin Eddie who lives in the US.

There's a lot about traveling I don't know.

I don't know why we men would rather floss a crocodile than ask for directions. I don't know why vacation pictures aren't used to treat insomnia, and I don't know when I'll learn not to eat food whose names I can't pronounce.

But most of all, I don't know how to travel light.

But I need to learn. You're wondering why I can't. *Loosen up!* you're thinking. *You can't enjoy a journey carrying so much stuff. Why don't you just drop all that luggage?* Funny you should ask. I'd like to inquire the same of you. Haven't you been known to pick up a few bags?

Odds are, you did this morning. Somewhere between the first step on the floor and the last step out the door, you grabbed some luggage. You stepped over to the baggage carousel and loaded up. Don't remember doing so? It's because you did it without thinking. Don't remember seeing a baggage terminal? That's because the carousel is not the one in the airport; it's the one in the mind. The bags we grab are not made of leather; they're made of burdens.

The suitcase of guilt. A sack of discontent. You drape a duffel bag of weariness on one shoulder and a hanging bag of grief on the other. Add on a backpack of doubt, an overnight bag of loneliness, and a trunk of fear. Pretty soon you're pulling more stuff than a skycap. No wonder you're so tired at the end of the day. Lugging luggage is exhausting.

What you were saying to me, God is saying to you. *Set that stuff down! You're carrying burdens you don't need to bear.* "Come to me," he invites, "all of you who are weary and carry heavy burdens, and I will give you rest" (Matthew 11:28 NLT).[10]

— **PRAYER** —

Dear Father, I don't know how to travel light. I go through my days burdened by doubts, fears, loneliness, and grief. Show me how to be free from these earthly cares. Throughout this week, teach me, Lord, to come to you. Teach me to unburden myself. Teach me to seek your rest. Amen.

— **MEMORY VERSE** —

"So if the Son sets you free, you are truly free."

JOHN 8:36 NLT

Week 16: THE LUGGAGE OF LIFE

To get an idea of the freedom found in Jesus Christ, imagine yourself donning the literal pieces of luggage (all overpacked) that were just described. You're carrying a suitcase of guilt in one hand and a sack of discontent in the other. There's a duffel bag of weariness slung over one shoulder and bag of grief on the other. A backpack of doubt is strapped on your back.

Let that mental picture linger for a moment. The exhaustion. The stretched muscles. The strain on your cramped fingers and your aching back. Now, imagine dropping each piece. Feel the release. Take in a deep breath. Finally, you are free!

If we let him, God will lighten our loads. But how do we let him? May I invite an old friend to show us? The Twenty-third Psalm. You know how it starts: "The LORD is my shepherd, I lack nothing. He makes me lie down in green pastures, he leads me beside quiet waters, he refreshes my soul. He guides me along the right paths for his name's sake" (verses 1–3).

Does a more beloved psalm exist? Framed and hung in hospital halls, scratched on prison walls, quoted by the young, and whispered by the dying. In these lines sailors have found a harbor, the frightened have found a Father, and strugglers have found a friend. It's been set to music in a hundred songs, translated into a thousand tongues, domiciled in a million hearts.

One of those hearts might be yours. What kinship do you feel with this psalm? Where do its verses transport you? To a fireside? Bedside? Graveside?

This passage is to the minister what balm is to the physician. I recently applied them to the heart of a dear friend. I was summoned to his house with the words, "the doctors aren't giving him more than a few days." I looked at him and understood. Face pale. Lips stretched and parched. Skin draping between bones like old umbrella cloth between spokes. The cancer had taken so much: his appetite, his strength, his days. But the cancer hadn't touched his faith. Pulling a chair to his bed and squeezing his hand, I whispered, "Bill, 'The Lord is my shepherd; I shall not want.'" He rolled his head toward me as if to welcome the words.

Reaching the fourth verse, fearful that he might not hear, I leaned forward until I was a couple of inches from his ear and said, "Even though I walk through the darkest valley, I will fear no evil, for you are with me; your rod and your staff, they comfort me." He didn't open his eyes, but he arched his brows. He didn't speak, but his thin fingers curled around mine. I wondered if the Lord was helping him set down some luggage: the fear of dying.

Do you think God might use David's psalm to lighten your load? Traveling light means trusting God with the burdens that you were never intended to bear. He wants to use you. But how can he use you if you are exhausted?

It reminds me of a time I was preparing for a jog but couldn't decide what to wear. The sun was out, but the wind was chilly. The sky was clear, but the forecast said rain. Jacket or sweatshirt? The Boy Scout within me prevailed. I wore both.

I needed to stay in touch with my kids, so I carried a cell phone. I worried that someone might steal my car, so I pocketed my keys. As a precaution against thirst, I brought along some drink money in a pouch. I looked more like a pack mule than a runner! Within half a mile, I was peeling off the jacket and hiding it in a bush. That kind of weight will slow you down.

What's true in jogging is true in faith. God has a great race for you to run. Under his care, you will go where you've never been and serve in ways you've never dreamed. But you will first have to drop some stuff. After all, how can you share grace with others if you are full of guilt? How can you offer comfort to someone in need if you are disheartened? How can you lift someone else's load if your arms are full with your own?

Have you ever considered the impact that excess baggage you are carrying has had on your relationships? We've made this point at our church by virtue of a drama.

A wedding is reenacted in which we hear the thoughts of the bride and groom. The groom enters, laden with luggage. A bag dangles from every appendage. And each bag is labeled: guilt, anger, arrogance, insecurities. This fellow is loaded. As he stands at the altar, the audience hears him thinking, *Finally, a woman who will help me carry all my burdens. She's so strong, so stable, so . . .*

As his thoughts continue, hers begin. She enters, wearing a wedding gown but, like her fiancé, is covered with luggage. Pulling a hanging bag, shouldering a carry-on, hauling a makeup kit, paper sack—everything you could imagine and everything labeled. She has her own bags: prejudice, loneliness, disappointments.

And her expectations? Just listen to what she is thinking: *Just a few more minutes and I've got a husband. No more counselors. No more group sessions. So long, discouragement and worry. I won't be seeing you anymore. He's going to fix me.*

They stand at the altar, lost in a mountain of luggage. They smile their way through the ceremony. But when given the invitation to kiss each other, they can't. Their arms are so full of bags that they can't embrace each other.

For the sake of the God you serve, travel light.

For the sake of those you love, travel light.

For the sake of your own joy, travel light.

There are certain weights in life you simply cannot carry. Your Lord is asking you to set them down and trust him. He is the father at the baggage claim. When a dad sees his five-year-old son trying to drag the family trunk off the carousel, what does he say? The father will say to his son what God is saying to you.

"Set it down, child. I'll carry that one."

What do you say we take God up on his offer? We just might find ourselves traveling a little lighter.

By the way, I may have previously overstated my packing problems. (I don't usually take snowshoes when I'm traveling.) But I can't overstate God's promise: "Throw the whole weight of your anxieties upon him, for you are his personal concern" (1 Peter 5:7 PHILLIPS).

THE HEART OF THE MATTER

- Jesus invites you to drop the baggage you try to carry through life.
- Give him the burdens you were never intended to bear.
- You cannot reach out to others if your hands are already full.
- Take Jesus up on his offer and learn how to travel light.

MEMORY VERSE

Take a few moments to review your Bible memory verse for this unit, and then write out the words of John 8:36 by heart in the space below.

The Heart of Jesus

Mary, like the rest, stood amazed at the appearance of Jesus in the room. She had been weeping since Friday, when news of his capture and trial had reached her. Her heart had been pierced at the sight of him, beaten almost beyond recognition. But a mother always knew her son. She had longed to run to his side, to clean the blood from his face and soothe his tattered back. She had wanted to stand between him and the Roman soldiers, to protect him from his executioners. When the nails had pierced his hands, she'd turned her eyes from the scene, but she'd stood her ground. She would not abandon her precious Son. Though it had broken her heart, she'd stayed nearby until he was gone. She had seen him die. Yet here he was, alive! And in his resurrection, she found freedom. She was free from the disapproval of the temple leaders, free from all her motherly worries about him, free from the sibling rivalries within her family, and free from the sorrow that had pierced her heart like a sword (see Luke 2:35).

WEEKLY BIBLE STUDY

READ: PSALM 23:1–3 AND LUKE 21:34–36

1. Traveling light means trusting God with the burdens you were never meant to bear. What does it mean for you to trust God as your "shepherd" (see Psalm 23:1)?

2. Shepherds lead their sheep into the "green pastures" where they can find nourishment and rest (see verses 2–3). How does your heavenly Shepherd do this for you?

3. Shepherds also guide their sheep "along the right paths" so they do not stray and get lost (see verse 3). How has your heavenly Shepherd guided you in life?

4. The baggage of life can weigh you down and impede you from pursuing God's plans. What does Jesus warn about "the anxieties of life" (see Luke 21:34)?

5. Jesus instructs his followers to stay focused on their mission as they wait for his return (see verses 34–35). Why is it so important for followers of Jesus to stay focused in this way?

6. What instruction does Jesus give his followers as it relates to the day of his return? For what are his followers to pray as they do this (see verse 36)?

7. For the sake of the God you serve . . . travel light. What kinds of "baggage" from your past do you sense that God is calling you to set down today?

Week 17: FREEDOM FROM WANT

Come with me to the most populated prison in the world. The facility has more inmates than bunks. More prisoners than plates. More residents than resources.

Come with me to the world's most oppressive prison. Just ask the inmates; they will tell you. They are overworked and underfed. Their walls are bare and bunks are hard.

Come with me to not only the most populated and oppressive prison but also the most permanent one. Most inmates never leave. They never escape. They never get released. They serve a life sentence in this over-crowded, under-provisioned facility.

The name of the prison? You'll see it over the entrance. Rainbowed over the gate are four cast-iron letters that spell out its name: W-A-N-T.

The prison of want. You've seen her prisoners. They are "in want." They want something. They want something bigger. Nicer. Faster. Thinner. They want. They don't want much, mind you. They want just one thing. One new job. One new car. One new house. One new spouse. They don't want much. They want just one.

They tell you that when they have that "one" thing, they will be happy. And they are right—they are happy. They leave the prison. But then it happens. The new-car smell passes. The new job gets old. The neighbors buy a larger television set. The new spouse has bad habits. The sizzle fizzles, and before you know it, another ex-con breaks parole and returns to jail.

Are you in the prison of want? You are if you feel better when you have more and worse when you have less. You are if joy is one delivery away, one transfer away, one award away, or one makeover away. If your happiness comes from something you deposit, drive, drink, or digest, then face it—you are in the prison of want.

That's the bad news. The good news is that you have a visitor. And your visitor has a message that can get you paroled. So make your way to the receiving room. Take your seat in the chair. Look across the table at the psalmist David. See him there? He is motioning for you to lean forward. "I have a secret to tell you," he whispers, "the secret of satisfaction. 'The LORD is my shepherd; I shall not want'" (Psalm 23:1 NKJV).

David has found the pasture where discontent goes to die. It's as if he is saying, "What I have in God is greater than what I don't have in life." Think for just a moment about the things you own. Think about the house you have, the car you drive, the money you've saved. Think about the jewelry you've inherited and the stocks you've traded and the clothes you've purchased. Envision all your stuff. Now let me remind you of two biblical truths.

First, your stuff isn't yours. Ask any funeral-home director. No one takes anything with him. When one of the wealthiest men in history, John D. Rockefeller, died, his accountant was asked, "How much did John D. leave?" The accountant's reply? "All of it."[11]

Second, all that stuff is not you. Who you are has nothing to do with the clothes you wear or the car you drive. Jesus said, "Life is not defined by what you have, even when you have a lot" (Luke 12:15 MSG). Heaven does not know you as the fellow with the nice suit or the woman with the big house or the kid with the new bike. Heaven knows your heart. "The LORD does not look at the things people look at. People look at the outward appearance, but the LORD looks at the heart" (1 Samuel 16:7). When God thinks of you, he may see your compassion, your devotion, your tenderness or quick mind, but he doesn't think of your things.

And when you think of you, you shouldn't either. Define yourself by your stuff, and you'll feel good when you have a lot and bad when you don't. Contentment comes when we can honestly say with Paul: "I have learned to be satisfied with the things I have. . . . I know how to live when I am poor, and I know how to live when I have plenty" (Philippians 4:11–12 NCV).

Doug McKnight could say those words. At the age of thirty-two, he was diagnosed with multiple sclerosis. Over the next sixteen years, it took his career, his mobility, and eventually his life. Because of the disease, he couldn't feed himself or walk. He battled depression and fear.

But Doug never lost his sense of gratitude. Evidence of this was seen in his prayer list. Friends asked him to compile a list of requests so they could intercede for him. His response included eighteen blessings for which to be grateful and six concerns for which to be prayerful. His blessings outweighed his needs by three times. Doug McKnight had learned to be content.[12]

Are you hoping that a change in circumstances will bring a change in your attitude? If so, you are in prison and you need to learn a secret of traveling light. *What you have in your Shepherd is greater than what you don't have in life.*

So, what is the one thing separating you from joy? How do you fill in this blank: "I will be happy when _____"? When I am healed. When I am promoted. When I am married. When I am single. When I am rich. How would you finish that statement?

If your ship never comes in, if your dream never comes true, if the situation never changes, can you be happy? If not, then you are sleeping in the cold cell of discontent. You are in prison. And you need to know what you have in your Shepherd.

Paul says that "godliness with contentment is great gain" (1 Timothy 6:6). When we surrender to God the cumbersome sack of discontent, we don't just give up something; we gain something. God replaces it with a lightweight, tailor-made, sorrow-resistant attaché of gratitude.

What will you gain with contentment? You may gain your marriage. You may gain precious hours with your children. You may gain your self-respect. You may gain joy. You may gain the faith to say, "The Lord is my shepherd; I shall not want."

Try saying it slowly. "The Lord is my shepherd; I shall not want."

Again, "The Lord is my shepherd; I shall not want."

Again, "The Lord is my shepherd; I shall not want."

Shhhhhhh. Did you hear something? I think I did.

I'm not sure . . . but I think I heard the opening of a jail door.

THE HEART OF THE MATTER

- *Want* is a prison with many inmates in our world today.
- You do not own the stuff you possess—and it does not define you.
- Don't wait for a change in circumstances to change your attitude.
- Gratitude is a sign of freedom from want and contentment in Christ.

MEMORY VERSE

Your verse to memorize for this unit is John 8:36. Take a few moments to review this verse, and then write it out from memory in the space below.

The Heart of Jesus

He had it made. His family was well-connected and well-to-do. His home was a showplace—marble floors, columned porches, airy upper rooms for entertaining, splashing fountains in the courtyard, and a staff of servants. He was bright, educated, well-liked, and respected. His neighbors admired him for his devotion to the Law and his righteous lifestyle. His behavior was beyond reproach. The community counted him as an upstanding citizen—courteous, dependable, and benevolent. What more could a young man want? So when the rich young ruler came before Jesus, his friends expected the Teacher to acknowledge the man's goodness, perhaps setting him up as an example. But instead, Jesus looked into his eyes and saw his discontentment. Jesus held out to the man an offer of freedom. There was just one change that needed to happen. He had but one thing to do. *Give it all away.* The house, the staff, the status, the money—it would all have to go. And with astonishment, the rich young ruler was confronted with his own lack of faith. Though it pained him, he turned and walked away, ashamed by his need to cling to earthly possessions (see Luke 18:18–25).

WEEKLY BIBLE STUDY

READ: LUKE 12:13–21 AND 1 TIMOTHY 6:6–10

1. Want is an overcrowded, oppressive, and often permanent prison. What warning did Jesus give the man who came to him with a request regarding his inheritance (see Luke 12:13–15)?

2. Jesus went on to tell a parable to the man who had approached him. What did the rich farmer in the story say to himself (see verses 16–17)?

3. What plans did the rich man develop to solve his storage problem? What were the motives of his heart in deciding to take this particular course (see verses 18–19)?

4. What did God say to the rich man when he heard about his plans and assessed his attitude? What was the moral of this story according to Jesus (see verses 20–21)?

5. God desires to give his children freedom from want. What does the apostle Paul say is "great gain"? With what should all God's followers be content (see 1 Timothy 6:6–8)?

6. What does Paul say are the dangers for those who want to get rich? What does he say happens to many of those who lust after money (see verses 9–10)?

7. What are your main takeaways from the passages you've studied this week about the dangers of desiring money? What would it look like in your life to be *content*?

Week 18: FREEDOM FROM HOPELESSNESS

I wonder if you could imagine yourself in a jungle. A dense jungle. A dark jungle. Your friends convinced you it was time for a once-in-a-lifetime trip, and here you are. You paid the fare. You crossed the ocean. You hired the guide and joined the group. And you ventured where you had never ventured before—into the thick, strange world of the jungle.

Sound interesting? Let's take it a step further. Imagine that you were in the jungle, lost and alone. You paused to lace your boot, and when you looked up, no one was near. You took a chance and went to the right; now you're wondering if the others went to the left. (Or did you go left and they go right?)

You have a problem. First, you were not made for this place. Drop you in the center of avenues and buildings, and you could sniff your way home. But here in sky-blocking foliage? You are out of your element. You weren't made for this jungle. Who could blame you for sitting on a log (better check for snakes first), burying your face in your hands, and thinking, *I'll never get out of here*. You have no direction, no equipment, no hope.

Can you freeze-frame that emotion for a moment? Can you sense, for just a second, how it feels to be out of your element? Out of solutions? Out of ideas and energy? Can you imagine, just for a moment, how it feels to be out of hope?

For many people, life is—well, life is a jungle. Not a jungle of trees and beasts. Would that it were so simple. Would that our jungles could be cut with a machete or our adversaries trapped in a cage. But our jungles are comprised of the thicker thickets of failing health, broken hearts, and empty wallets. Our forests are framed with hospital walls and divorce courts. We don't hear the screeching of birds or the roaring of lions, but we do hear the complaints of neighbors and the demands of bosses. Our predators are our creditors, and the brush that surrounds us is the rush that exhausts us.

It's a jungle out there.

And for some, even for many, hope is in short supply. Hopelessness is an odd bag. Unlike the others, it isn't full. It is empty, and its emptiness creates the burden. Unzip the top and examine all the pockets. Turn it upside down and shake it hard. The bag of hopelessness is painfully empty.

Not a very pretty picture, is it? Let's see if we can brighten it up. We've imagined the emotions of being lost; you think we can do the same with being rescued? What would it take to restore your hope? What would you need to reenergize your journey?

Though the answers are abundant, three come quickly to mind. The first would be a *person*. Not just any person. You don't need someone equally confused. You need someone who knows the way out. And from him you need some *vision*. You need someone to lift your spirits. You need someone to look you in the face and say, "This isn't the end. Don't give up. There is a better place than this. And I'll lead you there."

And, perhaps most important, you need *direction*. If you have only a person but no renewed vision, all you have is company. If he has a vision but no direction, you have a dreamer for company. But if you have a person with direction—who can take you from this place to the right place—ah, then you have one who can restore your hope.

Have you ever met someone like the type of person we just described? David has. And in his words, this person "restores my soul." David, of course, is talking about his Shepherd. Our Shepherd. He majors in restoring hope to the soul. Whether you are a lamb lost on a craggy ledge or a city slicker alone in a deep jungle, everything changes when your rescuer appears.

Your loneliness diminishes, because you have fellowship.

Your despair decreases, because you have vision.

Your confusion begins to lift, because you have direction.

You still haven't left the jungle. The trees still eclipse the sky and the thorns still cut the skin. Animals lurk and rodents scurry. The jungle is still a jungle. It hasn't changed, but you have. You have changed because you have hope. And you have hope because you have met someone who can lead you out.

Your Shepherd knows that you were not made for this place. He knows you are not equipped for this place. So he has come to guide you out. He has come to restore your soul. He is the perfect one to do so.

The story is told of a man on an African safari deep in the jungle. The guide had a machete and was whacking away the thick underbrush. The traveler, wearied and hot, asked in frustration, "Where are we? Do you know where you are taking me? Where is the path?!" The seasoned guide stopped and looked back at the man and replied, "I am the path."

We ask the same questions, don't we? We ask God, "Where are you taking me? Where is the path?" And he, like the guide, doesn't tell us. Oh, he may give us a hint or two, but that's all. If he did, would we understand? Would we comprehend our location? No, like the traveler, we are unacquainted with this jungle. So rather than give us an answer, he gives us a far greater gift. He gives us Jesus.

We often think freedom in the midst of a trial translates as having the answers we need. Instead, God offers all the Jesus we need to get through the trial.

We all need that reminder. For all of us need hope at some point in our lives.

Some of us don't need it right now. Our jungle has become a meadow and our journey a delight. If such is the case, congratulations. But remember—we do not know what tomorrow holds. We do not know where this road will lead. We could be one turn from a cemetery, from a hospital bed, from an empty house. We may be one bend in the road from a jungle. And though we might not need our hope restored today, we may need to restored tomorrow. So we need to know to whom to turn.

Or perhaps you do need hope today. You know you were not made for this place. You know you are not equipped. You want someone to lead you out. If so, call out for your Shepherd. He knows your voice. And he's just waiting for your request.

THE HEART OF THE MATTER

- For many people in the world today, life is a jungle.
- Jesus gives you hope because he knows the way you should go.
- Jesus, your Shepherd, has come to guide you through life.
- God offers all the Jesus you need to get through the trial.

MEMORY VERSE

Your verse to memorize for this unit is John 8:36. Take a few moments to review this verse, and then write it out from memory in the space below.

The Heart of Jesus

Peter faced the growing crowds, waiting for the milling mob to settle down enough so that he would be heard. He should be fighting butterflies in his stomach. Here he was, an uneducated fisherman, ready to address this great assembly. He was no orator. No scholar. No learned man. He had no training. No prior experience. His hands were used to pulling at oars and hefting nets. He could gut a fish, hoist an anchor, and trim a sail—but this? Even so, Peter stood calmly. He was no slave to the doubts that tried to plague his mind. He was free in Christ. Nothing would turn him away from telling these people the good news. So Peter cleared his throat and lifted his voice. The crowds fell into rapt silence as the words poured out over them. Words of life. Words of hope. Words of salvation. An invitation to freedom (see Acts 2).

WEEKLY BIBLE STUDY

READ: LAMENTATIONS 3:19–25 AND ROMANS 5:1–5

1. Jeremiah is believed to have written Lamentations after the Israelites were exiled from their homeland. What does he remember about that time (see Lamentations 3:19–20)?

2. Jeremiah writes that his soul was "downcast" when he considered what had happened to his people. But in what was he able to find hope (see verses 21–22)?

3. What does Jeremiah say is the nature of God's mercies and compassions? What did Jeremiah resolve to do because of his hope in God (see verses 23–25)?

4. Jesus has come to restore your soul. What does Paul say that you have because of your faith in Christ? What can you now "boast" about (see Romans 5:1–2)?

5. Paul often endured what could only be described as *hopeless* situations in which his very life was in peril. What does Paul say about these sufferings (see verses 3–4)?

6. Paul states that God used his sufferings to ultimately produce hope in his life. What does Paul say about this hope that he now has gained (see verse 5)?

7. What situations are causing you to lose hope right now? How might God be using those situations to develop perseverance, character, and hope within you?

Week 19: FREEDOM FROM FEAR

It's the expression of Jesus that puzzles us. We've never seen his face like this. Jesus smiling, yes. Jesus weeping, absolutely. Jesus stern, even that. But Jesus anguished? Cheeks streaked with tears? Face flooded in sweat? Rivulets of blood dripping from his chin?

The Bible I carried as a child contained a picture of Jesus in the garden of Gethsemane. His face was soft, hands calmly folded as he knelt beside a rock and prayed. Jesus seemed peaceful. One reading of the Gospels disrupts that image. Mark says Jesus "fell to the ground" (Mark 14:35). Matthew tells us that Jesus was "sorrowful and troubled . . . to the point of death" (Matthew 26:37–38). According to Luke, Jesus was "in anguish" (Luke 22:44).

What do we do with this image of Jesus? Simple. We turn to it when we look the same. We read it when we feel the same. We read it when we feel afraid. For isn't it likely that fear is one of the emotions Jesus felt? One might even argue that fear was the primary emotion. He saw something in the future so fierce and foreboding that he begged for a change of plans.

What causes you to pray this prayer? Boarding an airplane? Public speaking? Driving on a highway? The source of your fear may seem small to others. But to you, it freezes your feet, makes your heart pound, and brings blood to your face.

That's what happened to Jesus. He was so afraid that he bled. Doctors describe this condition as *hematidrosis*. Severe anxiety causes the release of chemicals that break down the capillaries in the sweat glands. When this occurs, sweat comes out tinged with blood.

Jesus was more than anxious; he was afraid. Isn't it remarkable to discover that Jesus felt such fear? But how kind that he told us about it. We tend to do the opposite. Gloss over our fears. Cover them up. Keep our sweaty palms in our pockets, our nausea and dry mouths a secret. Not so with Jesus. We see no mask of strength. But we do hear a request for strength.

"Father, if you are willing, take away this cup of suffering" (Luke 22:42 NCV). The first one to hear Jesus' fear is his Father. He could have gone to his mother. He could have confided in his disciples. He could have assembled a prayer meeting. All would have been appropriate, but none were his priority. He went *first* to his Father.

We tend to go everywhere else. First to the bar, to the counselor, to the self-help book or the friend next door. Not Jesus. The first one to hear his fear was his Father in heaven.

David did the same. He could make the claim "I will fear no evil" because he knew where to look. "You are with me; your rod and your staff, they comfort me" (Psalm 23:4). Rather than turn to the other sheep, David turned to the Shepherd. Rather than stare at the problems, he stared at the rod and staff. He knew where to look.

I know a fellow who has a fear of crowds. When encircled by large groups, his breath grows short, panic surfaces, and he begins to sweat like a sumo wrestler in a sauna. He received some help, curiously, from a golfing buddy. The two were at a movie theater, waiting to enter, when the fear struck. The crowd closed in like a forest. His buddy told him to take a few deep breaths. Then he helped manage the crisis by reminding him of the golf course.

"When you are hitting your ball out of the rough, and you are surrounded by trees, what do you do?"

"I look for an opening."

"You don't stare at the trees?"

"Of course not. I find an opening and focus on hitting the ball through it."

"Do the same in the crowd. When you feel the panic, don't focus on the people; focus on the opening." Good counsel in golf. Good counsel in life. Rather than focus on the fear, focus on the solution. That's what Jesus did. That's what David did. And that's what the writer of Hebrews urges us to do. "Let us run with endurance the race that is set before us, looking unto Jesus, the author and finisher of our faith" (Hebrews 12:1–2 NKJV).

The author of Hebrews speaks of a runner and a forerunner. The forerunner is Jesus, the "author and finisher of our faith." He is the author—that is to say, he wrote the book on salvation. And he is the finisher—he not only charted the map but also blazed the trail. He is the forerunner, and we are the runners. And we runners are urged to keep our eyes on Jesus.

The counsel of the Hebrew epistle is that we remain "looking unto Jesus." What was the focus of David? "You are with me; your rod and your staff, they comfort me." The discovery of David is indeed the message of Scripture—the Lord is with us. And, since the Lord is near, everything is different. Everything!

You may be facing death, but you aren't facing death alone; the Lord is with you. You may be facing unemployment, but you aren't facing unemployment alone; the Lord is with you. You may be facing marital struggles, but you aren't facing them alone; the Lord is with you. You may be facing debt, but you aren't facing debt alone; the Lord is with you.

Underline these words: you are not alone. Your family may turn against you, but God won't. Your friends may betray you, but God won't. You may feel alone in the wilderness, but you are not. He is with you. And because he is, everything is different. You are different.

Don't avoid life's gardens of Gethsemane. Enter them. Just don't enter them alone. And while there, be honest. Pounding the ground is permitted. Tears are allowed. And if you sweat blood, you won't be the first. Do what Jesus did; open your heart.

And be specific. Jesus was. "Take this cup," he prayed. Give God the number of the flight you fear. Tell him the length of the speech. Share the details of the job transfer. He has plenty of time. He also has plenty of compassion. He doesn't think your fears are foolish or silly. He won't tell you to "buck up" or "get tough." He's been where you are. He knows how you feel.

And he knows what you need. That's why we punctuate our prayers as Jesus did. "If you are willing . . ." Was God willing? Yes and no. He didn't take away the cross, but he took away the fear. God didn't still the storm, but he calmed the sailor.

Who's to say he won't do the same for you? So don't measure the size of the mountain; talk to the one who can move it. Instead of carrying the world on your shoulders, talk to the one who holds the universe on his. Hope is a look away.

Now, what were you looking at?

THE HEART OF THE MATTER

- *Fear* is one of the emotions Jesus felt in the garden of Gethsemane.
- Jesus went *first* to his heavenly Father in the face of his fears.
- Keep your eyes on Jesus when fears surround you in your life.
- Remember that God is always with you in every fearful situation.

MEMORY VERSE

Your verse to memorize for this unit is John 8:36. Take a few moments to review this verse, and then write it out from memory in the space below.

The Heart of Jesus

The was nothing for Paul to be proud of when he considered his past. He'd tried to root the "heresy" of Christianity out of the land. He'd badgered men and women into confessions. He'd separated families, burned down homes, infiltrated churches, and brought charges against countless individuals. He'd turned households over to the authorities and seen Christians fined, persecuted, imprisoned, and killed. He was a Pharisaical bounty hunter, obsessed with catching his prey. Christians spoke of him in whispers and feared the very sound of his name. But then Paul met the risen Jesus on one of his outings to destroy the church— and everything changed. He became the tender Christian father to dozens of churches he planted throughout the known world. Jesus had forgiven Paul, and Paul was able to do the work of the ministry, unburdened by his past and the guilt and shame it held. He left those cares at Jesus' feet and kept his eyes firmly on the prize that lies ahead. Paul had experienced the freedom of Jesus (see Acts 9).

WEEKLY BIBLE STUDY

READ: LUKE 22:39–45 AND PSALM 23:4–6

1. Luke describes Jesus' state of mind in the garden of Gethsemane right before he was arrested. Why had Jesus gone there (see Luke 22:39–41)?

2. Jesus instructed his disciples to pray and then went a "stone's throw" beyond to pray himself. What impassioned plea did he make to his heavenly Father (see verses 41–42)?

3. The image of Jesus that Luke relates is not one of peaceful serenity. What detail does Luke add that describes the depth of Jesus' anguish (see verse 44)?

4. David also knew what it meant to be afraid at times. How does he describe fear? What does he acknowledge about God in spite of his fears (see Psalm 23:4)?

5. What does David say about God's provision even in the midst of fearsome enemies? What does God do for those who come to him with their fears (see verse 5)?

6. Don't avoid life's gardens of Gethsemane. Enter them. Just don't enter them alone! What does David say will happen when you do this (see verse 6)?

7. Jesus went *first* to his heavenly Father when he was feeling anxiety and fear. How will you follow Christ's example? What fears and anxieties will you take to your heavenly Father?

Week 20: FREEDOM FROM SHAME

See the fellow in the shadows? That's Peter. Peter the apostle. Peter the impetuous. Peter the passionate. He once walked on water. Stepped right out of the boat onto the lake. He'll soon preach to thousands. But tonight he has hurried into hiding. The one who will speak with power is weeping in pain. Bawling. His howl echoing in the Jerusalem night. What hurts more? The fact that he did it? Or the fact that he swore he never would?

One of the next times we see Peter interact with Jesus is on the shore of Lake Galilee. Peter is back in the fishing boat. We know why he goes to Galilee—he had been told the risen Christ would meet the disciples there. The arranged meeting place is not the sea, however, but a "mountain where Jesus had told them to go" (Matthew 28:16). No one told the disciples to go fishing, but that's what they did. Two years earlier, when Jesus called him to fish for men, he dropped his net. We haven't seen him fish since. So why now? Jesus had risen from the dead. Peter had seen the empty tomb. Who could fish at a time like this?

Were the disciples hungry? Perhaps that's the sum of it. Maybe the expedition was born out of growling stomachs. Or then again, maybe it was born out of a broken heart.

You see, Peter could not deny his denial. The empty tomb did not erase the crowing rooster. Christ had returned, but Peter must have wondered, *After what I did, would he return for someone like me?* We've wondered the same. Rather than resist the flirting, we return it. Rather than ignore the gossip, we share it. Rather than stick to the truth, we shade it. And the rooster crows, the conviction pierces, and Peter has a partner in the shadows.

We weep as Peter wept, and we do what Peter did. We go back to our old lives. We return to our pre-Jesus practices. We do what comes naturally rather than what comes spiritually. And we question whether Jesus has a place for folks like us.

Jesus answers that question for you and all who tend to "Peter out" on Christ. His answer came on the shore of the sea in a gift to Peter. You know what Jesus did?

He invited Peter to breakfast. Jesus prepared a meal.

Of course, the breakfast was one special moment among several that morning. There was the great catch of fish and the recognition of Jesus. The plunge of Peter and the paddling of the disciples. And there was the moment they reached the shore and found Jesus next to a fire of coals. The fish were sizzling, the bread was waiting, and the defeater of hell and the ruler of heaven invited his friends to sit down and have a bite to eat.

If you find yourself awash in the whirlpool of sorrow, hiding in the shadows of shame, continually reliving your failures, Jesus' invitation is for you. He wants face time with you—not to scold you but to hold you. He wants you to come back to his heart. Let him set you free.

No one could have been more grateful than Peter. The one Satan had sifted like wheat was eating bread at the hand of God. Right there for the devil and his tempters to see, Jesus "prepared a table in the presence of his enemies." Okay, the Gospel writer didn't say it that way. But David did. "You prepare a table before me in the presence of my enemies" (Psalm 23:5 NKJV). What the shepherd did for the sheep sounds a lot like what Jesus did for Peter.

When David writes this line, it's as if his mind is lingering in the high country with the sheep. The shepherd, after guiding the flock through the valley to the lands with greener grass, has an added responsibility. He must "prepare" the pasture.

This is new land, so he must be careful. Ideally, the grazing area will be flat—a mesa or tableland. The shepherd searches for poisonous plants and ample water. He looks for signs of wolves, coyotes, and bears.

Of special concern is the adder, a small brown snake that lives underground. Adders are known to pop out of their holes and nip the sheep on the nose. The bite often infects and can even kill. As a defense against the snake, the shepherd pours a circle of oil at the top of each adder's hole.

He also applies the oil to the noses of the animals. The oil on the snake's hole lubricates the exit, preventing the snake from climbing out. The smell of the oil on the sheep's nose drives the serpent away. The shepherd, in a very real sense, has prepared the table.[13]

What if your Shepherd did for you what the shepherd did for his flock? Suppose he dealt with your enemy, the devil, and prepared for you a safe place of nourishment? What if Jesus did for you what he did for Peter? Suppose he, in the hour of your failure, invited you to a meal? What would you say if I told you he has done exactly that?

On the night before his death, "Jesus sent two of his followers and said to them, 'Go into the city and a man carrying a jar of water will meet you. Follow him. When he goes into a house, tell the owner of the house, "The Teacher says: Where is my guest room in which I can eat the Passover meal with my followers?" The owner will show you a large room upstairs that is furnished and ready. Prepare the food for us there'" (Mark 14:13–15 TEV).

Notice who did the "preparing" here. Jesus reserved a large room and arranged for the guide to lead the disciples. Jesus made certain the room was furnished and the food set out. What did the disciples do? They faithfully complied and were fed.

Not only that, but Jesus also dealt with the snakes. Remember that only one of the disciples didn't complete the meal that night. "The devil had already prompted Judas, the son of Simon Iscariot, to betray Jesus" (John 13:2). Judas started to eat, but Jesus didn't let him finish. On the command of Jesus, he left the room. "'What you are about to do, do quickly.' . . . As soon as Judas had taken the bread, he went out" (John 13:27, 30).

There is something dynamic in this dismissal. Judas was allowed to see the supper, but he wasn't allowed to stay there. *This table is for my children. You may tempt them. You may trip them. But you will never sit with them.* This is how much he loves us.

Lest there be any "Peters" who wonder if there is a place at the table for them, Jesus issued a tender reminder as he passed the cup.

"Drink from it, all of you" (Matthew 26:27). Those who feel unworthy, drink this. Those who feel ashamed, drink this. Those who feel embarrassed, drink this. Jesus has prepared a table for you.

THE HEART OF THE MATTER

- Your failures can leave you mired down in guilt and shame.
- Jesus calls you to come not for a scolding but to welcome you back.
- Jesus has dealt with your enemy and made a safe place for you.
- Jesus has prepared a place for you at his table and invites you to come.

MEMORY VERSE

This is it . . . one last review of your memory verse. Write out the words of John 8:36 from memory in the space below. Reflect on what these words mean to you.

The Heart of Jesus

They expected him to perform wonders. They expected him to tell stories. They expected him to put the uppity Pharisees in their place. They expected him to have all the answers. They expected him to give them bread when they were hungry. They expected him to heal their sick. They expected him to come when they called. They expected him to overthrow the Roman Empire. They expected him to become their king here on earth. Jesus didn't worry about those things. He never tried to live up to anyone's agenda. Jesus was free from the expectations of others. He kept his ear tuned to heaven and remained true to his Father's calling.

WEEKLY BIBLE STUDY

READ: LUKE 22:54–62 AND JOHN 21:4–19

1. Peter understood what it meant to feel the sting of shame. What was he doing as Jesus was being seized by the authorities and led to the home of the high priest (see Luke 22:54–55)?

2. Peter was quickly identified as being associated with Christ. How did he respond to the accusations of the servant girl and others who questioned him (see verses 55–60)?

3. Peter had vowed that he would never abandon Jesus. Now he was doing exactly that. What happened next that caused Peter to weep bitterly (see verses 61–62)?

4. Fortunately, this was not the end of the story for Peter. Later, we find him back fishing with the other disciples. What did Jesus instruct them to do (see John 21:4–6)?

5. What did Peter do when he realized that the Man calling out to them from the beach was the Lord? What did he see when he reached Jesus (see verses 7–9)?

6. It was Jesus who extended the invitation for restoration to Peter. What three questions did Jesus ask Peter? How did Peter respond (see verses 15–17)?

7. Jesus offers you the same freedom from shame that he offered to Peter. What burdens of guilt have you been carrying that you need to set at Jesus' feet today?

EXPERIENCING THE
JOY OF JESUS

No man had more reason to be miserable than this one—yet no man was more joyful. His first home was a palace. Servants were at his fingertips. The snap of his fingers changed the course of history. His name was known and loved. He had everything—wealth, power, respect.

And then he had nothing.

Students of the event still ponder it. Historians stumble as they attempt to explain it. How could a king lose everything in one instant?

One moment he was royalty; the next he was in poverty. His bed became, at best, a borrowed pallet—and usually the hard earth. He never owned even the most basic mode of transportation and was dependent on handouts for his income. He was sometimes so hungry that he would eat raw grain or pick fruit off a tree. He knew what it was like to be rained on, to be cold. He knew what it meant to have no home.

His palace grounds had been spotless; now he was exposed to filth. He had never known disease, but was now surrounded by illness.

In his kingdom he had been revered; now he was ridiculed. His neighbors tried to lynch him. Some called him a lunatic. His family tried to confine him to their house.

Those who didn't ridicule him tried to use him. They wanted favors. They wanted tricks. He was a novelty. They wanted to be seen with him—that is, until being with him was out of fashion. Then they wanted to kill him.

He was accused of a crime he never committed. Witnesses were hired to lie. The jury was rigged. No lawyer was assigned to his defense. A judge swayed by politics handed down the death penalty. He left as he came—penniless. He was buried in a borrowed grave, his funeral financed by compassionate friends. Though he once had everything, he died with nothing.

He should have been miserable. He should have been bitter. He had every right to be a pot of boiling anger. But he wasn't. He was joyful.

He was joyful when he was poor. He was joyful when he was abandoned. He was joyful when he was betrayed. He was even joyful as he hung on a tool of torture, his hands pierced with six-inch Roman spikes.

Jesus embodied a stubborn joy. A joy that refused to bend in the wind of hard times. A joy that held its ground against pain. A joy whose roots extended into the bedrock of eternity.

What type of joy is this? What is this cheerfulness that dares to wink at adversity? What is this bird that sings while it is still dark? What is the source of this peace that defies pain?

I call it sacred delight.

It is sacred because it is not of this earth. What is sacred is God's. And this joy is God's. It is delight because delight can both satisfy and surprise.

Sacred delight is good news coming through the back door of your heart. It's what you'd always dreamed but never expected. It's the too-good-to-be-true coming true. It's having God as your pinch-hitter, your lawyer, your dad, your biggest fan, and your best friend. God on your side, in your heart, out in front, and protecting your back. It's hope where you least expected it: a flower in life's sidewalk.

It's no accident that the same word used by Jesus to promise sacred delight is the word used by Paul to describe God: "The blessed God . . ." (1 Timothy 1:11); "God . . . who is blessed forever . . ." (2 Corinthians 11:31 NKJV); "God, the blessed and only Ruler . . ." (1 Timothy 6:15).

Think about God's joy. What can cloud it? What can quench it? What can kill it? Is God ever in a bad mood because of bad weather? Does God get ruffled over long lines or traffic jams? Does God ever refuse to rotate the earth because his feelings are hurt?

No. His is a joy that consequences cannot quench. His is a peace that circumstances cannot steal. There is a delicious gladness that comes from God. A holy joy. A sacred delight. And it is within your reach. You are one decision away from joy.[14]

— PRAYER —

Dear Father, help me to know the joy that is at the heart of Jesus. I know that the joy you give cannot be affected by circumstances, other people, or my own emotions. Show me how I can experience this same joy in my own life. Amen.

— MEMORY VERSE —

"Rejoice and be glad, because great is your reward in heaven."

MATTHEW 5:12

Week 21: SACRED DELIGHT

Delight is the Bethlehem shepherds dancing a jig outside a cave. Delight is Mary watching God sleep in a feed trough. Delight is white-haired Simeon praising God, who is about to be circumcised. Delight is Joseph teaching the Creator of the world how to hold a hammer.

Delight is the look on Andrew's face at the lunch pail that never came up empty. Delight is the dozing wedding guests who drank the wine that had been water. Delight is Jesus walking through waves as casually as you walk through curtains.

Delight is a leper seeing a finger where there had been only a nub . . . a widow hosting a party with food made for a funeral . . . a paraplegic doing somersaults. Delight is Jesus doing impossible things in crazy ways: healing the blind with spit, paying taxes with a coin found in a fish's mouth, and coming back from the dead disguised as a gardener.

What is sacred delight? It is God doing what the gods of the day would be doing only in people's wildest dreams—wearing diapers, riding donkeys, washing feet, dozing in storms. Delight is the day the critics accused God of having too much fun, attending too many parties, and spending too much time with the happy-hour crowd.

Sacred delight is the day's wage paid to workers who had worked only one hour . . . the father scrubbing the pig smell off his son's back . . . the shepherd throwing a party because a lost sheep had been found. Delight is a discovered pearl, a multiplied talent, a heaven-bound beggar, a criminal in the kingdom. Delight is the surprise on the faces of street folks who learned that they had been invited to a king's banquet. Delight is the Samaritan woman big-eyed and speechless, the adulteress walking out of the stone-cluttered courtyard, and a skivvy-clad Peter plunging into cold waters to get close to the one whom he had cursed.

The apostle John wrote, "See what great love the Father has lavished on us, that we should be called children of God!" (1 John 3:1). Certain things about God are easy for us to imagine. God creating the world and suspending the stars. God as almighty, all-powerful, and in control. We can fathom a God who knows us, made us, and even a God who hears us. But a God who has *lavished* love on us? A God who is crazy for us? A God who cheers for us?

But that is the message of the Bible. Our Father is relentlessly in pursuit of his children. He takes delight in us. He has called us home with his word, paved the path with his blood, and is longing for our arrival. God's love for his children is the message of the Bible.

Truly, it's difficult for us to imagine. Perhaps this is because it is so easy for us to just know *about* God without actually *knowing* him at all. We read the Bible and listen to sermons *about* God—which are good things. But unless we *experience* God and what it means to be in his presence, can we ever really *know* him? Experiencing God radically changes what we think we know about him. All it takes is hearing that first beat of his heart.

I remember experiencing this when I would go into the girls' playroom at the end of a busy day to write. I would sit in the stillness accompanied by the tap of a computer keyboard, the aroma of coffee, and the rhythm of the dishwasher. What was a playroom thirty minutes ago was now a study. And what was a study became a sanctuary. The quietness slowed my pulse, the silence opened my ears, and something sacred happened. The soft slap of sandaled feet broke the stillness, a pierced hand extended a quiet invitation, and I followed.

I wish I could say it happened every night. It doesn't. Some nights he would ask, but I wouldn't listen. Other nights he would ask, but I wouldn't go. But some nights I heard his poetic whisper, "Come to me, all you who are weary and burdened . . ." and I followed. I left behind the budgets, bills, and deadlines to walk the narrow trail up the mountain with him.

You've been there. You've escaped the sandy foundations of the valley and ascended his grand outcropping of granite. You've turned your back on the noise and sought his voice. You've stepped away from the masses and followed the Master as he led you up the winding path to the summit. *His* summit. Clean air. Clear view. Crisp breeze. The roar of the marketplace down there . . . the perspective of the peak up there.

Gently, your guide invited you to sit on the rock above the tree line and look out with him at the ancient peaks. "What is necessary is still what is sure," he would say to you. "Just remember: you'll go nowhere tomorrow that I haven't already been. Truth will still triumph. Death will still die. The victory is yours. And delight is one decision away—seize it."

The sacred summit. A place of permanence in a world of transition.

Think about the people in your world. Can't you tell the ones who have been to his mountain? Oh, their problems aren't any different. Their challenges are just as severe. But there is a stubborn peace that enshrines them. A confidence that life isn't toppled by unmet budgets or rerouted airplanes. A serenity that softens the corners of their lips. A contagious delight sparkling in their eyes. And in their hearts reigns a fortress-like confidence that the valley can be endured, even enjoyed, because the mountain is only a decision away.

I read recently about a man who had breathed the summit air. His trips up the trail began early in his life and sustained him to the end. A few days before he died, a priest went to visit him in the hospital. As the priest entered the room, he noticed an empty chair beside the man's bed. The priest asked him if someone had been by to visit.

The old man smiled. "I place Jesus on that chair," he said, "and I talk to him."

The priest was puzzled, so the man explained. "Years ago, a friend told me that prayer was as simple as talking to a good friend. So every day I pull up a chair, invite Jesus to sit, and we have a good talk."

Some days later, the daughter of the man came to the parish house to inform the priest that her father had just died. "Because he seemed so content," she said, "I left him in his room alone for a couple of hours. When I got back to the room, I found him dead. I noticed a strange thing, though: his head was resting, not on the pillow, but on an empty chair that was beside his bed."[15]

Learn a lesson from the man with the chair. Take a trip with the King to the mountain peak. It's pristine, uncrowded, and on top of the world. Stubborn joy begins by breathing deep up there before you go crazy down here.

THE HEART OF THE MATTER

- *Sacred delight* is an inner exuberance that comes from God.
- God the Father is in pursuit of his children and takes delight in them.
- There is no place you can go that God hasn't already been.
- Those who share the joy of Jesus have an unshakable peace.

MEMORY VERSE

Take a few moments to review your Bible memory verse for this unit, and then write out the words of Matthew 5:12 by heart in the space below.

The Heart of Jesus

The woman followed the men who carried her son's body. Mourners wailed all around her, filling the air with mournful shrieks she couldn't bring herself to make. She was alone now. Bereft. Her husband had died years ago, and she had no other children. How would she survive? Suddenly, she realized the procession had stopped. She looked around. What was going on? Then she saw the cause of the interruption—a man was making his way through the crowd. She didn't think she knew him—not a neighbor or an acquaintance. But then he spoke and touched her son. She gasped as she watched her son take a breath and then sit up. She ran to him as the men lifted him from the pallet—then danced for sheer joy (see Luke 7:11–17).

WEEKLY BIBLE STUDY

READ: NEHEMIAH 8:9–17 AND PSALM 16:5–11

1. When the exiled Israelites returned home and heard the words of the book of the law, they started to weep. What did Nehemiah instruct them to do (see Nehemiah 8:9–10)?

2. Nehemiah understood this was a day to be joyful in what the Lord had done and not a day to mourn over the past. How did the people respond (see verses 11–12)?

3. The exiled Israelites were able to once again celebrate the Festival of Booths in their homeland. What was the result of their celebrating this festival (see verse 17)?

4. King David often took delight in God's presence. How does he describe the Lord? What does he say about the "boundary lines" that God had given to him (see Psalm 16:5–6)?

5. David praised the Lord for his counsel and vowed to always keep his eyes on God (see verses 7–8). How did knowing that God was always with him make him feel (see verses 9–11)?

6. God invites you to take a trip with him to the mountain peak—a sacred summit where you can experience his presence. How are you taking up God on that offer?

7. As you look at your life today, what reasons do you have to be joyful in the Lord? How will you determine to praise God in spite of your circumstances?

Week 22: GOD'S GLADNESS

It is sacred delight that Jesus promises in the Sermon on the Mount. *Nine times* he promises it. And he promises it to an unlikely crowd.

"The poor in spirit" (Matthew 5:3). Beggars in God's soup kitchen.

"Those who mourn" (verse 4). Sinners Anonymous bound together by the truth of their introduction: "Hi, I am me. I'm a sinner."

"The meek" (verse 5). Pawnshop pianos played by Van Cliburn. (He was so good that no one noticed the missing keys.)

"Those who hunger and thirst" (verse 6). Famished orphans who know the difference between a TV dinner and a Thanksgiving feast.

"The merciful" (verse 7). Winners of the million-dollar lottery who share the prize with their enemies.

"The pure in heart" (verse 8). Physicians who love lepers and escape infection.

"The peacemakers" (verse 9). Architects who build bridges with wood from a Roman cross.

The "persecuted" (verse 10). Those who manage to keep an eye on heaven while walking through hell on earth.

It is to this band of pilgrims that God promises a special blessing. A heavenly joy. A sacred delight. But this joy is not cheap. What Jesus promises is not a gimmick to give us goose bumps nor a mental attitude that has to be pumped up at pep rallies. No, what Jesus is describing is God's radical reconstruction of the heart. Observe the sequence.

First, we recognize we are in need (we're poor in spirit). Next, we repent of our self-sufficiency (we mourn). We surrender control to God (we're meek). So grateful are we for his presence that we yearn for more of him (we hunger and thirst). We recognize God alone will fill our cavernous needs, trust him to do it, and rejoice when he does it. As we grow closer to him, we become more like him. We forgive others (we're merciful). We change our outlook (we're pure in heart). We love others (we're peacemakers). We endure injustice (we're persecuted).

What we call the Beatitudes, the text of Jesus' words in Matthew 5:3–16, is not a list of proverbs nor a compilation of independent sayings. Rather, it is a step-by-step description of how God rebuilds the believer's heart.

The first step is to ask for help—to become "poor in spirit" and admit our need for a Savior. The next step is sorrow: "Blessed are those who mourn." Those who mourn are those who know they are wrong and say they are sorry. No excuses. No justification. Just tears.

The first two steps are admittance of inadequacy and repentance for pride. The next step is the one of renewal: "Blessed are the meek. " Realization of weakness leads to the source of strength—God. And renewal comes when we become meek—when we give our lives to God to be his tool. The first two beatitudes pass us through the fire of purification; the third places us in the hands of the Master.

The result of this process? Courage: "They will inherit the earth." No longer shall the earth and its fears dominate us, for we follow the one who dominates the earth. This leads to joy: "Rejoice and be glad, because great is your reward in heaven" (verse 12).

Fear is the thief of joy.

Back in the late 1800s, there was man whose name stirred fear in people's hearts as the desert wind stirs tumbleweeds. He terrorized the Wells Fargo stage line for years, roaring like a tornado in and out of the Sierra Nevadas, spooking the most rugged frontiersmen. In journals from San Francisco to New York, his name became synonymous with the danger of the frontier. During his reign of terror between 1875 and 1883, he is credited with stealing the bags and the breath away from twenty-nine different stagecoach crews.

And he did it all without firing a shot. His weapon was his reputation. His ammunition was intimidation. A hood hid his face. No victim ever saw him. No artist ever sketched his features. No sheriff could ever track his trail. He never fired a shot or took a hostage.

He didn't have to. His presence was enough to paralyze.

Black Bart. A hooded bandit armed with a deadly weapon.

He reminds us of another thief. You know him. You've never seen his face, either, and couldn't describe his voice or sketch his profile. But when he's near, you know it in a heartbeat.

If you've ever been in the hospital, you've felt the leathery brush of his hand against yours. If you've ever sensed someone was following you, you've felt his cold breath down your neck. If you've awakened late at night in a strange room, it was his husky whisper that stole your slumber. You know him.

It was this thief who left your palms sweaty as you went for the job interview. It was this con man who convinced you to swap your integrity for popularity. And it was this scoundrel who whispered in your ear as you left the cemetery, "You may be next."

Fear is the Black Bart of the soul. He doesn't want your money. He doesn't want your diamonds. He won't go after your car. He wants something far more precious. He wants your peace of mind—your joy. His task is to take your courage and leave you timid and trembling. His modus operandi is to manipulate you with the mysterious, to taunt you with the unknown.

Fear of death, fear of failure, fear of God, fear of tomorrow—his arsenal is vast. His goal? To create cowardly, joyless souls.

If you are in Christ, the promises that God makes to you in his Word are not only a source of joy but are also a foundation of true courage. You are guaranteed that your sins will be filtered through, hidden in, and screened out by the sacrifice of Jesus. When God looks at you, he doesn't see you; he sees the one who surrounds you. This means that failure is not a concern for you. Your victory is secure. How could you not be courageous?

Here is where the journey of joy begins to take shape: having the courage to believe God has forgiven you and wants to bestow joy on your life. Receiving his sacred delight begins with accepting his complete and total salvation.

THE HEART OF THE MATTER

- Joy is the result of a radical reconstruction of your heart.
- The more you allow God to change you, the greater your joy will be.
- Fear is an enemy of the soul that will try to steal your joy away.
- Joy begins with having the courage to believe that you are forgiven.

MEMORY VERSE

Your memory verse for this unit is Matthew 5:12. Take a few moments to review this verse, and then write it out from memory in the space below.

The Heart of Jesus

The two men set a quick pace, talking with each other about the events that had transpired over the past few days. They were eager to get out of Jerusalem and to the town of Emmaus, where they could put everything that had happened behind them. Along the way they were joined by a third traveler, and they quickly struck up a conversation with him.

They began with the usual small talk, but the conversation soon turned to the Passover feast in Jerusalem. The two men were depressed and sullen. They spoke with the third man about the execution of Jesus and the downfall of their hopes that the Messiah had finally come. The third man then questioned them about their understanding of Jesus' teachings and his subsequent death. Surprisingly, the traveler was well acquainted with the Scriptures and began to draw fascinating comparisons between the requirements of Messiah and the life of Jesus.

When they reached Emmaus, the two travelers begged their companion to join them for a meal to finish their discussion. Their hearts were being stirred with something akin to hope, and they wanted to see where it would lead. Suddenly, the two from Emmaus felt a stirring of understanding—of recognition—that this stranger was Jesus himself! And with this sudden illumination, all their previous glumness evaporated into shining joy (see Luke 24:13–35).

WEEKLY BIBLE STUDY

READ: MATTHEW 5:1–12 AND DEUTERONOMY 31:1–8

1. Jesus' Sermon on the Mount can be seen as a step-by-step description of how God rebuilds a believer's heart. What are the first two steps in this process (see Matthew 5:3–4)?

2. The first two steps are admittance of inadequacy and repentance for pride. What is the third step? What is the result of this three-step process (see verse 5)?

3. What does it mean to "hunger and thirst" for righteousness? What does Jesus say about those who are merciful, who are pure in heart, and who make peace (see verses 6–9)?

4. What is the ultimate promise for those who choose to follow God's rebuilding plan? What kind of reward does Jesus say they will obtain (see verses 3, 10, 12)?

5. Fear is the thief of joy. What fears did Moses try to allay when he told the Israelites he would not be accompanying them into Canaan (see Deuteronomy 31:1–8)?

6. What promise and command did Moses then make to the people? What did he say to Joshua, his successor, in the presence of the people (see verses 6–8)?

7. What do you sense God is leading you to do this week as it relates to hungering and thirsting for his righteousness? Where do you need more godly courage in your life?

Week 23: THE STATE OF THE HEART

I can still remember the first time I saw one. I had gone to work with my dad—a big thrill for a ten-year-old whose father worked in the oil fields. The countryside was flat and predictable, boasting nothing taller than pumpjacks and windmills. Maybe that is why the thing seemed so colossal. It stood out on the horizon like a science-fiction city.

My dad told me it was a refinery—a jungle of pipes and tanks and tubes and generators. It looked like a giant Tinker Toy set. I soon learned the function of that maze of machinery is defined by its name: it *refines*. Gasoline, oil, chemicals—the refinery takes whatever comes in and purifies it so that it's ready to go out.

The refinery does for petroleum and other products what your "heart" should do for you. It takes out the bad and utilizes the good. We tend to think of the heart as the seat of emotion. We speak of "heartthrobs," "heartaches," and "broken hearts." But when Jesus said "Blessed are the pure in heart" (Matthew 5:8), he was speaking in a different context.

To Jesus' listeners, the heart was the totality of the inner person—the control tower and flight deck. The heart was thought of as the seat of character—the origin of desires, affections, perceptions, thoughts, reasoning, imagination, conscience, intentions, purpose, will, and faith.

Thus a proverb admonished, "Above all else, guard your heart, for everything you do flows from it" (Proverbs 4:23). To the Hebrew mind, the heart was a freeway cloverleaf where all emotions and prejudices and wisdom converged. It was a switch house that received freight cars loaded with moods, ideas, emotions, and convictions and put them on the right track.

The heart is the center of the spiritual life. If the fruit of a tree is bad, you don't try to fix the fruit; you treat the roots. And if a person's actions are evil, it's not enough to change habits; you have to go deeper. You have to go to the heart of the problem, which is the problem of the heart. That is why the state of the heart is so critical. What's the state of yours?

When someone barks at you, do you bark back or bite your tongue? That depends on the state of your heart.

When your schedule is too tight or your to-do list too long, do you lose your cool or keep it? That depends on the state of your heart.

When you are offered a morsel of gossip marinated in slander, do you turn it down or pass it on? That depends on the state of your heart.

Do you see the homeless person on the street as a burden on society or as an opportunity for God? That, too, depends on the state of your heart.

The state of your heart dictates whether you harbor a grudge or give grace, seek self-pity or seek Christ, drink human misery or taste God's mercy.

Jesus' statement rings true: "Blessed are the pure in heart, for they will see God" (verse 8). Note the order of this beatitude: first, purify the heart, and then you will see God. We usually reverse the order. We try to change the inside by altering the outside.

We do it all the time. A young woman battles with depression. What is the solution suggested by some well-meaning friend? Buy a new dress. A husband is involved in an affair that brings him as much guilt as it does adventure. What is his solution? Change peer groups. Hang out with people who don't make you feel guilty! A young professional is plagued with loneliness. His obsession with success has left him with no friends. His boss gives him an idea: Change your style. Get a new haircut. Flash some cash.

Case after case of treating the outside while ignoring the inside—polishing the case while ignoring the interior. What is the result?

The young woman gets a new dress, and the depression disappears . . . for a day, maybe. Then the shadow returns. The husband finds a bunch of buddies who sanction his adultery. The result? Peace . . . until the crowd is gone. Then the guilt is back. The young professional gets a new look and the people notice . . . until the styles change. Then he has to scurry out and buy more stuff so he won't appear outdated.

The exterior polished; the interior corroding. The outside altered; the inside faltering. One thing is clear: cosmetic changes are only skin-deep.

By now you could write the message of the Beatitude. It's a clear one: you change your life by changing your heart. Jesus gave the plan for changing your heart on the mountainside. Back away from the Beatitudes once more and view them in sequence.

The first step is an admission of poverty: "Blessed are the poor in spirit . . ." God's gladness is not received by those who earn it but by those who admit they don't deserve it.

The second step is sorrow: "Blessed are those who mourn . . ." Joy comes to those who are sincerely sorry for their sin. They discover gladness when they leave the prison of pride and repent of their rebellion.

Sorrow is followed by meekness. The meek are those who are willing to be used by God. Amazed that God would save them, they are just as surprised that God could use them. They are a junior-high-school clarinet section playing with the Boston Pops. They don't tell the maestro how to conduct; they're just thrilled to be part of the concert.

The result of the first three steps? Hunger. Never have you seen anything like what is happening! You admit sin—you get saved. You confess weakness—you receive strength. You say you are sorry—you find forgiveness. It's a zany, unpredictable path full of pleasant encounters. For once in your life you're addicted to something positive—something that gives you life instead of draining it. And you want more. Then comes mercy. The more you receive, the more you give. You find it easier to give grace because you realize you have been given so much. What has been done to you is nothing compared to what you did to God.

For the first time in your life, you have found a joy that is not dependent on your whims and actions. It's a joy from God, a joy no one can take away from you.

A sacred delight is placed in your heart. It is sacred because only God can grant it. It is a delight because you would never expect it. And though your heart isn't perfect, it isn't rotten. And though you aren't invincible, at least you're plugged in. And you can bet that he who made you knows just how to purify you—from the inside out.

THE HEART OF THE MATTER

- The heart is where your thoughts, desires, and faith are found.
- The state of your heart dictates how you will act toward others.
- You can change your life by allowing God to change your heart.
- He who made you knows how to purify you—from the inside out.

MEMORY VERSE

Your memory verse for this unit is Matthew 5:12. Take a few moments to review this verse, and then write it out from memory in the space below.

The Heart of Jesus

He had followed every tradition. He had met every requirement. His clothes fit every standard of stylish righteousness, right down to the long, blue, tasseled fringe that dusted the ground as he walked. He attended morning and evening prayers faithfully. He had memorized great portions of the Scriptures. He engaged in rousing discussions of the law of Moses with his colleagues. He had been elected to the ruling leaders of the faith. People nodded respectfully whenever he passed by, and he was used to being given preference wherever he went. Yet the words of Jesus had stung Nicodemus deeply. He and his associates had been reprimanded—called a brood of vipers and whitewashed tombs. How had Jesus known of his emptiness? His restlessness? His dissatisfaction? Though he kept up appearances, Nicodemus knew no joy. So he had arranged to meet this traveling Teacher discreetly. Under cover of darkness, he plied Jesus with all his questions. And Nicodemus was astonished to discover that not only did Jesus hold all the answers he sought, but he also promised him joy (see John 3:1–21).

WEEKLY BIBLE STUDY

READ: MATTHEW 15:10–20 AND 1 SAMUEL 16:4–8

1. Jesus spoke of the heart as being the seat of character and the center of spiritual life. What does Jesus say about the heart as it relates to your words (see Matthew 15:10–11)?

2. The Jewish religious leaders (the Pharisees) were offended at Jesus' remarks about the state of their hearts. What did Jesus say about them (see verses 12–14)?

3. Peter asked Jesus to explain the parable that he had just given them. What further insights does Jesus reveal about the heart (see verses 15–20)?

4. The anointing of David reveals that God is more interested in the heart than outward appearances. What prompted Samuel to seek out David (see 1 Samuel 16:1)?

5. What concerns did Samuel have about anointing one of Jesse's sons to be the next king of Israel? What course did the Lord tell Samuel to take (see verses 2–5)?

6. When Samuel arrived in Bethlehem and saw Jesse's impressive oldest son, he thought surely God would anoint him as king. But what did God say (see verses 6–7)?

7. As you consider the passages you've studied, how would you describe the state of *your* heart? What steps do you need to take to be more of a person after *God's* heart?

Week 24: THE KINGDOM OF THE ABSURD

The kingdom of heaven. Its citizens are drunk on wonder. Consider Sarai. She is in her golden years, but God promises her a son. She visits the maternity shop. She plans her shower and remodels her tent. But no son. She eats a few birthday cakes and goes through a decade of wall calendars . . . but still no son.

Finally, fourteen years later, when her husband, Abram, is pushing a century of years and she ninety . . . when the wallpaper in the nursery is faded and the baby furniture out of date . . . when the topic of the promised child brings tears and long looks into a silent sky . . . God pays them a visit and tells them they had better select a name for their new son.

Abram and Sarai have the same response: laughter. They laugh partly because it is too good to happen and partly because it might. They laugh because they have given up hope. They laugh at the lunacy of it. Abram looks at Sarai—snoring in her rocker, head back and mouth wide open, as fruitful as a pitted prune and just as wrinkled. And he cracks up. He tries to contain it, but he can't. He has always been a sucker for a good joke.

Sarai is just as amused. When she hears the news, a cackle escapes before she can contain it. She mumbles something about her husband needing a lot more than what he's got and then laughs again. They laugh because that is what you do when someone says he can do the impossible. They laugh a little at God, and a lot with God—for God is laughing, too. Then, with the smile still on his face, God gets busy doing what he does best—the unbelievable.

We need to see people like Sarai and Abram, who have been through the stuff of life and come out rejoicing at the wonder of God. These flesh-and-blood examples inspire us. They help us realize it is possible to make the decision for joy despite the odds against us.

People like Beverly Sills. Even though she was an incredibly talented singer, she went unrecognized for years. Prestigious opera circles closed their ranks when she tried to enter. American critics ignored her compelling voice. She was repeatedly rejected for parts for which she easily qualified. It was only after she went to Europe and won the hearts of tough-to-please European audiences that Stateside opinion leaders acknowledged her talent.

Not only was her professional life a battle, but her personal life was also marked by challenges. She was the mother of two children with disabilities, one of whom had a severe mental disability. Years ago, in order to escape the pace of New York City, she purchased a home on Martha's Vineyard. It burned to the ground two days before she was to move in.

Professional rejection. Personal setbacks. Perfect soil for the seeds of bitterness. A receptive field for the roots of resentment. But in this case, anger found no home. Her friends didn't call her bitter; they called her "Bubbles." How could a person handle such professional rejection and personal trauma and still be known as "Bubbles"?

"I choose to be cheerful," she said. "Years ago I knew I had little or no choice about success, circumstances, or even happiness; but I knew I could choose to be cheerful."

Or people like Glyn. Her husband, Don, sat in the chair next to her. It had been a year since Glyn and Don had first learned of Glyn's condition—amyotrophic lateral sclerosis (Lou Gehrig's disease). The cause and the cure remain a mystery. But the result doesn't. Muscle strength and mobility steadily deteriorate, leaving only the mind and the faith.

The three of us had come together to plan a funeral—hers. And now, with that task done, Glyn spoke. "We have prayed for healing. God has not given it. But he has blessed us. He has given us strength we did not know. He gave it when we needed it and not before."

I wondered what it would be like to have my life taken from me at age forty-five. I wondered what it would be like to say goodbye to my children and spouse. I wondered what it would be like to be a witness to my own death. "God has given us peace in our pain. He covers us all the time. Even when we are out of control, he is still there."

It was the coming together of Glyn's mind and faith that caused me to realize I was doing more than planning a funeral. I was beholding holy jewels she had quarried out of the mine of despair. "We can use any tragedy as a stumbling block or a steppingstone. I hope this will not cause my family to be bitter. I hope I can be an example that God is wanting us to trust in the good times and the bad. For if we don't trust when times are tough, we don't trust at all."

Don held her hand. He wiped her tears. He wiped his own.

Who are these two? I asked myself as I watched him touch a tissue to her cheek. *Who are these, who, on the edge of life's river, can look across with such faith?* The moment was solemn and sweet. I said little. One is not bold in the presence of the sacred.

Or people like Robert Reed. He had cerebral palsy. His hands were twisted and his feet useless. He couldn't feed or bathe himself. He couldn't brush his teeth, comb his hair, or put on his underwear. His shirts were held together by strips of Velcro. His speech was labored. The condition had kept him from driving a car, riding a bike, and going for a walk.

But it hadn't kept him from graduating from high school or attending Abilene Christian University, from which he graduated with a degree in Latin. Having cerebral palsy didn't keep him from teaching at a St. Louis junior college or from venturing overseas on five mission trips. And his condition didn't prevent him from becoming a missionary in Portugal.

I went to hear Robert speak one time. I watched other men carry him in his wheelchair onto the platform. I watched them lay a Bible in his lap. I watched his stiff fingers force open the pages. And I watched people in the audience wipe away tears of admiration from their faces.

Robert could have asked for sympathy or pity, but he did just the opposite. He held his bent hand up in the air and boasted, "I have everything I need for joy."

The jewel of joy is given to the impoverished spirits, not the affluent. God's delight is received upon surrender, not awarded upon conquest.

Those who taste God's presence have declared spiritual bankruptcy and are aware of their spiritual crisis. Their cupboards are bare. Their pockets are empty. Their options are gone.

Oh, the irony of God's delight—born in the parched soil of destitution rather than the fertile ground of achievement.

THE HEART OF THE MATTER

- God brings joy by doing what he does best—the unbelievable.
- You can choose to be joyful even when the odds are against you.
- God has given you everything that you need for joy.
- God's gift of delight is given to those who know they are needy.

MEMORY VERSE

Your memory verse for this unit is Matthew 5:12. Take a few moments to review this verse, and then write it out from memory in the space below.

The Heart of Jesus

Peter's feet pounded the dust of the path. When he and John had started out, they had speculated about the strange news that the women had brought. *The body was gone.* Could the Roman soldiers have taken their Lord away? *An angel's announcement.* Could Jesus really be alive again? What if it were true! At that thought, John had picked up his pace. Peter's enthusiasm equaled John's, but he couldn't match the younger man's speed. When he did finally catch up, he saw John puffing outside the entrance to the tomb. The stone certainly had been rolled away. Peter barreled through the door and slid to a stop before the stone shelf. The wrappings were there, undisturbed, but they were empty! Soldiers wouldn't have taken such care if they had stolen Jesus' body. Maybe the women were right! Then a heavenly light struck their eyes, and they, too, received angelic confirmation. Jesus was alive! Though he had just run to the tomb, joy gave Peter's feet wings for the return trip (see John 20:1–10).

WEEKLY BIBLE STUDY

READ: GENESIS 21:1–7 AND PSALM 126:1–6

1. The kingdom of heaven . . . its citizens are drunk on wonder. What remarkable promise did God fulfill in the lives of Abraham and Sarah (see Genesis 21:1–2)?

2. The name that Abraham gave to the newborn was *Isaac*, which in Hebrew means "he laughs." How did Sarah indicate this was an appropriate name (see verses 3–6)?

3. Abraham was "a hundred years old" when Isaac was born (verse 5). Sarah was ninety. What did she say about the absurdity of what God had done (see verse 7)?

4. Sacred delight is born in the soil of destitution. The Israelites who returned after the exile experienced this delight. How did the psalmist describe this moment (see Psalm 126:1)?

5. The Israelites who had been taken into exile had endured much grief and loss. What does the psalmist say they were experiencing now (see verses 2–3)?

6. What does the psalmist say about "sowing" with weeping and tears? What type of harvest does he say the Lord had produced for the people (see verses 4–6)?

7. What are some of the more unbelievable—and even downright absurd—things that God has done in your life? How did those moments bring you joy?

Week 25: THE APPLAUSE OF HEAVEN

I'm almost home. After five days, four hotel beds, eleven restaurants, and twenty-two cups of coffee, I'm almost home. After eight airplane seats, five airports, two delays, one book, and 513 packages of peanuts, I'm almost home. The plane resonates under me. A baby cries behind me. Businessmen converse around me. Cool air blows from a hole above me. But all that matters is what is before me—home.

Home. There is a leap of the heart as I exit the plane. I almost get nervous as I walk up the ramp. I step past people. I grip my satchel. My stomach tightens. My palms sweat. I walk into the lobby like an actor walking onto a stage. The curtain is lifted, and the audience stands in a half-moon. Most of the people see that I'm not the one they want and look past me.

But from the side, I hear the familiar shriek of two little girls. "Daddy!" I turn and see them—faces scrubbed, standing on chairs, bouncing up and down in joy as the man in their life walks toward them. Jenna stops bouncing just long enough to clap. She applauds! I don't know who told her to do that, but you can bet I'm not going to tell her to stop. Faces of home.

That is what makes the promise at the end of the Beatitudes so compelling: "Rejoice and be glad, because great is your reward in heaven" (Matthew 5:12). What is our reward? Home. A heavenly reward for obedience to Christ!

The book of Revelation could be titled the book of Homecoming, for in it we are given a picture of our heavenly home. In this final mountaintop encounter, God pulls back the curtain and allows the warrior to peek into the homeland. When John is given the task of writing down what he sees, he chooses the most beautiful comparison earth has to offer. The Holy City, John says, is like "a bride beautifully dressed for her husband" (21:2).

A bride. A commitment robed in elegance. "I'll be with you forever." Tomorrow bringing hope to today. Promised purity faithfully delivered. When you read that our heavenly home is similar to a bride, tell me, doesn't it make you want to go home? When you look at this world, stained by the curse of sin, doesn't it make you want to go home?

John tells us that when we get home, God "will wipe every tear" from our eyes (verse 4). When I was a young man, I had plenty of people to wipe away my tears. I had two big sisters who put me under their wings. I had a dozen or so aunts and uncles. I had a mother who worked nights as a nurse and days as a mother—exercising both professions with tenderness. I even had a brother three years my elder who felt sorry for me occasionally.

But when I think about someone wiping away my tears, I think about Dad. His hands were callused and tough, his fingers short and stubby. And when my father wiped away a tear, he seemed to wipe it away forever. There was something in his touch that took away more than the drop of hurt from my cheek. It also took away my fear.

God will wipe away your tears. The same hands that stretched the heavens will touch your cheeks. The same hands that formed the mountains will caress your face. The same hands that curled in agony as the

Roman spike cut through will someday cup your face and brush away your tears. Forever. When you think of a world where there will be no reason to cry, ever, doesn't it make you want to go home?

"There will be no more death" John declares (verse 4). Can you imagine it? A world with no hearses or morgues or cemeteries or tombstones? A world with no spades of dirt thrown on caskets? No names chiseled into marble? No funerals? No black dresses? No black wreaths?

In the next world, John says, "goodbye" will never be spoken.

The most hopeful words of that passage from Revelation are those of God's resolve: "I am making everything new" (verse 5). It's hard to see things grow old. The town in which I grew up is growing old. I was there recently. Some of the buildings are boarded up. Some of the houses are torn down. Some of my teachers are retired; some are buried.

I wish I could make it all new again. I wish I could blow the dust off the streets. I wish I could walk through the familiar neighborhood, and wave at the familiar faces, and pet the familiar dogs, and hit one more home run in the Little League park. I wish I could walk down Main Street and call out the merchants that have retired and open the doors that have been boarded up.

I wish I could make everything new . . . but I can't.

But God can. "He restores my soul" (Psalm 23:3 NKJV). He doesn't reform; he restores. He doesn't camouflage the old; he restores the new. The Master Builder will pull out the original plan and restore it. He will restore the vigor. He will restore the energy. He will restore the hope. He will restore the soul.

When you see how this world grows stooped and weary and then read of a home where everything is made new, tell me, doesn't that make you want to go home?

And what would you give in exchange for a home like that? Would you really rather have a few possessions on earth than eternal possessions in heaven? Would you really choose a life of slavery to passion over a life of freedom? Would you honestly give up all of your heavenly mansions for a second-rate, sleazy motel on earth?

Jesus said, "Great is your reward in heaven" (Matthew 5:12). He must have smiled when he said that line. His eyes must have danced, and his hand must have pointed skyward. For he should know. It was his idea. It was his home.

Experiencing the joy of Jesus makes us different. Knowing what we know, and seeing what we've seen, it just doesn't make sense for us to choose fleeting moments of earthly pleasures over eternal joy. It is no longer appealing to grow bitter over our hurts instead of better. We find ourselves where the Beatitudes said we would be—hungry for more of Jesus.

You may not have noticed it, but you are closer to home than ever before. Each moment is a step taken. Each breath is a page turned. Each day is a mile marked, a mountain climbed. You are closer to home than you've ever been. Before you know it, your appointed arrival time will come; you'll descend the ramp and enter the Holy City. You'll see faces that are waiting for you. You'll hear your name spoken by those who love you. And, maybe, just maybe—in the back, behind the crowds—the one who would rather die than live without you will remove his pierced hands from his heavenly robe and applaud.

THE HEART OF THE MATTER

- Heaven is the reward for those who remain faithful to God.
- The promise of heaven in the future brings joy in the here and now.
- Heaven is a place of rejoicing—for there will be no more death.
- The promise of heaven should make you hungry for more of Jesus.

MEMORY VERSE

This is it . . . one last review of your memory verse. Write out the words of Matthew 5:12 from memory in the space below. Reflect on what these words mean to you.

The Heart of Jesus

The cell was unpleasant—dank, musty, and infested. The soldiers who had shackled Paul and Silas had not been especially gentle. The heavy chains prevented them from finding a comfortable position in which to rest. The evening's chill was seeping through the walls. With aching muscles and weary heads, the two men faced a long night of darkness. But Paul was not a man to wallow in his circumstances. He was not beaten down and hopeless. In the midst of the prison cell in Philippi, he and Silas lifted up prayers to their Savior. And when God met them there in the cell, they experienced such joy that their surroundings faded away. Ushered into worship, the two rusty voices took up a tune, and soon the whole prison was filled with songs of praise to Jesus. Paul and Silas sang for the joy of their salvation (see Acts 16:16–40).

WEEKLY BIBLE STUDY

READ: HEBREWS 11:8–16 AND REVELATION 21:1–5

1. Followers of God look beyond this earthly existence to their eternal home. How did Abraham follow God? What was he looking forward to (see Hebrews 11:8–10)?

2. Abraham and Sarah considered God to be faithful and trusted in him. What does the author of Hebrews state happened as a result (see verses 11–12)?

3. What did Abraham and Sarah admit about their status and position on earth? What were they actually longing to receive (see verses 13–16)?

4. God doesn't just camouflage the old. He restores the new. What does John say that he saw in his vision? What is unique about this place (see Revelation 21:1)?

5. How does John describe the appearance of the Holy City? What does the voice from the throne call out to the people of heaven (see verses 2–3)?

6. What does God say will *not* be in the Holy City that he has prepared for his people? How does God describe what he is doing (see verses 4–5)?

7. How does it make you feel to know that God is preparing an eternal home for his faithful followers? How does that help you to follow after him today?

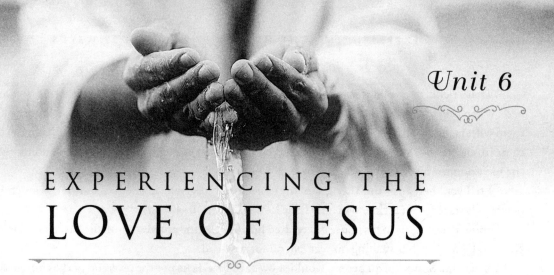

Unit 6

EXPERIENCING THE
LOVE OF JESUS

Could two people be more different? He is looked up to. She is looked down on. He is a church leader. She is a streetwalker.

He makes a living promoting standards. She's made a living breaking them.

He's hosting the party. She's crashing it.

Ask the other residents of Capernaum to point out the more pious of the two, and they'll pick Simon. After all, he's a student of theology, a man of the cloth. Anyone would pick him. Anyone, that is, except Jesus. Jesus knew them both. And Jesus would pick the woman. Jesus does pick the woman. And, what's more, he tells Simon why.

Not that Simon wants to know. His mind is elsewhere. *How did this prostitute get into my house?* He doesn't know whom to yell at first, the woman or the servant who let her in. After all, this dinner is a formal affair. Invitation only. Upper crust. Crème de la crème. Who let the riffraff in?

Simon is angry. *Just look at her—groveling at Jesus' feet. Kissing them, no less! Why, if Jesus were who he says he is, he would have nothing to do with this woman.*

One of the lessons Simon learned that day was this: don't think thoughts you don't want Jesus to hear. For Jesus heard them, and when he did, he chose to share a few of his own.

"'Simon,' he said to the Pharisee, 'I have something to say to you.'

"'Go ahead, Teacher,' Simon replied.

"Then Jesus told him this story: 'A man loaned money to two people—500 pieces of silver to one and 50 pieces to the other. But neither of them could repay him, so he kindly forgave them both, canceling their debts. Who do you suppose loved him more after that?'

"Simon answered, 'I suppose the one for whom he canceled the larger debt.'

"'That's right,' Jesus said. Then he turned to the woman and said to Simon, 'Look at this woman kneeling here. When I entered your home, you didn't offer me water to wash the dust from my feet, but she has washed them with her tears and wiped them with her hair. You didn't greet me with a kiss, but from the time I first came in, she has not stopped kissing my feet. You neglected the courtesy of olive oil to anoint my head, but she has anointed my feet with rare perfume.'

"'I tell you, her sins—and they are many—have been forgiven, so she has shown me much love. But a person who is forgiven little shows only little love'" (Luke 7:40–47 NLT).

Simon invited Jesus to his house but treated him like an unwanted step-uncle. No customary courtesies. No kiss of greeting. No washing his feet. No oil for his head.

You'd think Simon, of all people, would show such love. Is he not the reverend of the church, the student of Scripture? But he is so harsh and distant. You'd think the woman would avoid Jesus. Is she not the woman of the night, the town hussy? But she can't resist him. Simon's "love" is calibrated and stingy. Her love, on the other hand, is extravagant and risky.

How do we explain the difference between the two? Training? Education? Money? No, for Simon has outdistanced her in all three.

But there is one area in which the woman leaves him eating dust. Think about it. What one discovery has she made that Simon hasn't? What one treasure does she cherish that Simon doesn't? Simple. God's love. We don't know when she received it. We aren't told how she heard about it. But we know this: she came thirsty. Thirsty from guilt. Thirsty from regret. Thirsty from countless nights of making love and finding none. She came thirsty.

And when Jesus hands her the goblet of grace, she drinks like the parched pilgrim she is. She drinks until the mercy flows down her chin and onto her neck and chest. She drinks until every inch of her soul is moist and soft. She comes thirsty and she drinks. She drinks deeply.

Could it be that the secret to loving is receiving? We give love by first receiving it. "We love, because He first loved us" (1 John 4:19 NASB).

Long to be more loving? Begin by accepting your place as a dearly loved child. "Follow God's example, therefore, as dearly loved children and walk in the way of love, just as Christ loved us" (Ephesians 5:1–2).[16]

— PRAYER —

Dear Jesus, I pray that your love—its depth, its steadfastness, and its cost—will be made evident to me. Help me to understand how I am able to pass your love on to others. Cause me to rest in the assurance that nothing can separate me from your love. Amen.

— MEMORY VERSE —

May you experience the love of Christ, though it is too great to understand fully. Then you will be made complete with all the fullness of life and power that comes from God.

EPHESIANS 3:19 NLT

Week 26: WHERE LOVE AND JUSTICE MEET

Paul wrote, "The wrath of God is being revealed from heaven against all the godlessness and wickedness" (Romans 1:18). He also wrote, "For it is by grace you have been saved, through faith—and this is not from yourselves, it is the gift of God" (Ephesians 2:8). So, how can God punish the sin but give grace to the sinner? Does God lower his standard so we can be forgiven?

No. God "does not change like shifting shadows" (James 1:17), and he "judges all people in the same way" (Romans 2:11 NCV). Besides, to ignore our sin would be to endorse our sin. If our sin had no price, then we should just "do evil that good may result" (Romans 3:8). But this is not the aim of God. He does not compromise his holiness to enable our evil.

Yet the dilemma remains. Holiness demands that sin be punished. Mercy compels that the sinner be loved. How can God do both?

An illustration might shed some light. Imagine being arrested and brought before a judge for a speeding violation—your third in two years. You admit your wrongdoing. You were speeding. Your palms are sweaty as you are called to enter the judge's chamber. Once there, you wait for him render his decision.

"I have found a way to deal with your mistakes," he says. "I can't overlook them; to do so would be unjust. I can't pretend you didn't commit them; to do so would be a lie. But here is what I can do. In our records, we have found a person with a spotless past. He has never broken a law. He has volunteered to trade records with you. We will take your name and put it on his record. We will take his name and put it on yours. We will punish him for what you did. You, who did wrong, will be made right. He, who did right, will be made wrong."

Who is this person? What fool would do such a thing? For the sake of illustration, imagine if it were the judge himself. He is the one willing to substitute his spotless record for your flawed one. In the same way, Jesus loves you so much that he was willing to give you his own "perfect driving record" (a sinless life) so that he could take on the punishment for your imperfect one. Like the judge in this illustration, he had no reason to do you a favor. He certainly wasn't indebted to you. You were guilty, remember?

But he chose to take the penalty for your sin because of his love for you. This is a love born from within him, not from what he found in you. His love is uncaused and spontaneous. He did not love you because of *your* goodness, or kindness, or great faith. No, he loves you because of *his* goodness, kindness, and great faith. John says it like this: "This is love: not that we loved God, but that he loved us" (1 John 4:10).

Doesn't this thought comfort you? God's love does not hinge on yours. The abundance of your love does not increase his. The lack of your love does not diminish his. Your goodness does not enhance his love, nor does your weakness dilute it. What Moses said to Israel is what God says to us: "The LORD did not set his heart on you and choose you because you were more numerous than other nations, for you were the smallest of all nations! Rather, it was simply that the LORD loves you" (Deuteronomy 7:7–8 NLT).

God loves you simply because he has chosen to do so. He loves you when you don't feel lovely. He loves you when no one else loves you. Others may abandon you, ignore you, and forget you, but God will love you. Always. No matter what.

This is his sentiment: "I'll call nobodies and make them somebodies; I'll call the unloved and make them beloved" (Romans 9:25 MSG).

This is his promise: "I have loved you, my people, with an everlasting love. With unfailing love I have drawn you to myself" (Jeremiah 31:3 NLT).

God's love goes the distance—and Jesus traveled from limitless eternity to be confined by time in order to become one of us.

He didn't have to. He could have given up. At any step along the way, he could have called it quits.

When he saw the size of the womb, he could have stopped. When he saw how tiny his hands would be, how soft his voice would be, how hungry his tummy would be, he could have stopped. At the first whiff of the stinky stable, at the first gust of cold air. The first time he scraped his knee or blew his nose or tasted burnt bagels, he could have turned and walked out.

When he saw the dirt floor of his Nazareth house. When Joseph gave him a chore to do. When his fellow students were dozing off during the reading of the Torah, *his* Torah. When the neighbor took his name in vain. When the lazy farmer blamed his poor crop on God. At any point Jesus could have said, "That's it! That's enough! I'm going home." But he didn't.

He didn't, because he is love. And his love "always perseveres" (1 Corinthians 13:7). He endured the distance. "For the joy set before him he endured the cross, scorning its shame, and sat down at the right hand of the throne of God" (Hebrews 12:2).

We have done nothing to earn God's love. Remember, as Paul said, "it is the gift of God" (Ephesians 2:8). Given this, it only stands to reason that we do not need to live in fear of losing God's love. After all, if we did nothing to gain it, how could our performance (or lack thereof) lead to us losing it? Many people live in fear of God's justice because they have never reckoned his justice with his love. Grace is where the two meet together, forming an insoluble bond.

Are you aware that the most repeated command from the lips of Jesus was "Fear not"? Are you aware that the command from heaven not to be afraid appears in every book of the Bible? The apostle Paul points to the cross as our guarantee of God's love: "But God demonstrates his own love for us in this: While we were still sinners, Christ died for us" (Romans 5:8). God proved his love for us by sacrificing his only Son.

Formerly, God had sent prophets to preach. Now he has sent his Son to die. Earlier God commissioned angels to aid. Now he has offered his Son to redeem. When we tremble, he points us to the splattered blood on the splintered beams and says, "Don't be afraid."

THE HEART OF THE MATTER

- God cannot simply compromise his holiness to enable your sin.
- God instead took the penalty for your sin because of his love for you.
- God loves you simply because that is what he has chosen to do.
- Nothing will ever be able to separate you from the love of God.

MEMORY VERSE

Take a few moments to review your Bible memory verse for this unit, and then write out the words of Ephesians 3:19 by heart in the space below.

The Heart of Jesus

He had places to go, things to do, people to see. He was on a road trip, speaking in local synagogues, seaside venues, and country hillsides throughout the region. He had a message to communicate, questions to answer, parables to compose. And when he wasn't talking, he was listening. His chosen disciples, his closest friends, and even the religious rulers were vying for his time and attention. Jesus was a busy man. How could he possibly take on one more responsibility? Where would he find the time to commit to one more ministry opportunity? Didn't he deserve some downtime, some time off, some me-time? In the same situation, the last thing we would want to face is a crowd of needy people. Yet there he was, listening to stories of stiff joints and dimming sight. Holding the hand of the depressed and weary. Touching the faces of the desperate and dying. And did Jesus grit his teeth and smile through these interruptions to his schedule? Was he bored by hearing the same sorts of stories again and again? Did it bother him that nobody seemed to care about his feelings, his problems, his needs? No, he understood that his mission was "to proclaim good news to the poor . . . and recovery of sight for the blind" (Luke 4:18). Though confronted with a sea of faces, Jesus saw every individual heart, every precious life, every eternal soul through the eyes of love.

WEEKLY BIBLE STUDY

READ: JOHN 3:16–21 AND 1 JOHN 4:7–12

1. God's holiness demands that sin be punished, but his mercy compels him to love the sinner. How did God resolve this dilemma (see John 3:16)?

2. God *so* loved the sinners in this world that he sent his only Son to pay the price of their sin. What promise is given to those who believe in Jesus (see verses 17–18)?

3. John declares, "Light has come into the world" (verse 19). How do people respond to that light? What in their hearts determines how they react (see verses 20–21)?

4. John writes that "love comes from God" (1 John 4:7). What, then, is true of his followers? What is true of those who do *not* love others (see verses 7–8)?

5. God revealed his love by sending Jesus into the world. What does Jesus' sacrifice provide to you? What should you do as a response to God's love (see verses 9–11)?

6. John notes that "no one has ever seen God" (verse 12). Given this reality, how can people experience his love? What part do you play in this?

7. What do the passages you've studied this week reveal about the nature of God's love? Why is it so critical for followers of Jesus to actively love others?

Week 27: HONEST HEARTS

Once we experience Jesus' love, we know what it is like to live in freedom. Jesus knows everything about us—the good and the bad—yet he loves us entirely. We are free to be honest with him about who we are and who we are not. His love for us will not change.

From the beginning, God has called us to such honesty. He never demanded perfection of his people, but he expected truthfulness from them. As far back as the days of Moses, God said, "If they will confess their sins and the sins of their ancestors—their unfaithfulness and their hostility toward me, which made me hostile toward them so that I sent them into the land of their enemies—then . . . I will remember my covenant with Jacob and my covenant with Isaac and my covenant with Abraham, and I will remember the land" (Leviticus 26:40–42).

Honesty is something that would have greatly helped a young man named Charles Robertson. Strapped for cash, the nineteen-year-old went to a bank on a Wednesday afternoon, filled out a loan application, and left. Apparently, he changed his mind about the loan and opted for a quicker plan. He returned within a couple of hours with a pistol, a bag, and a note demanding money. The teller complied, and all of a sudden Robertson was holding a sack of loot.

He was halfway to his car when he realized that he'd left the note. Fearing it could be used as evidence against him, he ran back into the bank and snatched it from the teller. Now holding the note and the money, he ran a block to his parked car. That's when he realized he'd left his keys on the counter when he'd returned for the note. Total panic set in.

Robertson ducked into the restroom of a fast-food restaurant. He dislodged a ceiling tile and hid the money and the handgun. Scampering through alleys and creeping behind cars, he finally reached his apartment where his roommate, who knew nothing of the robbery, greeted him with the words, "I need my car." Yes, Robertson's getaway vehicle was a *loaner*. But rather than confess to the crime and admit the bungle, Robertson shoveled yet another spade of dirt deeper into the hole. "Uh, your car was stolen," he lied.

This led to the roommate calling the police to inform them of the stolen vehicle. About twenty minutes later, an officer spotted the "stolen" car a block from the recently robbed bank. Word was already on the police radio that the robber had forgotten his keys. The officer put two and two together and tried the keys on the car. They worked.

Detectives went to the address of the person who'd reported the missing car. There they found Robertson. He confessed, was charged with robbery, and put in jail.

Some days it's hard to do anything right. But it's even harder to do anything *wrong* right. Robertson's not alone. We've done the same. Perhaps we didn't take money, but we've taken leave of our senses, and then, like the thief, we've taken off. Dashing down alleys of deceit. Hiding behind buildings of work to be done or deadlines to be met. Though we try to act normal, anyone who looks closely can see we are on the lam. Eyes darting and hands fidgeting, we chatter nervously. Committed to the cover-up, we scheme and squirm, changing the topic and changing direction. We don't want anyone to know the truth, especially God.

God asks us to be honest and confess our sins to him. "Whoever conceals their sins does not prosper, but the one who confesses and renounces them finds mercy" (Proverbs 28:13). The act of confession brings us closer to our heavenly Father. We know we are loved by the only one who can help us with our weaknesses.

Confession does for the soul what preparing the land does for the field. Before the farmer sows the seed, he works the acreage, removing the rocks and pulling the stumps. He knows that seed grows better if the land is prepared. Confession is the act of inviting God to walk the acreage of our hearts. "There is a rock of greed over here, Father. I can't budge it. And that tree of guilt near the fence? Its roots are long and deep. And may I show you some dry soil, too crusty for seed?" God's seed grows better if the soil of the heart is cleared.

And so the Father and the Son walk the field together, digging and pulling, preparing the heart for fruit. Confession invites the Father to work the soil of the soul.

Confession seeks pardon from God—not amnesty. Pardon presumes guilt; amnesty, derived from the same Greek word as *amnesia*, "forgets" the alleged offense without imputing guilt. Confession admits wrong and seeks forgiveness; amnesty denies wrong and claims innocence.

Many mouth a prayer for forgiveness while in reality claiming amnesty. I don't think I am out of line when I say that many of us *spend our lives on the run*. But God's grace means that we don't have to run anymore. We can go to God and be honest about our failings.

This is what Peter discovered.

Remember Peter? "Flash the sword and deny the Lord" Peter? The apostle who boasted one minute and bolted the next? He snoozed when he should have prayed. He denied when he should have defended. He cursed when he should have comforted. He ran when he should have stayed. We remember Peter as the one who turned and fled, but do we remember Peter as the one who returned and confessed? We should.

I've got a question for you. How did the New Testament writers know of his sin? Who told them of his betrayal? How did they know the details? Who told them of the girl at the gate and the soldiers at the fire? How did Matthew know it was Peter's accent that made him a suspect? How did Luke learn of Jesus' stare? Who told them of the crowing rooster and tears?

The Holy Spirit? I suppose. It could be that each writer learned by divine inspiration. Or, more likely, each learned by an honest confession. Peter turned himself in. Like the bank robber, he had bungled it and ran. Unlike the robber, somewhere in the Jerusalem shadows he quit running, fell to his knees, and gave up.

But not only did he *give* up; he *opened* up. He went back to the room where Jesus had broken the bread and shared the wine. (It says a lot about the disciples that they let Peter back in the door.) There he was, every burly bit of him filling the doorframe. "Fellows, I've got something to get off my chest." And that's when they learned of the fire and the girl and the look from Jesus. That's when they heard of the cursing mouth and the crowing rooster.

May I ask a frank question? Are you keeping any secrets from God? Are any parts of your life off limits? If so, learn a lesson from the robber: the longer you run, the worse it gets. And learn a lesson from Peter: the sooner you speak to Jesus, the more you'll speak for Jesus.

Once you're in the grip of grace, you're free to be honest. So turn yourself in before things get worse. You'll be glad you did.

THE HEART OF THE MATTER

- You can be honest with God about who you are and who you are not.
- God's seed grows better if the soil of the heart is cleared by confession.
- God's grace means you can go to him and be honest about your failings.
- Don't hide your sins from God; confess them so he can forgive them.

MEMORY VERSE

Your memory verse for this unit is Ephesians 3:19. Take a few moments to review this verse, and then write it out from memory in the space below.

The Heart of Jesus

She looked annoyed to find him there. When he'd asked her for water, she'd been polite enough, but he'd seen her back stiffen. Was she upset at having to do more work? Surprised he would ask her for a drink? Afraid of a Jewish man who ignored society's conventions? He'd listened as she bluffed through his words and questions. But now he had cut to the heart of the matter. She knew that *he* knew her past, her present circumstances, and her greatest need. He had seen the deep longing inside. In fact, he had gone out of his way—taken the scenic route south and passed through unfriendly territories—just for her. He'd rearranged his life to be at that well, on that day, at that time, because he loved the woman whom he would find there. She needed to experience the love of Jesus. And she did (see John 4:1–42).

WEEKLY BIBLE STUDY

READ: 1 JOHN 1:5–10 AND PSALM 51:1–9

1. God never demanded perfection of his people, but he expected truthfulness from them. What will be true of you if you have fellowship with God (see 1 John 1:5–6)?

2. What is also true if you "walk in the light" of Jesus just as "he is in the light"? How will this influence your interactions with others (see verse 7)?

3. John states that if you claim to be without sin, you are only deceiving yourself. But what does God promise to do if you are honest and confess your sins (see verses 8–10)?

4. David was a man who sinned but was honest with God and confessed those sins. What request did he make of God regarding his transgressions (see Psalm 51:1–2)?

5. What does David acknowledge about God's right to judge him for his sins? What does he say that God had given him to help him not to sin (see verses 3–6)?

6. David desired for God to make him "whiter than snow" and to hear God's "joy and gladness." What other request did David make concerning his sins (see verse 9)?

7. What do the passages you've studied this week reveal about the importance of being honest with God about your sins? What do you need to confess to God today?

Week 28: THE HEAVINESS OF HATRED

Each week, Kevin Tunell was required to mail a dollar to a family he'd rather forget. They sued him for $1.5 million but settled for $936, to be paid a dollar at a time. The family expected the payment each Friday so Tunell would not forget what happened on the first Friday of 1982.

That's the day their daughter was killed. Tunell was convicted of manslaughter and drunken driving. He was seventeen. She was eighteen. The weekly restitution was to last for eighteen years. Tunell would make the check out to the victim, mail it to her family, and they would deposit the money into a scholarship fund.

Tunell served a court sentence. He also spent seven years campaigning against drunk driving—six years more than his sentence required. But he kept forgetting to send the dollar.

The family took him to court four times for failure to comply. After one appearance, Tunell spent thirty days in jail. He insisted that he was not defying the order but was haunted by the girl's death and tormented by the reminders. He offered the family two boxes of checks covering the payments until the year 2001, one year more than required.

They refused. It was not money they sought, but penance. Quoting the mother, "We want to receive the check every week on time. He must understand we are going to pursue this. . . . We will go back to court every month if we have to."[17]

Few would question the anger of the family. It's only natural to want to settle the score. However, God calls us to be *super*natural. God's grace toward us requires—and actually enables—us to be gracious toward others. If we experience his love through Christ, he requires us to act lovingly toward others, however undeserving they may appear to be.

Paul wrote, "Forgive as the Lord forgave you" (Colossians 3:13). Hatred is so out of place in the Christian life. After we have been forgiven so much, how could we not forgive others? Hatred makes no sense. But the 7:47 Principle does. What is the 7:47 Principle?

It is found in verse 47 of Luke chapter 7: "The person who is forgiven only a little will love only a little" (NCV). Just like the 747 jumbo jet, the 7:47 Principle has wide wings. Just like the aircraft, this truth can lift you to another level. Read it one more time: "The person who is forgiven only a little will love only a little." In other words, we can't give what we've never received. If we've never received love, it won't be possible for us to love others.

But, oh, how we try! We try to conjure up love by sheer force of will, as if there is within us a distillery of affection that lacks only a piece of wood or a hotter fire. We poke it and stoke it with resolve. What's our typical strategy for treating a troubled relationship? Try harder.

"My spouse needs my forgiveness? I don't know how, but I'm going to give it."

"I don't care how much it hurts, I'm going to be nice to that man."

"I'm supposed to love my neighbor? Okay. By golly, I will."

So we try. Teeth clenched. Jaw firm. We're going to love if it kills us! And it may do just that. But could it be that we are missing a step? Could it be that the first step of love is not toward *them* but toward *him*? Could it be that the secret to loving is receiving?

Jesus' love is the key to forgiveness. As we grow to experience and relish the love of Christ, one of the results is a growing love for other people. An irrational, inexplicable desire to love and forgive them replaces time-worn bitterness. We experience God's great forgiveness ourselves and are able, in turn, to love and forgive others all the more (the 7:47 Principle). But if we never realize the weight of our own indebtedness to God, we will be stingy with our love.

Of course, to believe that we are totally and eternally debt free is seldom easy. Even if we've stood before the throne and heard it from the King himself, we still doubt. As a result, many are forgiven only a little—not because the grace of the King is limited, but because the faith of the sinner is small. God is willing to forgive *all*. He is willing to wipe the slate completely clean for every person. He guides us to a pool of mercy and invites us to bathe. Some of us plunge in, but others among us just touch the surface. We leave feeling unforgiven.

As a result, because we haven't been willing to receive God's love, we find it nearly impossible to love and forgive others. Apart from God, "the heart is deceitful above all things" (Jeremiah 17:9). A marriage-saving love is not within us. A friendship-preserving devotion cannot be found in our hearts. We need help from an outside source . . . a transfusion. If we want to love as God loves, then we must start by receiving God's love.

We preachers have been guilty of skipping the first step. "Love each other!" we tell our churches. "Be patient, kind, forgiving," we urge. But instructing people *to* love without telling them they *are* loved is like telling them make a withdrawal from their bank account without first making a deposit into it. No wonder so many relationships are overdrawn. Hearts have insufficient love. The apostle John models the right sequence. He makes the deposit before he instructs us to make the withdrawal.

First, the deposit: "God showed how much he loved us by sending his one and only Son into the world so that we might have eternal life through him. This is real love—not that we loved God, but that he loved us and sent his Son as a sacrifice to take away our sins" (1 John 4:9–10 NLT). Then, John calls on us to pull out the debit card: "Dear friends, since God loved us that much, we surely ought to love each other" (verse 11 NLT).

Your friend broke his promises? Your boss didn't keep her word? Before you take action, answer this question: *How did God react when you broke your promises to him?* You've been lied to? It hurts to be deceived. But before you double your fists, think, *How did God respond when you lied to him?* You've been left behind? Rejection hurts. But before you get even, get honest with yourself. Have you ever neglected God? Have you always been attentive to his will? None of us have. *How did he react when you neglected him?*

The key to forgiving others is to quit focusing on what they did to you and start focusing on what God did for you. But, Max, that's not fair! Somebody has to pay for what he did.

I agree. Someone must pay, and someone already has. Jesus' love is love in action. It effects change. It promotes healing. It gives the debtor the freedom to forgive other debtors.

THE HEART OF THE MATTER

- God's grace toward you requires you to be gracious toward others.
- God asks you to forgive others in the same way that he has forgiven you.
- Receiving God's love makes it possible for you to love and forgive others.
- Jesus' love gives the debtor the freedom to forgive other debtors.

MEMORY VERSE

Your memory verse for this unit is Ephesians 3:19. Take a few moments to review this verse, and then write it out from memory in the space below.

The Heart of Jesus

Jesus had the chance to surround himself with the best and the brightest the world had to offer. When he started ministry, he could have created the ultimate Dream Team of service-minded men and women. He could have taken applications to find the most energetic, dedicated team players. He could have made a job requirement for applicants to have teachable hearts and the ability to follow through. A quick peek into hearts could have revealed those with the natural gifts of preaching, teaching, evangelism, and missions. He could have signed on a youth leader, a children's ministry coordinator, and even an administrative pastor for good measure. But he didn't. Take a look at the men and women who surrounded Jesus. They kept missing the point. They couldn't seem to trust their leader. They were always blowing it. And, finally, they all bailed on him. Hardly what we'd expect in a ministry team. So why did Jesus pick this bunch of people for his closest companions? Because he loved them—and he knew how his love would change them into the kind of people God could use mightily.

WEEKLY BIBLE STUDY

READ: LUKE 7:36–47 AND I JOHN 2:1–6

1. Jesus was attending a dinner at the home of Simon, a Pharisee, when an unexpected visitor arrived. How is this visitor described? What did she do (see Luke 7:36–38)?

2. Simon questioned Jesus' status as a prophet because he deemed that Christ did not know about this "sinner" in their midst. How did Jesus respond to him (see verses 39–43)?

3. What charge did Jesus make against Simon? What did Jesus say the woman with the alabaster jar did that Simon did not do (see verses 44–46)?

4. Jesus was drawing a distinction between Simon's heart and the heart of the woman. What had the woman recognized that Simon had failed to grasp (see verse 47)?

5. The woman who had lived a sinful life was willing to admit her need for God's forgiveness. What promise are you given when you likewise confess your sins (see 1 John 2:1–2)?

6. What does John say then happens to those who confess their sins and come to know God? What is the connection between obeying God and loving God (see verses 3–6)?

7. What do the passages you've studied this week reveal about just how much God loves you and has forgiven you? How will you extend this same love and forgiveness to others?

Week 29: A LOVE WORTH GIVING

Many people tell us to love. We know what God wants us to do: "This is what God commands . . . that we love each other" (1 John 3:23 NCV). But how can we? How can we be kind to the vow breakers? How can we be patient with people who have the tenderness of a porcupine? How can we forgive the moneygrubbers and backstabbers we meet, love, and marry? How can we love as God loves?

We want to. We long to. But how can we?

By following the 7:47 Principle: receive first, love second.

Let's carry this principle up the Mount Everest of love writings: 1 Corinthians 13. No words get to the heart of loving people like these verses. And no verses get to the heart of the chapter like verses 4 through 8: "Love is patient, love is kind. It does not envy, it does not boast, it is not proud. It does not dishonor others, it is not self-seeking, it is not easily angered, it keeps no record of wrongs. Love does not delight in evil but rejoices with the truth. It always protects, always trusts, always hopes, always perseveres. Love never fails."

Several years ago, someone challenged me to replace the word *love* in this passage with my name. I did and became a liar. "Max is patient, Max is kind. Max does not envy, he does not boast, he is not proud . . ." That's enough! Those words are false. Max is not patient. Max is not kind. Ask my wife and kids. Max can be an out-and-out clod! That's my problem.

And for years, that was my problem with this paragraph. It set a standard I could not meet. No one can meet it! No one, that is, except Christ. Does this passage not describe the measureless love of God? "Jesus is patient, Jesus is kind. Jesus does not envy, he does not boast, he is not proud. Jesus does not dishonor others, he is not self-seeking, he is not easily angered, he keeps no record of wrongs. Jesus does not delight in evil but rejoices with the truth. Jesus always protects, always trusts, always hopes, always perseveres. Jesus never fails."

Jesus loves you. That's why he came. That's why he endured the distance between you. Love "always perseveres" (1 Corinthians 13:7). That's why he endures the resistance from you. That's why he went the final step of the Incarnation: "God made him who had no sin to be sin for us, so that in him we might become the righteousness of God" (2 Corinthians 5:21). Why did Jesus do that? Only one answer: *love*. And the love of Christ "bears all things, believes all things, hopes all things, endures all things" (1 Corinthians 13:7 CSB).

Think about that for a moment. It's time to let his love cover all things in your life. All secrets. All hurts. All hours of evil, minutes of worry. Every promise broken, drug taken, penny stolen. Every cross word, cuss word, and harsh word. His love covers all things.

Let it. Discover, along with the psalmist, how he "loads me with love and mercy" (Psalm 103:4 NCV). Picture a giant dump truck full of love. There you are, behind it. God lifts the bed until the love starts to slide. Slowly at first, then down, down, down until you are hidden, buried, covered in his love. Let his love cover all things. Do it for his sake. To the glory of his name. Do it for your sake. For the peace of your heart. And do it for the sake of others—for the people in your life. Let his love fall on you so yours can fall on them.

Besides, the alternate is not appealing. Jesus once told a parable in which he described an unmerciful servant. Even though the servant had been forgiven a great debt by his master, he couldn't bring himself to forgive a smaller debt owed to him by a fellow servant. When the master found out, he said, "You wicked servant. . . . Shouldn't you have had mercy on your fellow servant just as I had on you?"

Then Jesus said, "In anger his master handed him over to the jailers to be tortured, until he should pay back all he owed" (Matthew 18:32–34).

Unforgiving servants always end up in prison. Prisons of anger, guilt, and depression. God doesn't have to put us in a jail; we create our own.

Oh, the gradual grasp of hatred. Its damage begins like a crack I once had in my windshield. Thanks to a speeding truck on a gravel road, my window was chipped. With time the nick became a crack and the crack became a winding tributary. Soon the windshield was a spiderweb of fragments.

I couldn't drive without thinking of the jerk who had driven too fast. Though I'd never seen him, I could describe him. He was a deadbeat who cheated on his wife, drove with a six-pack on the seat, and kept the television so loud the neighbors couldn't sleep. His carelessness blocked my vision. (Didn't do much for my view out the windshield either.)

Ever heard the expression "blind rage"? Hatred will sour your outlook and break your back. The load of bitterness is simply too heavy. Your knees will buckle under the strain and your heart will break beneath the weight. The mountain before you is steep enough without the heaviness of hatred on your back. The wisest choice—the *only* choice—is for you to drop the anger. You will never be called to give anyone more grace than God has already given you.

During World War I, a German soldier plunged into an out-of-the-way shell hole. There he found a wounded enemy. The fallen soldier was soaked with blood and only minutes from death. Touched by the plight of the man, the German soldier offered him water. Through this small kindness, a bond was developed. The dying man pointed to his shirt pocket; the German soldier took from it a wallet and removed some family pictures. He held them so the wounded man could gaze at his loved ones one final time. With bullets raging over them and war all around them, these two enemies were, but for a few moments, friends.

What happened in that shell hole? Did all evil suddenly cease? Were all the wrongs that had been committed made right?

No. What happened was simply this: two enemies saw each other as humans in need of help. This is forgiveness. Forgiveness begins by rising above the war, looking beyond the uniform, and choosing to see the other not as a foe or even as a friend, but simply as a fellow fighter longing to make it home safely.

So, rather than allowing 1 Corinthians 13 to remind you of a love you cannot produce, let it remind you of a love you cannot resist—God's love. Some of us are so thirsty for this type of love. Those who should have loved us didn't. Those who could have loved us didn't. We were left at the hospital. Left at the altar. Left with an empty bed. Left with a broken heart. Left with the question, "Does anybody love me?"

Listen to heaven's answer: God loves you. Personally. Powerfully. Passionately. Others have promised and failed. But God has promised and succeeded. He loves you with an unfailing love. And his love—if you will let it—can fill you and leave you with a love worth giving.

THE HEART OF THE MATTER

- Allow Jesus' love to cover all your secrets, hurts, hours of evil, and worries.
- Unforgiving servants end up in prisons of anger, guilt, and depression.
- Forgiveness begins by looking at the other person as a fellow fighter.
- God's love can fill you and leave you with a love worth giving.

MEMORY VERSE

Your memory verse for this unit is Ephesians 3:19. Take a few moments to review this verse, and then write it out by heart in the space below.

The Heart of Jesus

Jesus welcomed them with open arms. Sure, sometimes they clung too close to him. Sure, they often asked outlandish questions. But when the disciples tried to turn them away, Jesus said, "Let the little children come to me, and do not hinder them" (Matthew 19:14). Jesus had time for children. He listened to them. He took their wonderings seriously. He gave great bear hugs. Kids couldn't understand why they had to share Jesus with their parents. They didn't care if the adults wanted to discuss other things. All they wanted was one more piggyback ride. Just one more story. Wide-eyed, energetic, trusting children—Jesus loves them, too!

WEEKLY BIBLE STUDY

READ: 1 CORINTHIANS 13:1–8 AND 1 JOHN 4:19–21

1. How does Paul compare possessing love to possessing other gifts in the church such as tongues, prophecy, and service (see 1 Corinthians 13:1–3)?

2. What are some of the qualities of love that Paul describes (see verses 4–7)? What are some ways that you have seen these qualities of love demonstrated to you?

3. What does Paul say about the endurance of love as compared to other gifts in the church such as prophecies, tongues, and knowledge (see verse 8)?

4. Only Jesus can perfectly meet this standard of love—and he shows you how to love. What reason does John give as to why you can show love (see 1 John 4:19)?

5. Bitterness and resentment is a too-heavy load for anyone to bear through life. What else does John say about a person who "hates" others (see verse 20)?

6. God *requires* his children to let go of any unforgiveness toward others. How does John make it clear that this is not just a suggestion from the Lord (see verse 21)?

7. Is there any anger, bitterness, or resentment that you are holding against another person? If so, what steps will you take today to move toward forgiving that person?

Week 30: WHAT WE REALLY WANT TO KNOW

It was her singing that did it. Sara was about God. Singing to God. Head back, chin up, and lungs full, she filled the car with music. Heaven's harps paused to listen. *Is that my daughter?* I thought. *She sounds older. She looks older. She is becoming a young lady. Somewhere in the night a page had turned and, well . . . look at her!*

If you're a parent, you know what I mean. Just yesterday, diapers. Today, the car keys. Suddenly, your child is halfway to the dormitory, and you're running out of chances to show your love. So you speak.

That's what I did. "Sara," I said, "you're something special."

She turned and smiled tolerantly. "Someday, some hairy-legged boy is going to steal your heart and sweep you into the next century. But right now, you belong to me." She tilted her head, looked away for a minute, then looked back and asked, "Daddy, why are you acting so weird?"

I suppose such words would sound strange to a six-year-old. The love of a parent falls awkwardly on the ears of a child. But that didn't keep me from speaking—just as our inability to comprehend the love of God didn't stop him from coming.

And we, too, have tilted our heads. Like Sara, we have wondered what our heavenly Father is doing. We've pondered his love. What *can* you say to that kind of emotion? Upon learning that God would rather die than live without you, how do you react? How can you begin to explain such passion?

If you're Paul the apostle, you don't. You make no statements. You offer no explanations. You ask a few questions. Five questions, to be exact.

Question 1: "If God is for us, who can be against us?" (Romans 8:31). The question is not simply "Who can be against us?" You could answer that one. Who is against you? Disease, inflation, corruption, exhaustion. Rather, the question is *If GOD IS FOR US, who can be against us?* Indulge me for a moment. Four words in this verse deserve your attention: "God is for us."

God is for you. Others may have forgotten you, neglected you, or been ashamed of you, but within reach of your prayers is the Maker of the oceans. God!

God *is* for you. Not "may be," "has been," or "was." He is for you. Today. His loyalty won't increase if you are better nor lessen if you are worse. He is for you.

God is *for* you. God is cheering you on. Applauding your steps. Shouting your name. Too tired to continue? He'll carry you. Too discouraged to fight? He's picking you up. God is for you.

God is for *you.* If he drove a car, your name would be on his bumper. We know he has a tattoo, and we know what it says: "I have written your name on my hand" (Isaiah 49:16 NCV).

Question 2: "He who did not spare his own Son, but gave him up for us all—how will he not also, along with him, graciously give us all things?" (Romans 8:32). Paul's question is "Would he who gave his Son not meet our needs?"

Still, we worry. We worry about the IRS and the SAT and the FBI. We worry that we won't have enough money, and when we have money, we worry that we won't manage it well. We worry what the dog thinks if he sees us step out of the shower. We worry that someday we'll learn that fat-free yogurt was fattening.

Honestly, now. Did God save you so you could fret? Would he teach you to walk just to watch you fall? Would he be nailed to the cross for your sins and then disregard your prayers? Is Scripture teasing us when it reads, "He will command his angels concerning you to guard you in all your ways" (Psalm 91:11)?

I don't think so either.

Questions 3 and 4: "Who can accuse the people God has chosen? No one, because God is the One who makes them right. Who can say God's people are guilty? No one, because Christ Jesus died, but he was also raised from the dead, and now he is on God's right side, appealing to God for us" (Romans 8:33–34 NCV).

Paul's questions are about *guilt* and *grace*. Every moment of your life, your accuser is filing charges against you. He has noticed every error and marked each slip. Neglect your priorities, and he will jot it down. Abandon your promises, and he will make a note. Try to forget your past, and he'll remind you. Try to undo your mistakes, and he will thwart you.

He rails, "This one you call your child is not worthy. Greed lingers within. He often only thinks of himself. He'll go days without prayer. Why, even this morning he chose to sleep rather than spend time with you. I accuse him of laziness, egotism, worry, distrust."

As he speaks, you hang your head. You have no defense. His charges are fair. "I plead guilty, Your Honor," you mumble. "The sentence?" Satan asks.

"The wages of sin is death," explains the Judge, "but in this case the death has already occurred. For this one died with Christ."

Satan is suddenly silent. And you are suddenly jubilant. You realize that Satan cannot accuse you. No one can accuse you! Fingers may point, but the charges glance off like arrows hitting a shield. Once the Judge has released you, you need not fear the court.

Question 5: "Who shall separate us from the love of Christ?" (Romans 8:35). There it is. This is the question! We want to know how long God's love will endure.

Does God really love us forever? Not just on Easter Sunday when our shoes are shined and our hair is fixed. We want to know, "How does God feel about me when I'm a jerk? Not when I'm peppy and positive and ready to tackle world hunger. How does God feel about me when I snap at anything that moves, when my thoughts are gutter-level, when my tongue is sharp enough to slice a rock?"

That's the concern. Did I drift too far? Wait too long? Slip too much?

To these questions God replies, "Can anything make me stop loving you? Watch me speak your language, sleep on your earth, and feel your hurts. You wonder if I understand how you feel? Look into the dancing eyes of the kid in Nazareth; that's God walking to school. Ponder the toddler at Mary's table; that's God spilling his milk. You wonder how long my love will last? Find your answer on a splintered cross, on a craggy hill. That's me you see up there, your maker, nail-stabbed, bleeding, covered in spit, and sin-soaked. That's your sin I'm feeling. That's your death I'm dying. That's your resurrection I'm living. That's how much I love you."

That's what we really want to know. Will his love last forever? When we really believe the answer is *yes*, our lives open up to the potential for significant change.

THE HEART OF THE MATTER

- God is for you—cheering you, applauding you, shouting your name.
- God did not teach you how to walk just so he could watch you fall.
- *No one* can accuse you once the Judge has released you.
- There is nothing that can make God stop loving you!

MEMORY VERSE

This is it . . . one last review of your memory verse. Write out the words of Ephesians 3:19 from memory in the space below. Reflect on what these words mean to you.

The Heart of Jesus

His humiliation was complete. One of his closest friends had betrayed him. His other friends had abandoned him. He'd been bullied and beaten. They'd mocked him, then mauled him. Their cruelty was unspeakable. The pain was so great he could hardly stand. Whips had cracked over his head and back, and the blood loss made him dizzy. The thorns in his scalp were hard to ignore whenever the cross on his back had bumped them. They'd stripped him, forcing him to stand in complete nakedness, then the nails had pierced him and the cross had been raised. Every breath was agony. Every muscle and nerve protested. And with his last breaths, he flung words out over the crowds. Not a backlash of curses. Not regrets. Not a promise of revenge. Jesus gasped out words of forgiveness. Though they had done their worst, Jesus still loved them—loved them enough to say, "Father, forgive them" (Luke 23:34).

WEEKLY BIBLE STUDY

READ: ROMANS 8:31–35 AND ISAIAH 49:14–19

1. In this world, it can seem at times as if everyone is against you. What does Paul say you can depend on when you feel this way (see Romans 8:31)?

2. Some days, it can seem as if no one cares about you. What does Paul say about the lengths God was willing to go to show his love for you (see verse 32)?

3. Satan will remind you of your past failings and bring accusations against you to shame you. Who does God say can bring a charge against you (see verses 33–34)?

4. You may wonder how long God's love will endure for you. How does Paul answer this question? What can separate you from God's love (see verse 35)?

5. The Israelites in exile wondered if God had forsaken or forgotten them. What images did God use to show his people just how much he cared for them (see Isaiah 49:14–15)?

6. What other image did God use to show that he had not forgotten his people (see verse 16)? What promise did he make to them concerning their enemies (see verses 17–19)?

7. How do the passages you've studied this week encourage you to trust that God will never abandon or forsake you? Which promises especially stand out to you?

EXPERIENCING THE
POWER OF JESUS

*I*magine it's a Saturday afternoon. What you needed to get done today, you've already done. Your afternoon lies before you with no obligations. Free afternoons don't come as often as they once did, so you consider your options for the day. You pick up a paper to get some ideas. A movie? Nothing good is showing. Television? You can do that anytime. Wait. What's this? An ad catches your eye.

Special Art Exhibit
"Bruised Reeds and Smoldering Wicks"
2:00 to 4:00 Saturday Afternoon
Lincoln Library

Hmm . . . It's been a while since you've seen some good art. Bruised Reeds and Smoldering Wicks? Probably some nature stuff. Besides, the walk would be nice. You'll do it. You lay down the paper, put on a coat, and grab some gloves.

You're greeted by the musty odor of books as you walk through the library doors. It's an intimate room—no larger than a nice den. Bookshelves cover the walls, and books line the shelves. A fire crackles in a fireplace, and a couple of high wingback chairs invite you to spend the afternoon with a good book. You start to pick up one when you see a sign that reminds you why you came. "Bruised Reeds and Smoldering Wicks," it reads and points you toward a door.

Maybe later on the book, you think. *First, the art.*

Placed around the room are the paintings. All set on easels, in pairs, and always back to back. You put your gloves in your coat pocket, hang your coat on a hook, and move toward the first painting.

It's a portrait of a leper, the center figure on the canvas. He stoops like a hunchback. His fingerless hand, draped in rags, extends toward you, pleading. A tattered wrap hides all of his face except two pain-filled eyes. The crowd around the leper is chaotic. A father is grabbing a curious child. A woman trips over her own feet as she scrambles to get away. A man glares over his shoulder as he runs. The painting is captioned with the leper's plea, "If You Will, You Can . . ."

The next painting portrays the same leper, but the scene has changed dramatically. The caption has only two words: "I Will." In this sketch, the leper is standing erect and tall. He is looking at his own outstretched hand—it has fingers! The veil is gone from his face and he is smiling. There is no crowd; only one other person is standing beside the leper. You can't see his face, but you can see his hand on the shoulder of the healed man.

"This is no nature exhibit," you whisper to yourself as you turn to the next painting.

The next portrait is surrealistic. A man's contorted face dominates the canvas. Orange hair twists against a purple background. The face stretches downward and swells at the bottom like a pear. The eyes are perpendicular slits in which a thousand tiny pupils bounce. The mouth is frozen open in a scream. You notice something odd—it's inhabited! Hundreds of spider-like creatures claw over each other. Their desperate voices are captured by the caption "Swear to God You Won't Torture Me!"

Fascinated, you step to the next painting. It is the same man, but now his features are composed. His eyes, no longer wild, are round and soft. The mouth is closed, and the caption explains the sudden peace: "Released." The man is leaning forward as if listening intently. His hand strokes his chin. And dangling from his wrist is a shackle and a chain—a broken chain.

Throughout the gallery the sequence repeats itself. Always two paintings, one of a person in trauma and one of a person in peace. "Before" and "after" testimonials to a life-changing encounter. Scene after scene of serenity eclipsing sorrow. Purpose defeating pain. Hope outshining hurt.

Throughout this week, we will stroll through the gallery together. We'll ponder the moments when Christ met people at their points of pain. We'll see the prophecy proven true. We'll see bruised reeds straightened and smoldering wicks ignited.[18]

— PRAYER —

Dear Father, your power is greater than my every need. Your power has conquered sin and death. Teach me to rest confidently in your strong hands. Help me to rely on your power, even when I do not understand why things are happening. Show me how Jesus can meet me at the point of my greatest weakness with his perfect power.

— MEMORY VERSE —

But he said to me, "My grace is sufficient for you, for my power is made perfect in weakness." Therefore I will boast all the more gladly about my weaknesses, so that Christ's power may rest on me.

2 CORINTHIANS 12:9

Week 31: EVERYONE NEEDS A MIRACLE

"A large crowd followed Jesus and pushed very close around him. Among them was a woman who had been bleeding for twelve years. She had suffered very much from many doctors and had spent all the money she had, but instead of improving, she was getting worse" (Mark 5:24–26 NCV).

She was a bruised reed. "Bleeding for twelve years." "Suffered very much." "Spent all the money she had." "Getting worse." A chronic menstrual disorder. A perpetual issue of blood. Such a condition would be difficult for any woman of any era. But for a Jewish woman, nothing could be worse. No part of her life was left unaffected.

Sexually . . . she could not touch her husband.

Maternally . . . she could not bear children.

Domestically . . . anything she touched was considered unclean. No washing dishes. No sweeping floors.

Spiritually . . . she was not allowed to enter the temple.

She was physically exhausted and socially ostracized. She had sought help "under the care of many doctors" (verse 26). The Talmud gives no fewer than eleven cures for such a condition. No doubt she had tried them all. Some were legitimate treatments. Others, such as carrying the ashes of an ostrich egg in a linen cloth, were hollow superstitions.

She "had spent all she had" (verse 26). To dump financial strain on top of the physical strain is to add insult to injury. A friend battling cancer told me the hounding of the creditors who demand payments for ongoing medical treatment is just as devastating as the pain.

But "instead of getting better she grew worse" (verse 26). She was a bruised reed. She awoke daily in a body that no one wanted. She was down to her last prayer. And on the day we encounter her, she was about to pray it.

By the time she got to Jesus, he was surrounded by people. He was on his way to help the daughter of Jairus, the most important man in the community. What were the odds that he would interrupt an urgent mission with a high official to help the likes of her? Very few. But what were the odds that she would survive if she didn't take a chance? Fewer still.

So she takes a chance. "If I just touch his clothes," she thinks, "I will be healed" (verse 28).

Risky decision. To touch him, she will have to touch the people. If one of them recognizes her . . . hello rebuke, goodbye cure. But what choice does she have? She has no money, no clout, no friends, no solutions. All she has is a crazy hunch that Jesus can help and a high hope that he will. Maybe that's all you have: a crazy hunch and a high hope. You have nothing to give. But you are hurting. And all you have to offer him is your hurt.

Maybe that has kept you from coming to God. Oh, you've taken a step or two in his direction. But then you saw the other people around him. They seemed so clean, so neat, so fit in their faith. And when you saw them, they blocked your view of him. So you stepped back.

If that describes you, note carefully, only one person was commended that day for having faith. It wasn't a wealthy giver. It wasn't a loyal follower. It wasn't an acclaimed teacher. It was a shame-struck, penniless outcast who clutched onto her hunch that he could and her hope that he would.

Which, by the way, isn't a bad definition of faith: *a conviction that he can and a hope that he will*. Sounds similar to the definition of faith given by the Bible. "Without faith it is impossible to please God, because anyone who comes to him must believe that he exists and that he rewards those who earnestly seek him" (Hebrews 11:6).

Not too complicated, is it? Faith is the belief that God is real and that God is good. Faith is not a mystical experience or a midnight vision or a voice in the forest . . . it is a choice to believe that the one who made it all hasn't left it all and that he still sends light into shadows and responds to gestures of faith.

There was no guarantee, of course. She hoped he'd respond . . . she longed for it . . . but she didn't know if he would. All she knew was that he was there and that he was good. That's faith. Faith is not the belief that God will do what you want. Faith is the belief that God will do what is right. "Blessed are the dirt-poor, nothing-to-give, trapped-in-a-corner, destitute, diseased," Jesus said, "for theirs is the kingdom of heaven" (Matthew 5:6, my paraphrase).

God's economy is upside down (or right-side up and ours is upside down!). God says that the more hopeless your circumstance, the more likely your salvation. The greater your cares, the more genuine your prayers.

A healthy lady never would have appreciated the power of a touch of the hem of his robe. But this woman was sick, and when her dilemma met his dedication, a miracle occurred.

Her part in the healing was very small. All she did was extend her arm through the crowd. "If only I can touch him."

Revisit the library gallery for a moment to see how the artist creatively portrays this story in the same pattern of a two-part series. The artist's brush has captured a woman in midair, jumping from one side of a canyon to another. Her clothes are ragged. Her body is frail, and her skin is pale. She looks anemic. Her eyes are desperate as she reaches for the canyon wall with both hands. On the ledge is a man. All you see are his legs, sandals, and the hem of a robe. Beneath the painting are the woman's words, "If Only . . ."

You step quickly to see the next scene. She is standing now. The ground beneath her bare feet is solid. Her face flushes with life. Her cautious eyes look up at the half-moon of people that surround her. Standing beside her is the one she sought to touch. The caption? His words. "Take Heart . . ."

God's help is near and always available, but it is only given to those who seek it. Nothing results from apathy. The great work in this story is the mighty healing that occurred. But the great truth is that the healing began with her touch. And with that small, courageous gesture, she experienced Jesus' tender power.

THE HEART OF THE MATTER

- Sometimes, all that you have to offer to God is your hurt.
- Faith is a conviction that Jesus *can* and a hope that he *will*.
- Faith is the belief that God is real and that God is good.
- God's help is near and always available to those who seek it.

MEMORY VERSE

Take a few moments to review your Bible memory verse for this unit, and then write out the words of 2 Corinthians 12:9 by heart in the space below.

The Heart of Jesus

The rumors had been flying for months now. Some people said that this wandering rabbi from Nazareth was a prophet. Some said he was a political reformer. But the greatest interest was roused by the rumors that this man could *heal*. The blind, the lame, the deaf, the diseased—all claimed to have been made whole by his touch. There were wilder stories of demons being cast out and the dead coming to life again. It was surely too good to be true, but the glimmer of hope was too much for the hurting ones to ignore. So wherever Jesus went, the seekers followed. They brought him all their sick. They begged him to let them touch just the edge of his coat. The weak and the needy longed to experience the power of Jesus.

WEEKLY BIBLE STUDY

READ: MARK 5:21–34 AND HEBREWS 11:1–3

1. Jesus was on another mission when the woman with the issue of blood encountered him in the crowd. What was Jesus on his way to do (see Mark 5:21–24)?

2. What prompted the woman to approach Jesus in the crowd and attempt to touch his cloak? What risk was she taking by doing this (see verses 25–28)?

3. What happened when the woman touched Jesus? How did the disciples—who were with Jesus in the midst of all the people—respond to him (see verses 29–31)?

4. All the woman knew was that Jesus was there and that he was good. What did Jesus say to the woman when she fell at his feet and said what she had done (see verses 32–34)?

5. Only one person is this story was commended that day for having faith. How does the author of Hebrews define *faith* (see Hebrews 11:1)?

6. This woman—like many of the other "ancients" in Scripture—was commended for her faith. What do we understand about God's power through faith (see verses 2–3)?

7. Is there anything today keeping you from approaching God? How does the story of the woman who had been bleeding for twelve years encourage you to come to him?

Week 32: THE POWER OF A TIMID PRAYER

If you struggle with prayer, I've got just the guy for you. Don't worry, he's not a monastic saint. He's not a callused-kneed apostle. Nor is he a prophet whose middle name is Meditation. He's just the opposite. A fellow crop duster. A parent with a sick son in need of a miracle.

The father's prayer isn't much. But the answer is, and the result reminds us, that the power is not in the prayer; it's in the one who hears it. He prayed out of desperation. His son, his only son, was demon possessed. Not only was he deaf, mute and epileptic, but he was also possessed by an evil spirit. Ever since the boy was young, the demon had thrown him into fires and water.

Imagine his pain. Other dads could watch their children grow and mature; he could only watch his suffer. While others were teaching their sons an occupation, he was just trying to keep his son alive.

What a challenge! He couldn't leave his son alone for a minute. Who knew when the next attack would come? The father had to remain on call, on alert twenty-four hours a day. He was desperate and tired, and his prayer reflects both.

"If you can do anything for him, please have pity on us and help us" (Mark 9:22 NCV). Listen to that prayer. Does it sound courageous? Confident? Strong? Hardly.

One word would have made a lot of difference. Instead of *if*, what if he'd said *since*? "*Since* you can do anything for him, please have pity on us and help us." But that's not what he said. He said *if*. The Greek is even more emphatic. The tense implies doubt. It's as if the man were saying, "This one's probably out of your league, but if you can . . ."

A classic crop duster appeal. More meek than mighty. More timid than towering. More like a crippled lamb coming to a shepherd than a proud lion roaring in the jungle. If the father's prayer sounds like yours, then don't be discouraged, for that's where prayer begins.

It begins as a yearning. An honest appeal. Ordinary people staring at Mount Everest. No pretense. No boasting. No posturing. Just prayer. Feeble prayer, but prayer nonetheless.

We are tempted to wait to pray until we know how to pray. We've heard the prayers of the spiritually mature. We've read of the rigors of the disciplined. And we are convinced we've a long way to traverse. And since we'd rather not pray than pray poorly, we don't pray. Or we pray infrequently. We are waiting to pray until we learn how to pray.

Good thing this man didn't make the same mistake. He wasn't much of a pray-er. And his wasn't much of a prayer. He even admits it! "I do believe!" he implored. "Help me to believe more!" (verse 24 NCV). This prayer isn't destined for a worship manual. No psalm will result from his utterance. His was simple—no incantation or chant. But Jesus responded. Not to the eloquence of the man but to the pain of the man.

Jesus had many reasons to disregard this man's request. Never has the arena of prayer been so poor.

Where is the faith in this picture? The disciples have failed, the scribes are amused, the demon is victorious, and the father is desperate (see verses 14–18). You'd be hard-pressed to find a needle of belief in that haystack.

You may even be hard-pressed to find one in your own. Perhaps your life is a long way from heaven, too. Noisy household—screaming kids instead of singing angels. Divisive religion—your leaders squabble more than they minister. Overwhelming problems. You can't remember when you didn't wake up to this demon.

Yet out of the din of doubt comes your timid voice. "If you can do anything for me . . ."

Does such a prayer make a difference? Let Mark answer that question: "When Jesus saw that a crowd was quickly gathering, he ordered the evil spirit, saying, 'You spirit that makes people unable to hear or speak, I command you to come out of this boy and never enter him again!' The evil spirit screamed and caused the boy to fall on the ground again. Then the spirit came out" (Mark 9:25–26 NCV).

This troubled the disciples. As soon as they got away from the crowds, they asked Jesus, "Why couldn't we force that evil spirit out?" (verse 28 NCV).

His answer? "That kind of spirit can only be forced out by prayer" (verse 29 NCV). What prayer? Was it the prayer of the disciples? No, they didn't pray. Must have been the prayers of the scribes. Maybe they went to the temple and interceded. No, the scribes didn't pray either. Then it must have been the people. Perhaps they had a vigil for the boy. Nope. The people didn't pray. They never bent a knee. Then what prayer led Jesus to deliver the demon?

There is only one prayer in the story. It's the honest prayer of a hurting man. And since God is more moved by our hurt than our eloquence, he responded. That's what fathers do.

That's exactly what Jim Redmond did. His son, Derek, was favored to win the 400-meter race in the 1992 Barcelona Olympics. Halfway into his semifinal heat, a fiery pain seared through his right leg. He crumpled to the track with a torn hamstring. As the medical attendants were approaching, Redmond fought to his feet. "It was animal instinct," he would later say. He set out hopping, pushing away the coaches in a crazed attempt to finish the race.

When he reached the stretch, a big man pushed through the crowd. He was wearing a T-shirt that read "Have you hugged your child today?" and a hat that challenged "Just Do It." The man was Jim Redmond, Derek's father.

"You don't have to do this," he told his weeping son.

"Yes, I do," Derek declared.

"Well, then," said Jim, "we're going to finish this together."

And they did. Jim wrapped Derek's arm around his shoulder and helped him hobble to the finish line. Fighting off security men, the son's head sometimes buried in the father's shoulder, they stayed in Derek's lane to the end. The crowd clapped, then stood, then cheered, and then wept as the father and son finished the race.

What made the father do it? What made the father leave the stands to meet his son on the track? Was it the strength of his child? No, it was the pain of his child. His son was hurt and fighting to complete the race. So the father came to help him finish.

God does the same. Our prayers may be awkward. Our attempts may be feeble. But since the power of prayer is in the one who hears it and not the one who says it, our prayers do make a difference.

THE HEART OF THE MATTER

- Even timid and less-than-faith-filled prayers are prayers nonetheless.
- God doesn't ask you to wait to pray until you know how to pray.
- God is more moved by your hurt than your eloquence in prayer.
- Your prayers may seem awkward or feeble, but they make a difference.

MEMORY VERSE

Your memory verse for this unit is 2 Corinthians 12:9. Take a few moments to review this verse, and then write it out from memory in the space below.

The Heart of Jesus

They were praying to God but probably never realized they were being overheard by God's Son. The first man, a Pharisee, was busy commending himself to God. "I tithe. I fast. I like me!" If that wasn't bad enough, he began to elaborate. "I'm glad you made me, me. The me that I am is so much better than anyone else." The little rant may have boosted the Pharisee's self-esteem, but it never reached God. The second man, a tax collector, had come to the temple with a very different attitude. He lingered near the entrance, not daring to go farther. His eyes were downcast, and the slope of his shoulders communicated sadness, regret, surrender. In humility, he acknowledged his sin. "God, have mercy on me, a sinner." His words were few, but his heart was sincere. Jesus announced that this second man's prayers had made all the difference in the world. He went home a forgiven man (see Luke 18:9–14).

WEEKLY BIBLE STUDY

READ: MARK 9:14–29 AND 2 CHRONICLES 7:11–15

1. The father in this story was a parent with a sick son in need of a miracle. What was the situation that brought the father into contact with Jesus (see Mark 9:14–18)?

2. How did Jesus respond when he learned his disciples could not drive the evil spirit out of the boy (see verse 19)? Why do you think he reacted in this way?

3. Jesus learned that the boy had been afflicted with the demon since childhood. What question did he ask the father? How did the father respond (see verses 20–22)?

4. Jesus told the father that "everything is possible for one who believes." What was the result of the man's small measure of faith in Christ (see verses 23–27)?

5. Everything that transpired with the man troubled the disciples. What question did they ask Jesus in private? Who prayed the prayer in the story (see verses 28–29)?

6. There is incredible power in prayer. What did God say to Solomon about his prayers? What did he say he would do if his people came to him in prayer (see 2 Chronicles 7:11–15)?

7. The power of prayer is in the one who hears it and not the one who says it. What do you need to take to your heavenly Father today in prayer?

Week 33: WHEN WE ARE OUT OF CHOICES

For the longest time, the story didn't make sense to me. It's about a man who had barely enough faith to stand on, but Jesus treated him as if he'd laid his son on the altar for God. Martyrs and apostles deserve such honor, but not some pauper who didn't know Jesus when he saw him. Or so I thought.

For the longest time, I thought Jesus was too kind. I thought the story was too bizarre. I thought the story was too good to be true. Then I realized something. This story isn't about an invalid in Jerusalem. This story is about you. It's about me. The fellow isn't nameless. He has a name—yours. He has a face—mine. He has a problem—just like ours.

Jesus encountered the man near a large pool north of the temple in Jerusalem. A colonnade with five porches overlooks the body of water. It's a monument of wealth and prosperity, but its residents are people of sickness and disease. It's called Bethesda. It could be called Central Park, Metropolitan Hospital, or even Joe's Bar and Grill. It could be the homeless huddled beneath a downtown overpass. It could be any collection of hurting people.

An underwater spring caused the pool to bubble occasionally. The people believed the bubbles were caused by the dipping of angels' wings. They also believed the first person to touch the water after the angel did would be healed. Did healing occur? I don't know. But I do know crowds of invalids came to give it a try.

On this day, Jesus must have sighed often as he walked along the poolside of Bethesda . . . and he sighed when he comes to you and me. Remember, I said I found our faces in the Bible. Here we are, filling the white space between the letters of John 5:5: "A man was lying there who had been sick for thirty-eight years" (NCV).

Maybe you don't like being described like that. Perhaps you'd rather find yourself in the courage of David or the devotion of Mary. But before we can be like them, we must admit we are like the paralytic. Invalids out of options. Can't walk. Can't work. Can't care for ourselves. Can't even roll down the bank to the pool to cash in on the angel water.

You may be holding this book with healthy hands and reading with strong eyes. You can't imagine what you and this four-decade invalid have in common. How could he be you? Simple: you share the same predicament and hope. What predicament? It is described in Hebrews 12:14: "Without holiness no one will see the Lord." That's our predicament: only the holy will see God. Holiness is a prerequisite to heaven. Perfection is a requirement for eternity.

We wish it weren't so. We act like it isn't so. We act like those who are "decent" will see God. Sounds right to us, but it doesn't sound right to God—and he sets the standard. And the standard is high. "Be perfect, therefore, as your heavenly Father is perfect" (Matthew 5:48). In God's plan, God is the standard for perfection. We don't compare ourselves to others; they are just as fouled up as we are. The goal is to be like him. Anything less is inadequate.

That's why the invalid is you and me. We, like the invalid, are paralyzed. We, like the invalid, are trapped. We, like the invalid, are stuck. We have no solution for our predicament.

When it comes to healing our spiritual condition, we don't have a chance. We might as well be told to pole-vault the moon. We don't have what it takes to be healed. Our only hope is that God will do for us what he did for the man at Bethesda—that he will step out of the temple and step into our ward of hurt and helplessness. Which is exactly what he has done.

Read Paul's description of what God has done for you: "When you were spiritually dead because of your sins and because you were not free from the power of your sinful self, God made you alive with Christ, and he forgave all our sins. He canceled the debt, which listed all the rules we failed to follow. He took away that record with its rules and nailed it to the cross. God stripped the spiritual rulers and powers of their authority. With the cross, he won the victory and showed the world that they were powerless" (Colossians 2:13–15 NCV).

Let's isolate some phrases. First, look at your condition: "When you were spiritually dead . . . and . . . you were not free." The invalid was better off than we are. At least he was alive. Paul says that if you and I are outside of Christ, then we are dead. Spiritually dead. Corpses. Lifeless. Cadavers. Dead. What can a dead person do? Not much.

But look what God can do with the dead: "God made you alive . . . forgave all our sins . . . canceled the debt . . . stripped the spiritual rulers . . . won the victory."

God's efforts are strongest when our efforts are useless.

Go back to Bethesda for a moment. Look at the brief but revealing dialogue between the paralytic and the Savior. Before Jesus healed him, he asked him a question: "Do you want to be well?" (John 5:6 NCV). The man replied, "Sir, there is no one to help me get into the pool when the water starts moving. While I am coming to the water, someone else always gets in before me" (verse 7 NCV).

Was the fellow complaining? Feeling sorry for himself? Or just stating the facts? Who knows. But before we think about it too much, look what happens next. "Jesus said, 'Stand up. Pick up your mat and walk.' And immediately the man was well" (verses 8–9 NCV).

I wish we would do that; I wish we would take Jesus at his word. I wish that we would learn that when he says something, it happens. What is this peculiar paralysis that confines us? What is this stubborn unwillingness to be healed? When Jesus tells us to stand, let's stand.

Is this your story? It can be. All the elements are the same. A gentle stranger has stepped into your hurting world and offered you a hand. Now it's up to you to take it.

THE HEART OF THE MATTER

- All of humanity is in the same predicament: only the holy will see God.
- The goal is to be like God . . . anything less is simply inadequate.
- The power of God can bring the spiritually dead back to life.
- Jesus has offered you his hand, but it's up to you to reach out and take it.

MEMORY VERSE

Your memory verse for this unit is 2 Corinthians 12:9. Take a few moments to review this verse, and then write it out from memory in the space below.

The Heart of Jesus

He was at his usual station, near a clump of shrubbery that gave him some relief from the heat. His mat was spread, and he sat cross-legged. He listened for the sound of hooves, the shuffle of feet, the plodding of camels, and then he would beg. Most folks never really saw him. Others turned their heads at his voice and were moved by compassion. They would drop a few coins into his bowl or offer him a bit of food or drink before moving along.

Then one morning, he heard the clamor of many voices. There seemed to be a parade going by—so many feet, so many voices. "What is this? What's going on?" he asked those nearest him. "I can see," commented another beggar nearby, "Jesus of Nazareth and his followers. They are passing by." The blind beggar paused for only a moment and then began to shout, "Jesus, Son of David, have mercy on me!" Again and again he called, as loudly as he could. Some of the others began to reprimand him. But the beggar did not stop, and Jesus turned his head. "Bring him to me," Jesus said.

So the blind beggar found himself trembling in the presence of the Son of God. "What do you want me to do for you?" he asked. Should he ask for bread? Should he ask for wine? Should he ask for a few coins? No. This was not some passing merchant. He faced the one who had the power to give even more. "I want to see," the beggar pleaded. Touched by the man's faith, Jesus touched him. Sight was restored, and God received the praise (see Luke 18:38–43).

WEEKLY BIBLE STUDY

READ: JOHN 5:1–15 AND ROMANS 7:14–25

1. Jesus traveled to the city of Jerusalem to attend a festival (likely the feast of Purim). What did he encounter when he went to the pool of Bethesda (see John 5:1–5)?

2. When Jesus saw a man lying there, he asked, "Do you want to get well?" (verse 6). Why do you think Jesus asked this question? How did the man respond (see verse 7)?

3. How did the Jewish religious leaders react when they learned that Jesus had healed the man on the Sabbath? What did the man say to them (see verses 8–11)?

4. When it comes to healing your spiritual condition . . . you don't have a chance. What does Paul say about the futility of living in your own strength (see Romans 7:14–17)?

5. Paul states that he has the desire to do what is good but cannot carry it out. What instead does he do? What does this indicate to him (see verses 18–20)?

6. The condition of all people is that they are each "a prisoner of the law of sin" (verse 23). What does Paul say is the only solution to this dilemma (see verses 24–25)?

7. The paralyzed man trusted Jesus and was healed. What do the passages you've studied this week reveal about trusting God for your healing—whether physical or spiritual?

Week 34: JESUS' POWER OVER DEATH

You are leaving the church building. The funeral is over. The burial is next. Ahead of you walk six men who carry the coffin that carries the body of your son. Your only son.

You're numb from the sorrow. Stunned. You lost your husband, and now you've lost your son. If you had any more tears, you'd weep. If you had any more faith, you'd pray. But both are in short supply, so you do neither. You just stare at the back of the wooden box.

Suddenly the pallbearers stop. A man has stepped in front of the casket.

You've never seen him. He wasn't at the funeral. You have no idea what he is doing. But before you can object, he steps up to you and tells you not to cry.

Don't cry? This is a funeral. My son is dead. Who is he to tell me not to cry?

Those are your thoughts, but they never become your words, because before you can speak, he acts. He places his hand on the coffin and says, "Young man, I tell you, get up!"

"Now, just a minute," one of the pallbearers objects. But the sentence is interrupted by a sudden movement in the casket. The men look at one another and lower it to the ground. It's a good thing they do, because as soon as it touches the sidewalk the lid slowly opens . . .

It sounds like something out of a science-fiction novel, but it's right out of the Gospel of Luke. "He went up and touched the coffin, and the people who were carrying it stopped. Jesus said, 'Young man, I tell you, get up!' And the son sat up and began to talk" (Luke 7:14–15 NCV).

Be careful now. Don't read that last line too fast. Try it again. Slowly.

"The son sat up and began to talk."

What's odd about that verse? You got it. Dead people don't sit up! Dead people don't talk! Unless Jesus shows up. Because when Jesus shows up, you never know what might happen.

Martha can tell you. She'd hoped Jesus would show up to heal Lazarus. He didn't. Then she'd hoped he'd show up to bury Lazarus. He didn't. By the time Jesus made it to Bethany, Lazarus was four-days buried and Martha was wondering what kind of friend Jesus was.

She heard he was at the edge of town, so she stormed out to meet him. "Lord . . . if you had been here, my brother would not have died" (John 11:21). There is hurt in those words. Hurt and disappointment. Jesus was the one man who could have made a difference. But he didn't come.

Lazarus got worse. She watched out the window. Jesus didn't show. Her brother drifted in and out of consciousness. "He'll be here soon, Lazarus," she promised. "Hang on."

But the knock at the door never came. Jesus never appeared. Not to help. Not to heal. Not to bury. And now, four days later, he finally showed up. The funeral was over. The body was buried and the grave sealed. And Martha was hurt.

Her words have been echoed in a thousand cemeteries. "If you had been here, my brother would not have died." *If you were doing your part, God, my husband would have survived. If you'd done what was right, Lord, my baby would have lived. If only you'd have heard my prayer, God, my arms wouldn't be empty.*

When we face death, our definition of God is challenged. Which, in turn, challenges our faith. Which leads me to ask a grave question. Why is it that we interpret the presence of death as the absence of God? Why do we think that if the body is not healed, then God is not near? Is healing the only way God demonstrates his presence?

Sometimes we think so. And as a result, when God doesn't answer our prayers for healing, we get angry. Blame replaces belief. "If you had been here, God, then this death would not have happened." It's distressing that this view of God has no place for death.

Some time ago, a visitor to our house showed my daughters some tricks. Simple sleight-of-hand stuff. I stood to the side and watched the girls' responses. They were amazed. When the coin disappeared, they gasped. When it reappeared, they were stunned.

At first, I was humored by their bewilderment. But with time, my bewilderment became concern. Part of me didn't like what was happening. He was tricking them. They, the innocent, were being buffaloed by him, the sneak. I didn't like that. I didn't like seeing my children fooled.

So I whispered to my daughters. "It's in his sleeve." Sure enough it was. "It's behind his ear." And what do you know, I was right! Maybe I was rude to interfere with the show, but I don't enjoy watching a trickster pull one over on my children. Neither does God.

Jesus couldn't bear to sit and watch the bereaved be fooled. Please understand, he didn't raise the dead for the sake of the dead. He raised the dead for the sake of the living.

"Lazarus, come out!" (verse 43). Martha was silent as Jesus commanded. The mourners were quiet. No one stirred as Jesus stood face to face with the rock-hewn tomb and demanded that it release his friend. No one, that is, except Lazarus. Deep within the tomb, he moved. His stilled heart began to beat again. Wrapped eyes popped open. Wooden fingers lifted. Want to know what happened next? Let John tell you: "The dead man came out, his hands and feet wrapped with strips of linen, and a cloth around his face" (verse 44).

There it is again. Did you see it? "The dead man came out."

Once again, what is wrong with this picture?

Dead men don't walk out of tombs.

Question: What kind of God is this?

Answer: The God who holds the keys to life and death.

The kind of God who rolls back the sleeve of the trickster and reveals death for the parlor trick it is. The kind of God you want present at your funeral.

He'll do it again, you know. He's promised he would. And he's shown that he can. "The Lord himself will come down from heaven, with a loud command" (1 Thessalonians 4:16). The same voice that awoke the boy near Nain and awakened the corpse of Lazarus—the same voice will speak again. The earth and the sea will give up their dead. There will be no more death.

Jesus made sure of that.

THE HEART OF THE MATTER

- When Jesus shows up, you never know what might happen!
- Facing the death of a loved one will reveal your view of God.
- The God you serve holds the keys to life and death.
- Jesus promises that when he returns, death will be no more.

MEMORY VERSE

Your memory verse for this unit is 2 Corinthians 12:9. Take a few moments to review this verse, and then write it out by heart in the space below.

The Heart of Jesus

They had sat there, side by side, clutching each other's hands even as fear clutched their hearts. Finally, her husband had left—off to find another doctor, she supposed. And so she clung to her daughter's hand instead, holding her breath until the girl drew another. She prayed, desperately and incoherently, "Please let Jairus bring help. Please don't let my baby die."

Family members stirred in the lower level of the house, occasionally coming to check on mother and daughter. So when the anguished cry reached their ears, they ran to her. Arms were ready to enfold the bereaved mother. Shoulders were offered to cry on. And quiet voices gave the orders that the funeral preparations should begin.

By the time Jairus returned with Jesus, the mourners had already gathered. Jairus gathered his wife into his arms. Jesus' command that the mourners be sent away barely registered. The couple moved woodenly as Jesus and a few of his disciples guided them toward their daughter's room. Jairus had hoped that Jesus would have the power to heal his daughter. Imagine his astonishment when Jesus' power proved enough to raise her from the dead! Sorrow was whisked away. Only joy and rejoicing remained (see Mark 5:21–24, 35–43).

WEEKLY BIBLE STUDY

READ: LUKE 7:11–17 AND JOHN 11:17–44

1. Jesus has the power over life and death. What happened when Jesus approached the town of Nain? What scene did he witness (see Luke 7:11–12)?

2. Jesus approached the grieving mother and told her not to cry. What happened next? What did Jesus demonstrate about his power in this moment (see verses 13–15)?

3. The mourners who were present with the mother were understandably awestruck when they saw her dead son sit up. What did they exclaim to each other (see verses 16–17)?

4. Jesus also demonstrated his power of death in the story of the raising of Lazarus. What was the situation when Jesus arrived in Bethany (see John 11:17–20)?

5. Facing death will challenge your definition of God. What questions did Martha and Mary have for Jesus when they met him (see verses 21–22, 32)?

6. Jesus couldn't bear to watch the bereaved be fooled. What did he instruct Martha to do when he came to the tomb? How did he reveal his power (see verses 38–44)?

7. What do the passages that you've studied this week reveal about Jesus' authority and power over death? How does this encourage you today?

Week 35: THE STONE MOVER'S GALLERY

Let's revisit the gallery we entered at the start of this unit. Alone in the center of the hall is a single painting. It is different from the others. There are no faces. No people. The artist has dipped his brush into ancient prophecy and sketched two simple objects—a reed and a wick. "A bruised reed he will not break, and a smoldering wick he will not snuff out" (Matthew 12:20).

Look at the bruised reed. A once slender and tall stalk of sturdy river grass, it is now bowed and bent. *Are you a bruised reed?* Was it so long ago that you stood so tall, so proud? You were upright and sturdy, nourished by the waters and rooted in the riverbed of confidence.

Then something happened. You were bruised by harsh words, a friend's anger, a spouse's betrayal, your own failure. And you were wounded, bent ever so slightly. Your hollow reed, once upright, now stooped and was hidden in the bulrush.

And the smoldering wick on the candle. Once aflame, it is now flickering and failing. *Are you a smoldering wick?* Was it that long ago you blazed with faith? You illuminated the path. Then came the wind . . . the cold wind, the harsh wind. They said your ideas were foolish. They told you your dreams were too lofty. They scolded you for challenging the time-tested.

The constant wind wore you down. Oh, you stood strong for a moment, but the endless blast whipped your flickering flame, leaving you one pinch away from darkness.

The bruised reed and the smoldering wick. Society knows what to do with you. The world has a place for the beaten. The world will break you off; the world will snuff you out. But the artists of Scripture proclaim that God won't. Painted on canvas after canvas is the tender touch of a Creator who has a special place for the bruised and weary of the world. A God who is the friend of the wounded heart. A God who is the keeper of your dreams.

Quite a gallery, don't you think? A room of pain-to-peace portraits. A ward of renewed strength. A forest of restored vigor. An exhibition of second chances.

Let me ask you a crucial question. *Why are these stories in the Bible?* Why are the Gospels full of such people? Such hopeless people?

Though their situations vary, their conditions don't. They are trapped. Estranged. Rejected. They have nowhere to turn. On their lips, a desperate prayer. In their hearts, desolate dreams. In their hands, a broken rope. But before their eyes a never-say-die Galilean who steps in when everyone else steps out.

Surprisingly simple, the actions of this man. Just words of mercy or touches of kindness. Fingers on sightless eyes. A hand on a weary shoulder. Words for sad hearts . . . all fulfilling the prophecy, "A bruised reed he will not break, and a smoldering wick he will not snuff out."

Again I ask. Why are these portraits in the Bible? So we could look back with amazement at what Jesus *did*? No. The purpose of these stories is to tell us what Jesus *does*. These are not just Sunday school stories. Not romantic fables. Not somewhere-over-the-rainbow illusions. They are historic moments in which a real God met real pain so we could answer the question, "Where is God when I hurt?"

Now that you've read their stories, reflect on yours. Stand in front of the canvases that bear your name and draw your portraits. It doesn't have to be on a canvas with paint. It could be on a computer with words, in a sculpture with clay, in a song with lyrics. It doesn't matter how you do it, but I urge you to do it. Record your drama. Retell your saga. Plot your journey.

Begin with "before." What was it like before you knew him? Do you remember? Perhaps it was yesterday. Maybe you know him well. Maybe you've just met him. Again, that doesn't matter. What matters is that you never forget what life is like without him.

But don't just portray the past; depict the present. Describe his touch. Display the difference he has made in your life. This task has its challenges, too. Whereas painting the "before" can be painful, painting the "present" can be unclear. He's not finished with you yet!

Ah, but look how far you've come! God has begun a work in your heart, and what God begins, God completes. "He who began a good work in you will carry it on to completion until the day of Christ Jesus" (Philippians 1:6). So chronicle what Christ has done. If he has brought peace, sketch a dove. If joy, splash a rainbow on a wall. When you're finished, put it where you can see it. Put it where you can be reminded, daily, of the Father's tender power.

Here's an idea. I know it's crazy, but what if, when we all get to our eternal home, we make a gallery? I don't know if they allow this kind of stuff in heaven. But something tells me the Father won't mind. After all, there's plenty of space and lots of time.

And somewhere in the midst of that arena of hope is your story. Person after person comes. Solomon asks you questions. Job compliments your stamina. Joshua lauds your courage. And when they all applaud, you applaud, too. For in heaven, everyone knows that all praise goes to one source. And speaking of this "source," he's represented in the heavenly gallery as well. There is one display elevated high on a platform above the others. Visible from any point in the gallery is a boulder. It's round. It's heavy. It used to seal the opening of a tomb.

But not anymore. Ask Mary and Martha. Ask Peter. Ask Lazarus. Ask anyone in the gallery. They'll tell you. Stones were never a match for God.

Will there be such a gallery in heaven? Who knows? But I do know there used to be a stone in front of a tomb. And I do know it was moved. And I also know that there are stones in your path. Stones that trip and stones that trap. Stones too big for you.

But those stones are no match for God. Not then, and not now. He still moves stones.

THE HEART OF THE MATTER

- The artists of Scripture proclaim that God will never overlook you.
- Jesus is the never-say-die Galilean who steps in when others step out.
- The purpose of the stories in the Bible is to tell us what God does.
- There will be stones in your path . . . but your God still moves stones.

MEMORY VERSE

This is it . . . one last review of your memory verse. Write out the words of 2 Corinthians 12:9 from memory in the space below. Reflect on what these words mean to you.

The Heart of Jesus

Thomas had seen it all. For three years he had watched Jesus feed the hungry, heal the sick, even raise the dead. The miracles had been amazing. Jesus had seemed to possess the very power of heaven. So why had he died? Jesus had been able to slip away from his pursuers before. What made him vulnerable now? Where had the power been when Judas betrayed him? When the soldiers beat him? When Pilate condemned him? Where had the power been when the cross was thrust onto his shoulders? When they nailed him to that cross? Now Jesus was dead, and the power was gone. That was that. Thomas felt duped, disappointed, and doubtful. He would be more careful about what he trusted in the future. So when the disciples came to him with the astonishing news that Jesus had returned, Thomas put his foot down. "No way. Unless I get a good look myself, I won't believe it. In fact, I want to touch the man, look into his eyes, see the scars." And so Jesus came. The power had never been gone, and Thomas was welcomed to experience it anew (see John 20:24–29).

WEEKLY BIBLE STUDY

READ: ISAIAH 40:28–31 AND EPHESIANS 6:10–20

1. Jesus never grew so weary that he could not help people out of hopeless situations. What does Isaiah say about God's strength and endurance (see Isaiah 40:28)?

2. What does Isaiah say that God provides to those who are in need? What promise is given to those who continue to put their hope in the Lord (see verses 29–31)?

3. Paul also encourages followers of Jesus to rely on his mighty power. Who is your enemy is this world? What has God given you to fight this enemy (see Ephesians 6:10–12)?

4. Paul states that God gives you his armor to stand against the enemy. What is the purpose of the belt, breastplate, and shoes that God provides (see verses 13–15)?

5. What is the purpose of the shield, helmet, and sword that God provides? Why do you think Paul adds the need for prayer after the list of armor (see verses 16–18)?

6. Paul closes his instructions to the believers with a request for prayer. What does Paul ask? What does he want the believers to pray that he will be able to do (see verses 19–20)?

7. What do the passages you've studied reveal about God's strength when you are weak? Which pieces of "armor" do you need to put on so you can stand against your enemy?

EXPERIENCING THE
FORGIVENESS OF JESUS

He deserves our compassion. When you see him, do not laugh. Do not mock. Do not turn away or shake your head. Just gently lead him to the nearest bench and help him sit down.

Have pity on the man. He is so fearful, so wide-eyed. He's a deer on the streets of Manhattan. Tarzan walking through the urban jungle.

Who is this forlorn creature? This ashen-faced orphan? He is—please remove your hats out of respect—he is the man in the women's department. Looking for a gift.

On this day, he has decided to buy his wife the gift of a purse. I thought it would be easy. What could be complicated about selecting a tool for holding cards and money? I've used the same money clip for eight years. What would be difficult about buying a purse?

Oh, naive soul that I am. Tell an attendant in the men's department that you want a wallet, and you're taken to a small counter next to the cash register. Your only decision is black or brown. Tell an attendant in the ladies' department you want a purse, and you are escorted to a room of shelves. Shelves with purses. Purses with price tags. Small but potent price tags . . . prices so potent they should remove the need for a purse, right?

Oh, the things we do to give gifts to those we love. But we don't mind, do we? We would do it all again. Fact is, we do it all again. Every Christmas, every birthday, every so often we find ourselves in foreign territory. Grown-ups are in toy stores. Dads are in teen stores. Wives are in the hunting department, and husbands are in the purse department.

Have you ever wondered why God gives so much? We could exist on far less. He could have left the world flat and gray; we wouldn't have known the difference. But he didn't. Instead, he splashed orange in the sunrise and cast the sky in blue.

If we give gifts to show our love, how much more does he? If we—speckled with foibles and greed—love to give gifts, how much more does God, pure and perfect God, enjoy giving gifts to us? Jesus asked, "If you hard-hearted, sinful men know how to give good gifts to your children, won't your Father in heaven even more certainly give good gifts to those who ask him for them?" (Matthew 7:11 TLB).

God's gifts shed light on God's heart—God's good and generous heart. James tells us, "Every desirable and beneficial gift comes out of heaven. The gifts are rivers of light cascading down from the Father of Light" (James 1:17 MSG). Every gift reveals God's love . . . but no gift reveals his love more than the gifts of the cross. They came wrapped, not in paper, but in passion. Not placed around a tree, but a cross. Not covered with ribbons, but sprinkled with blood. The gifts of the cross.

Much has been said about the gift of the cross itself, but what of the other gifts? What of the nails, the crown of thorns? The garments taken by the soldiers. The garments given for the burial. Have you taken time to open these gifts? He didn't have to give them, you know. The only act required for our salvation was the shedding of blood. Yet he did much more.

Could it be that the hill of the cross is rich with God's gifts? Let's examine some of them. Let's unwrap these gifts of grace as if—or perhaps—for the first time. And as you touch them—as you feel the timber of the cross and trace the braid of the crown and finger the point of the spike—pause and listen. Perchance you will hear him whisper: "I did it just for you."[19]

— PRAYER —

Dear Lord, take me to the cross this week. Help me see this precious gift of forgiveness with new eyes. Give me a glimpse of your fathomless love, the enormous price, and your perfect plan. Help me appreciate the cost of my forgiveness. And as I experience the forgiveness of Jesus this week, show me how to extend that same forgiveness to those around me. Amen.

— MEMORY VERSES —

He has rescued us from the dominion of darkness and brought us into the kingdom of the Son he loves, in whom we have redemption, the forgiveness of sins.

COLOSSIANS 1:13–14

Week 36: CONSIDER THE COST

You know the most amazing thing about the coming of Christ? You know the most remarkable part of the incarnation? Not just that he swapped eternity for calendars. Though such an exchange deserves our notice.

Scripture says that the number of God's years is unsearchable. "How great is God—beyond our understanding! The number of his years is past finding out" (Job 36:26). We may search out the moment the first wave slapped on a shore or the first star burst in the sky, but we'll never find the first moment when God was God, for there is no moment when God was not God. He has never not been, for he is eternal. God is not bound by time.

But when Jesus came to the earth, all this changed. He heard for the first time a phrase that was never used in heaven: "Your time is up." As a child, he had to leave the temple because his time was up. As a man, he had to leave his hometown of Nazareth because his time was up. And as a Savior, he had to die on the cross because his time was up. For thirty-three years, the stallion of heaven lived in the corral of time.

That's certainly remarkable, but there is something even more so.

You might think it was the fact that he lived in a body. One moment he was a boundless spirit; the next he was flesh and bones. Remember these words of King David? "Where can I go from your Spirit? Where can I flee from your presence? If I go up to the heavens, you are there; if I make my bed in the depths, you are there. If I rise on the wings of the dawn, if I settle on the far side of the sea, even there your hand will guide me, your right hand will hold me fast" (Psalm 139:7–10).

Our asking "Where is God?" is like a fish asking "Where is water?" or a bird asking "Where is air?" God is everywhere! Equally present in Peking and Peoria. As active in the lives of Icelanders as in the lives of Texans. The dominion of God is "from sea to sea and from the River to the ends of the earth" (Psalm 72:8). We cannot find a place where God is not.

Yet when God entered time and became a man, he who was boundless became bound. Imprisoned in flesh. Restricted by weary-prone muscles and eyelids. For more than three decades, his once limitless reach would be limited to the stretch of an arm, his speed checked to the pace of human feet.

Do you ever wonder, as I do, if he was ever tempted to reclaim his boundlessness? In the middle of a long trip, did he ever consider transporting himself to the next city? When the rain chilled his bones, was he tempted to change the weather? When the heat parched his lips, did he give thought to popping over to the Caribbean for some refreshment?

If ever he entertained such thoughts, he never gave in to them. Not once. Stop and think about this. Not once did Christ use his supernatural powers for personal comfort. With one word he could have transformed the hard earth into a soft bed, but he didn't. With a wave of his hand he could have boomeranged the spit of his accusers back into their faces, but he didn't. With a mere arch of his brow, he could have paralyzed the hand of the soldier as he braided the crown of thorns. But he didn't.

Remarkable. But was this the most remarkable part of his coming to earth? Many would argue not. Many, perhaps most, would point beyond the surrender of timelessness and boundlessness to the surrender of sinlessness. It's easy to see why.

Isn't this the message of the crown of thorns?

"Using thorny branches, they made a crown, put it on his head, and put a stick in his right hand. Then the soldiers bowed before Jesus and made fun of him, saying, 'Hail, King of the Jews!'" (Matthew 27:29 NCV). An unnamed Roman soldier took branches—mature enough to bear thorns, nimble enough to bend—and wove them into a crown of mockery for Jesus . . . a crown of thorns.

Throughout the Bible, thorns symbolize not sin but the consequence of sin. Remember Eden? After Adam and Eve sinned, God cursed the land: "Cursed is the ground because of you; through painful toil you will eat food from it all the days of your life. It will produce thorns and thistles for you, and you will eat the plants of the field" (Genesis 3:17–18). Brambles on the earth are the product of sin in the heart.

This truth is echoed in God's words to Moses. He urged the Israelites to purge the land of godless people. Disobedience would result in difficulties. "But if you do not drive out the inhabitants of the land, those you allow to remain will become barbs in your eyes and thorns in your sides" (Numbers 33:55).

Rebellion results in thorns. "Evil people's lives are like paths covered with thorns and traps" (Proverbs 22:5 NCV). Jesus even compared the lives of evil people to a thornbush. In speaking of false prophets, he said, "By their fruit you will recognize them. Do people pick grapes from thornbushes, or figs from thistles?" (Matthew 7:16).

The fruit of sin is thorns—spiny, prickly, cutting thorns. What exactly is the fruit of sin? Step into the briar patch of humanity and feel a few thistles. Shame. Fear. Disgrace. Discouragement. Anxiety. Haven't our hearts been caught in these brambles?

The heart of Jesus, however, had not. He had never been cut by the thorns of sin. What we face daily, he never knew. Anxiety? He never worried! Guilt? He was never guilty! Fear? He never left the presence of God! Jesus never knew the fruits of sin until he became sin for us.

And when he did, all the emotions of sin tumbled in on him like shadows in a forest. He felt anxious, guilty, and alone. Can't you hear the emotion in his prayer? "My God, my God, why have you forsaken me?" (Matthew 27:46). These are not the words of a saint. This is the cry of a sinner.

This prayer is one of the most remarkable parts of his coming. But I can think of something even greater. Want to know the coolest thing about the coming?

Not that the one who played marbles with the stars gave it up to play marbles with marbles. Or that the one who hung the galaxies gave it up to hang doorjambs to the displeasure of a cranky client who wanted everything yesterday but couldn't pay for anything until tomorrow.

Not that he refused to defend himself when blamed for every sin of every man and woman since Adam. Or that he stood silent as a million guilty verdicts echoed in the tribunal of heaven and the Giver of Light was left in the chill of a sinner's night.

Not even that after three days in a dark hole he stepped into the Easter sunrise with a smile and a swagger and a question for lowly Lucifer—"Is that your best punch?"

That was cool, incredibly cool. But want to know the coolest thing about the one who gave up the crown of heaven for a crown of thorns?

He did it for you. Just for you.

THE HEART OF THE MATTER

- God willingly chose to enter time and be imprisoned in flesh.
- The fruit of sin is thorns—spiny, prickly, cutting thorns.
- The heart of Jesus had never been cut by the thorns of sin.
- Jesus gave up the crown of heaven for a crown of thorns.

MEMORY VERSES

Take a few moments to review your Bible memory verses for this unit, and then write out the words of Colossians 1:13–14 from memory in the space below.

The Heart of Jesus

People brought him the sick. Jesus touched and healed people with every conceivable disease. He did not shrink from the outcasts and the unlovely. Blind eyes, shriveled limbs, pocked cheeks, decaying skin, twitching muscles, deaf ears . . . he had seen it all. But the outward ailments were only part of it. Jesus also knew what lay in the hearts of people. He could see it in their eyes—liars, cheaters, backstabbers, murderers, bigots, adulterers, gossips. He could heal their bodies, but he longed for the chance to heal their sin-sick souls. It was for this reason that he came to earth—for every selfish, angry, competitive, self-righteous, manipulative, cheating, stingy, ungrateful person who would come to him for forgiveness.

WEEKLY BIBLE STUDY

READ: PSALM 139:7–10 AND PHILIPPIANS 2:5–11

1. It is remarkable that God chose to be bound in human flesh and bones. What two questions does the psalmist ask about the Lord (see Psalm 139:7)?

2. What does the psalmist write about God's ability to be everywhere at all times? What comfort does he find in God's continual presence (see verses 8–10)?

3. Not once did Jesus use his supernatural powers for personal comfort. What does Paul say was Christ's mindset when he came into this world (see Philippians 2:5–6)?

4. Jesus provides a model for how every believer should think and behave. How does Paul say that Jesus demonstrated the quality of humility (see verse 7)?

5. What does Paul say was Jesus' ultimate act of humility for humankind? What happened as a result of Christ's obedience to his heavenly Father (see verses 8–11)?

6. Jesus triumphed over sin and death and has been exalted by God to "the highest place" (verse 9). What does this say about his authority over your life?

7. Jesus gave up the crown of heaven for a crown of thorns—and he did it *for you*. What do you want to say to Jesus right now for the incredible sacrifice he made for you?

Week 37: HIS CHOICE

He never should have asked me to keep the list. I dread showing it to him. He's a skilled builder, a fine friend. And he has built us a great house. But the house has a few mistakes.

Until this week, I didn't see them. But, then again, until this week, I didn't live in the house. Once you take up residence in a place, you see every flaw.

"Make a list of them," he told me.

If you say so, I thought.

A bedroom door won't lock. The storage room window is cracked. Someone forgot to install towel racks in the girls' bathroom. Someone else forgot the knobs to the den door. As I said, the house is nice, but the list is growing.

Looking at the list of the builder's mistakes caused me to think about God making a list of mine. After all, hasn't he taken up residence in my heart? And if I see flaws in my house, imagine what he sees in me. Oh, dare we think of the list he could compile?

The door hinges to the prayer room have grown rusty from underuse.

The stove called jealousy is overheating.

The attic floor is weighted with too many regrets.

The cellar is cluttered with too many secrets.

And won't someone raise the shutter and chase the pessimism out of this heart?

The list of our weaknesses. Would you like anyone to see yours? Would you like them made public? How would you feel if they were posted high so that everyone, including Christ himself, could see?

May I take you to the moment it was? Yes, there is a list of your failures. Christ has chronicled your shortcomings. And, yes, that list has been made public. But you've never seen it. Neither have I. Come with me to the hill of Calvary, and I'll tell you why.

Watch as the soldiers shove the carpenter to the ground and stretch his arms against the beams. One presses a knee against a forearm and a spike against a hand. Jesus turns his face toward the nail just as the soldier lifts the hammer to strike it.

Couldn't Jesus have stopped him? With a flex of the biceps, with a clench of the fist, he could have resisted. Is this not the same hand that stilled the sea? Cleansed the temple? Summoned the dead? But the fist doesn't clench . . . and the moment isn't aborted.

The mallet rings and the skin rips and the blood begins to drip, then rush. Then the questions follow. Why? Why didn't Jesus resist?

"Because he loved us," we reply. That is true, wonderfully true, but—forgive me—only partially true. There is more to his reason. He saw something that made him stay.

As the soldier pressed his arm, Jesus rolled his head to the side, and with his cheek resting on the wood he saw . . . a mallet? Yes. A nail? Yes. The soldier's hand? Yes.

But he saw something else. He saw the hand of God.

With a wave, this hand toppled Babel's tower and split the Red Sea. From this hand flew the locusts that plagued Egypt and the raven that fed Elijah. Is it any wonder the psalmist celebrated liberation by declaring, "You drove out the nations with Your hand. . . . It was Your right hand, Your arm, and the light of Your countenance" (Psalm 44:2–3 NKJV).

The hand of God is a mighty hand.

The crowd at the cross concluded that the purpose of the pounding was to skewer the hands of Christ to a beam. But they were only half right. We can't fault them for missing the other half. They couldn't see it. But Jesus could. And heaven could. And we can.

Through the eyes of Scripture, we see what others missed but what Jesus saw. "He canceled the record of the charges against us and took it away by nailing it to the cross" (Colossians 2:14 NLT). Between his hand and the wood was a list. A list of our mistakes: our lusts and lies and greedy moments and prodigal years. A list of our sins.

God has done with us what I am doing with our house. He penned a list of our faults. The list God has made, however, cannot be read. The mistakes are covered. The sins are hidden. Those at the top are hidden by his hand; those down the list are covered by his blood.

Your sins are "blotted out" by Jesus (TLB). "He has forgiven you all your sins: he has utterly wiped out the damning evidence of broken laws and commandments which always hung over our heads, and has completely annulled it by nailing it . . . on the cross" (Colossians 2:14 PHILLIPS).

This is why Jesus refused to close his fist. He saw the list! What kept him from resisting? This warrant, this tabulation of your failures. He knew the price of those sins was death. He knew the source of those sins was you, and since he couldn't bear the thought of eternity without you, he chose the nails.

Even as we progress more and more to a paperless society—one where a person wonders how we ever existed without online bill paying and the convenience of texting and social media—we still have not lost our esteem for recordkeeping. In the business world, we may no longer jot our lists of creditors and debtors on paper, but we are still scrupulous when it comes to data entry.

This leads us to the question. Based on what you have learned so far concerning the enormous charge Jesus paid, why didn't God keep our record of sin "on file"?

The hand squeezing the handle was not a Roman infantryman.

The force behind the hammer was not an angry mob.

The verdict behind the death was not decided by jealous Jews.

Jesus himself chose the nails.

So the hands of Jesus opened up. Had the soldier hesitated, Jesus himself would have swung the mallet. He knew how; he was no stranger to the driving of nails. As a carpenter he knew what it took. And as a Savior he knew what it meant. He knew that the purpose of the nail was to place your sins where they could be hidden by his sacrifice and covered by his blood.

THE HEART OF THE MATTER

- The list of every human's failures and shortcomings is a long one.
- Between Jesus' hand and the wood was the list of *your* mistakes.
- The blood of Jesus on the cross blotted out the list of your sins.
- Jesus himself chose the nails—to erase the record of sins.

MEMORY VERSES

Your verses to memorize for this unit are Colossians 1:13–14. Take a few moments to review these verses, and then write them out from memory in the space below.

The Heart of Jesus

The trap had been set and the ambush planned. As Jesus and his disciples were spending the evening in prayer, the soldiers were sharpening their swords and lighting their torches. Gethsemane was quiet except for the murmured prayers of Jesus and the snoring of his friends. Then, suddenly, noise. Tramping feet, crackling firebrands, shouted orders. The disciples leapt to their feet, momentarily dazed by the light. A surge of men entered their circle. Peter, James, and John stood before Jesus in order to protect him. Peter drew out a sword, and in one clumsy slash, cut off the ear of Malchus, the high priest's servant. A full-blown brawl was imminent. Jesus knew that the actions of this man would lead to him being carried off, beaten, taunted, bloodied, and nailed to a cross. He could have resisted. But instead, even in this tense moment, he had mercy on the man. He reached out and healed Malchus's ear (see John 18:3–11; Luke 22:47–53).

WEEKLY BIBLE STUDY

READ: ISAIAH 53:3–10 AND COLOSSIANS 2:9–15

1. The prophet Isaiah foretold the coming of the Messiah some seven hundred years before Jesus' birth. What did the prophet say he would endure (see Isaiah 53:3)?

2. Jesus could have halted his crucifixion at any time. What did he do instead? Why did he choose to go through with his painful execution (see verses 4–6)?

3. Jesus did not argue with his accusers or plead with the authorities to release him as he went to the cross. How does this fit what Isaiah said about him (see verses 7–8)?

4. Jesus was treated by the Romans in the same way that a criminal would be treated. But what does Isaiah say was different about him (see verses 9–10)?

5. Paul says "the fullness of the Deity" lived in bodily form in Christ (Colossians 2:9). What did Jesus' death on the cross allow you to "put off" (see verses 11–12)?

6. What did God do for you when you were spiritually dead in your sins? What was taken away when Jesus chose to be nailed to the cross (see verses 14–15)?

7. What do the passages you've studied this week reveal about the sins you've confessed to God? What does Jesus say about your sins that have been forgiven?

Week 38: OUR CHOICE

Meet Edwin Thomas, a master of the stage. During the latter half of the 1800s, this small man with the huge voice had few rivals. Debuting in *Richard III* at the age of fifteen, he quickly established himself as a premier Shakespearean actor.

In New York, he performed *Hamlet* for one hundred consecutive nights. In London, he won the approval of the tough British critics. When it came to tragedy on the stage, Edwin Thomas was in a select group.

When it came to tragedy in life, the same could be said as well.

Edwin had two brothers, John and Junius. Both were actors, although neither rose to his stature. In 1863, the three siblings united their talents to perform *Julius Caesar*. The fact that Edwin's brother John took the role of Brutus was an eerie harbinger of what awaited the brothers—and the nation—two years hence.

For this John who played the assassin in *Julius Caesar* is the same John who took the role of assassin in Ford's Theatre. On a crisp April night in 1865, he stole quietly into the rear of a box in the Washington theater and fired a bullet at the head of Abraham Lincoln. Yes, the last name of the brothers was Booth—Edwin Thomas Booth and John Wilkes Booth.

Edwin was never the same after that night. Shame from his brother's crime drove him into retirement. He might have never returned to the stage had it not been for a twist of fate at a New Jersey train station. Edwin was awaiting his coach when a well-dressed young man, pressed by the crowd, lost his footing and fell between the platform and a moving train.

Without hesitation, Edwin locked a leg around a railing, grabbed the man, and pulled him to safety. After the sighs of relief, the young man recognized the famous Edwin Booth.

Edwin, however, didn't recognize the young man whom he had just rescued. That knowledge came weeks later in a letter—a letter that he carried in his pocket to the grave. A letter from General Adams Badeau, chief secretary to General Ulysses S. Grant. A letter thanking Edwin Booth for saving the life of the child of an American hero, Abraham Lincoln. How ironic that while one brother killed the president, the other brother saved the president's son. The boy whom Edwin Booth yanked to safety? Robert Todd Lincoln.[20]

Edwin and John Booth. Same father, mother, profession, and passion—yet one chooses life, the other, death. How could it happen? I don't know, but it does. Though their story is dramatic, it's not unique.

Abel and Cain, both sons of Adam. Abel chooses God. Cain chooses murder. And God lets him.

Abraham and Lot, both pilgrims in Canaan. Abraham chooses God. Lot chooses Sodom. And God lets him.

David and Saul, both kings of Israel. David chooses God. Saul chooses power. And God lets him.

Peter and Judas, both deny their Lord. Peter seeks mercy. Judas seeks death. And God lets him.

In every age of history, on every page of Scripture, the truth is revealed: God allows us to make our own choices.

And no one delineates this more clearly than Jesus. According to him, we can choose a narrow gate or a wide one, a narrow road or a wide one, or the big crowd or the small crowd (see Matthew 7:13–14). We can choose to build on rock or sand (see verses 24–27), serve God or riches (see 6:24), or be numbered among the sheep or the goats (see 25:32–33).

God is omnipotent—meaning he is all-powerful. But he has chosen to limit his power in one area of his creation: our human will. He will not force himself or his ways upon us. He gave his creation the dignity of choice—choosing whether or not we will accept his offer of forgiveness, repent of our sin, and turn to him.

Jesus' forgiveness is a done deal, accomplished at Calvary. However, "Calvary's trio" of crosses reminds us that we must personally accept and embrace this gift in our lives.

Ever wonder why there were two crosses next to Christ? Why not six or ten? Ever wonder why Jesus was in the center? Why not on the far right or far left? Could it be that the two crosses on the hill symbolize one of God's greatest gifts? The gift of choice.

The two criminals have so much in common. Convicted by the same system. Condemned to the same death. Surrounded by the same crowd. Equally close to the same Jesus. In fact, they begin with the same sarcasm: "The two criminals also said cruel things to Jesus" (Matthew 27:44 CEV). But one changed.

"One of the criminals who hung there hurled insults at him: 'Aren't you the Messiah? Save yourself and us!' But the other criminal rebuked him. 'Don't you fear God,' he said, 'since you are under the same sentence? We are punished justly, for we are getting what our deeds deserve. But this man has done nothing wrong.' Then he said, 'Jesus, remember me when you come into your kingdom.' Jesus answered him, 'Truly I tell you, today you will be with me in paradise'" (Luke 23:39–43).

Much has been said about the prayer of the penitent thief, and it certainly warrants our admiration. But while we rejoice at the thief who changed, dare we forget the one who didn't? What about him, Jesus? Wouldn't a personal invitation be appropriate? Wouldn't a word of persuasion be timely?

There are times when God sends thunder to stir us. There are times when God sends blessings to lure us. But then there are times when God sends nothing but silence as he honors us with the freedom to choose where we spend eternity. Have we been given any greater privilege than that of choice? Not only does this privilege offset any injustice, but the gift of free will can also offset any mistakes.

Think about the thief who repented. Though we know little about him, we know this: he made some bad mistakes in life. He chose the wrong crowd, the wrong morals, the wrong behavior. But would you consider his life a waste? Is he spending eternity reaping the fruit of all the bad choices he made? No, just the opposite. He is enjoying the fruit of the one good choice he made. In the end all his bad choices were redeemed by a solitary good one.

How can two brothers be born of the same mother, grow up in the same home, and one choose life and the other choose death? I don't know, but they do.

How could two men see the same Jesus and one choose to mock him and the other choose to pray to him? I don't know, but they did.

And when one prayed, Jesus loved him enough to save him. And when the other mocked, Jesus loved him enough to let him. He allowed him the choice.

He does the same for you.

THE HEART OF THE MATTER

- God allows you to make your own choice when it comes to following him.
- God has chosen to limit his power over his creation in regard to human will.
- You must personally accept and embrace the gift of God's salvation.
- God honors you with the freedom to choose where you spend eternity.

MEMORY VERSES

Your verses to memorize for this unit are Colossians 1:13–14. Take a few moments to review these verses, and then write them out from memory in the space below.

The Heart of Jesus

Forgiveness was not a foreign concept to the Pharisees. After all, they obeyed the Law, attended the feasts, and brought their sacrifices to the Lord. In the heart of their city, the temple was a hubbub of priestly activity. The savory smoke of grilled meat filled the air as it rose toward heaven. Morning sacrifices. Evening sacrifices. Offerings brought for firstborn babies, for the new harvests, for thanksgiving, and as a tithe. Animal after animal took its place on the altar so that God would not be angry with the people. The prayers, the worship, the sacrifices—they were a familiar backdrop to every Jew's life in Jerusalem. But when the *perfect* sacrifice came through town, they missed him completely. In fact, their plotting brought about his capture, his trial, his sentence, and his sacrifice. But Jesus didn't hold it against them. He offered them the same choice he offers to everyone—forgiveness.

WEEKLY BIBLE STUDY

READ: MATTHEW 25:31–46 AND LUKE 23:39–43

1. Jesus once told a parable to explain what will happen at the end of the age when he returns in glory. What will Jesus do with the people before him (see Matthew 25:31–33)?

2. What will Jesus say to the "sheep" on his right who have faithfully followed after him? What reasons does he give for these blessings (see verses 34–40)?

3. What will Jesus say to the "goats" on his left who refused to follow after him? What reasons does he give for these judgments against them (see verses 41–46)?

4. What does Jesus' parable reveal about the consequences people face if they do not choose to accept his offer of salvation and follow him in loving and serving others?

5. The criminals who hung on the crosses near Jesus also had a choice to make regarding their salvation. What choice did the first criminal make (see Luke 23:39)?

6. The second criminal had a completely different attitude. What request did he make of Jesus? How did Christ respond to him (see verses 40–43)?

7. How do you respond to the fact that God leaves the choice of where you will spend eternity up to you? Who in your life do you need to encourage to follow after Jesus?

Week 39: CLOTHED IN CHRIST

The maître d´ wouldn't change his mind. He didn't care that this was our honeymoon. It didn't matter that the evening at the classy country club restaurant was a wedding gift. He couldn't have cared less that Denalyn and I had gone without lunch to save room for dinner.

All of this was immaterial in comparison to the looming problem.

I wasn't wearing a jacket.

Didn't know I needed one. I thought a sport shirt was sufficient. It was clean and tucked in. But Mr. Black-Tie with the French accent was unimpressed. He seated everyone else. Mr. and Mrs. Debonair were given a table. Mr. and Mrs. Classier-Than-You were seated. But Mr. and Mrs. Didn't-Wear-a-Jacket?

If I'd had another option, I wouldn't have begged. But the hour was late, other restaurants were closed or booked, and we were hungry. "There's got to be something you can do," I pleaded. He looked at me, then at Denalyn, and let out a long sigh that puffed his cheeks.

"All right, let me see." He disappeared into the cloakroom and emerged with a jacket. "Put this on."

I did. The sleeves were too short. The shoulders were too tight. And the color was lime green.

But I didn't complain. I had a jacket, and we were taken to a table. (Don't tell anyone, but I took it off when the food came.)

For all the inconvenience of the evening, we ended up with a great dinner and an even greater parable. I needed a jacket, but all I had was a prayer. The fellow was too kind to turn me away but too loyal to lower the standard. So the very one who required a jacket gave me a jacket, and we were given a table.

Isn't this what happened at the cross? Seats at God's table are not available to the sloppy. But who among us is anything but? Unkempt morality. Untidy with the truth. Careless with people. Our moral clothing is in disarray. Yes, the standard for sitting at God's table is high, but the love of God for his children is higher. So he offers a gift.

Not a lime-colored jacket but a robe. A seamless robe. Not a garment pulled out of a cloakroom but a robe worn by his Son, Jesus.

Scripture says little about the clothes Jesus wore. We know what his cousin John the Baptist wore. We know what the religious leaders wore. But the clothing of Christ is nondescript: neither so humble as to touch hearts nor so glamorous as to turn heads.

One reference to Jesus' garments is noteworthy. "They divided his clothes among the four of them. They also took his robe, but it was seamless, woven in one piece from top to bottom. So they said, 'Rather than tearing it apart, let's throw dice for it'" (John 19:23–24 NLT).

It must have been Jesus' finest possession. Jewish tradition called for a mother to make such a robe and present it to her son as a departure gift when he left home. Had Mary done this for Jesus? We don't know. But we do know the tunic was without seam, woven from top to bottom. Why is this significant?

Scripture often describes our behavior as the clothes we wear. Peter urges us to be "clothed with humility" (1 Peter 5:5 NKJV). David speaks of evil people who clothe themselves "with cursing" (Psalm 109:18 NKJV).

Garments can symbolize character, and like his garment, Jesus' character was seamless. Coordinated. Unified. Uninterrupted perfection.

"Woven . . . from top to bottom." Jesus wasn't led by his own mind; he was led by the mind of his Father. Listen to his words: "The Son can do nothing on his own but only what he sees the Father doing, for whatever the Father does, the Son does likewise" (John 5:19 NRSV). "I can do nothing on my own. As I hear, I judge" (John 5:30 NRSV).

The character of Jesus was a seamless fabric woven from heaven to earth . . . from God's thoughts to Jesus' actions. From God's tears to Jesus' compassion. From God's word to Jesus' response. All one piece. All a picture of the character of Jesus.

But when Christ was nailed to the cross, he took off his robe of seamless perfection and assumed a different wardrobe: the wardrobe of indignity. *The indignity of nakedness.* Stripped before his own mother and loved ones. Shamed before his family. *The indignity of failure.* For a few pain-filled hours, the religious leaders were the victors, and Christ appeared the loser. Worst of all, he wore *the indignity of sin.* "'He himself bore our sins' in his body on the cross, so that we might die to sins and live for righteousness" (1 Peter 2:24).

The clothing of Christ on the cross? Sin—yours and mine. The sins of all humanity.

I remember one time my father explaining to me the reason a group of men on the side of the road wore striped clothing. "They're prisoners," he said. "They have broken the law and are serving time." You want to know what stuck with me about these men? They never looked up. They never made eye contact. Were they ashamed? Probably so.

What they felt on the side of the road was what our Savior felt on the cross—disgrace. Every aspect of the crucifixion was intended not only to hurt the victim but to shame him. Crucifixion was so abhorrent that Cicero wrote, "Let the very name of the cross be far away, not only from the body of a Roman citizen, but even from his thoughts, his eyes, his ears."[21]

While on the cross, Jesus felt the indignity and disgrace of a criminal. No, he was not guilty. No, he had not committed a sin. And, no, he did not deserve to be sentenced. But you and I were, we had, and we did. We were left in the same position I was with the maître d´—having nothing to offer but a prayer.

Jesus willingly lifted our shame from our shoulders so he could don the burden on his way to the cross. Our shame is gone. Over. Finished. So why do we still insist on walking around our Father's world as if we are underdressed? Cowering in shame as if we had not been forgiven of each and every sin?

Jesus, however, goes further than the maître d´. Can you imagine the restaurant host removing his tuxedo coat and offering it to me?

Jesus does. We're not talking about an ill-fitting, leftover jacket. He offers a robe of seamless purity and dons my patchwork coat of pride, greed, and selfishness.

It wasn't enough for him to prepare you a feast.

It wasn't enough for him to reserve you a seat.

It wasn't enough for him to cover the cost and provide the transportation to the banquet. He did something more. He let you wear his own clothes so that you would be properly dressed.

He did that . . . just for you.

THE HEART OF THE MATTER

- God's standards of holiness are high, but his love for his children is even higher.
- Jesus' character, like his garment, was seamless, unified, uninterrupted perfection.
- Jesus wore the garment of humanity's sin and shame on the cross.
- Jesus let you wear his own clothes so you would be dressed in righteousness.

MEMORY VERSES

Your verses to memorize for this unit are Colossians 1:13–14. Take a few moments to review these verses, and then write them out from memory in the space below.

The Heart of Jesus

It was bad enough that Jesus hadn't asked for the woman to be thrown out of the house. It was bad enough that Jesus had allowed her to wet his feet with her tears, wipe them with her hair, kiss them, and pour perfume on them. It was bad enough that Jesus had then called out their friend Simon for his lack of hospitality. But when Jesus said that the woman's *sins* had been forgiven, it was just too much for the guests. They began to mutter among themselves. "Who is this who even forgives sins?" (Luke 7:49). It wasn't the first time Jesus had received such criticism. When Jesus forgave the sins of a paralyzed man before miraculously healing him, the religious leaders had cried out, "Who is this fellow who speaks blasphemy? Who can forgive sins but God alone?" (5:21). But these accusations from the religious elite didn't detract Jesus from his mission. He had come "to set the oppressed free" (4:18) from the prison of sin.

WEEKLY BIBLE STUDY

READ: GALATIANS 3:10–14 AND ISAIAH 61:8–11

1. The clothing of Christ on the cross was the sins of all humanity. What does Paul say about the curse that all people are placed under (see Galatians 3:10)?

2. What does Paul say is the problem with relying on the law—on trying to do good—to somehow achieve righteousness before God (see verses 11–12)?

3. What did Jesus do for you on the cross as it relates to living under the curse of the law? What did Jesus actually become for you (see verses 13–14)?

4. Jesus allows you to wear his own clothes so that you will be properly dressed before God. What does Isaiah say that the Lord loves and hates (see Isaiah 61:8)?

5. What did God say he would be faithful to do in regard to his people? What did he say that the other nations would recognize about them (see verses 8–9)?

6. In what kind of "garments" has the Lord clothed his people? What does Isaiah say that God will enable to "spring up" before all nations (see verses 10–11)?

7. What do the verses that you've studied this week say about the "clothes" that Jesus has provided to you? What garments of his nature do you need to wear today?

Week 40: LEFT AT THE CROSS

"Father, into your hands I commit my spirit" (Luke 23:46). With these words, Jesus took in his final breath and died on the cross. The earth gave a sudden stir. A rock rolled and a soldier stumbled. Then, as suddenly as the silence was broken, the silence returned.

And now, all is quiet. The mocking has ceased. There is no one to mock.

The soldiers are busy with the business of cleaning up the dead. Two men have come. Dressed well and meaning well, they are given the body of Jesus.

And we are left with the relics of his death. Three nails in a bin. Three cross-shaped shadows. A braided crown with scarlet tips.

Bizarre, isn't it? The thought that this blood is not man's blood but God's? Crazy, isn't it? To think that these nails held your sins to a cross? Absurd, don't you agree? That a scoundrel's prayer was offered and answered? Or more absurd that another scoundrel offered no prayer at all?

Absurdities and ironies. The hill of Calvary is nothing if not both.

We would have scripted the moment differently. Ask us how a God should redeem his world, and we will show you! White horses, flashing swords. Evil flat on his back. God on his throne. But God on a cross?

A split-lipped, puffy-eyed, blood-masked God on a cross?

Sponge thrust in his face? Spear plunged in his side? Dice tossed at his feet?

No, we wouldn't have written the drama of redemption this way. But, then again, we weren't asked to do so. These players and props were heaven-picked and God-ordained. We were not asked to design the hour. But we have been asked to respond to it. In order for the cross of Christ to be the cross of our lives, we need to bring something to the hill.

We have seen what Jesus brought. With scarred hands, he offered forgiveness. Through torn skin, he promised acceptance. He took the path to take us home. He wore our garment to give us his own. We have seen the gifts he brought.

Now we ask, "What will we bring?"

We aren't asked to paint the sign or carry the nails. We aren't asked to wear the spit or bear the crown. But we are asked to walk the path and leave something at the cross.

We don't have to, of course. Many don't. Many have done what we have done: More minds than ours have read about the cross; better minds than mine have written about it. Many have pondered what Christ left; fewer have pondered what we must leave.

May I urge you to leave something at the cross? You can observe the cross and analyze the cross. You can read about it, even pray to it. But until you leave something there, you haven't embraced the cross. You've seen what Christ left. Won't you leave something as well?

Why don't you start with your *bad moments*. Those bad habits? Leave them at the cross. Your selfish moods and white lies? Give them to God. Your binges and bigotries? God wants them all. Every flop, every failure. He wants every single one.

Why? Because he knows you can't live with them. Listen to his promise: "This is my commitment to my people: removal of their sins" (Romans 11:27 MSG). God does more than forgive your mistakes; he removes them! You simply have to take them to him.

Sometimes we want to remind Jesus of our past mistakes, even after we have confessed them and received his forgiveness. Their memory begins to bother us, and we feel the need to bring them up in conversation. We say, "Jesus, remember the time I . . . " as we go into the horrid details.

Jesus patiently interrupts us mid-sentence and says, "No, child. I don't remember that at all." When Jesus forgives us, he truly forgets. The past is just that—it has passed.

So start with your bad moments. Leave them there at the cross. While you are there, why not give God your *mad moments*? God wants your list. He inspired one servant to write, "Love does not keep a record of wrongs" (1 Corinthians 13:5 TEV). He wants you to leave the list at the cross. "Just look what they did to me!" you say as you point to your hurts. "Just look what I did for you," Jesus reminds you as he points to the cross.

You and I are commanded—not urged, *commanded*—to keep no list of wrongs. Besides, do you really want to keep one? Do you really want to catalog all your mistreatments? Do you really want to growl and snap your way through life? God doesn't want you to do so either.

Why not also take your *anxious moments* to the cross? The next time you're worried about your health, house, finances, or flights, take a mental trip up the hill. Spend a few moments looking at the pieces of passion. Run your thumb over the tip of the spear. Balance a spike in the palm of your hand. Read the wooden sign written in your own language. And as you do, touch the velvet dirt, moist with the blood of God.

Blood he bled for you. The spear he took for you. The nails he felt for you. He did all of this for you.

Knowing all he did for you *there*, don't you think he will look out for you *here*? As Paul wrote, "God did not keep back his own Son, but he gave him for us. If God did this, won't he freely give us everything else?" (Romans 8:32 CEV). If you don't believe God can provide for your daily needs, how will you believe that he can accomplish your salvation?

Do yourself a favor and take your anxious moments to the cross. And may I suggest one more to leave there? Your *final moments*. Barring the return of Christ first, you and I will have one. A final moment. A final breath. A final widening of the eyes and beating of the heart. In a split second, you will leave what you know and enter what you don't.

God promises to come at an unexpected hour and take us from the gray world we know to a golden world we don't. But since we don't, we aren't sure we want to go. We even get upset at the thought of his coming. But Jesus says, "Don't let your hearts be troubled. . . . I will come back and take you to be with me so that you may be where I am" (John 14:1, 3 NCV).

Jesus took your sins away at the cross. He offers you his perfect peace. So leave your bad moments, mad moments, and anxious moments behind. Of course, at this point you might be thinking, *You know, Max, if I leave all those moments at the cross—and truly experience the forgiveness of Jesus—I won't have any moments left but good ones.*

Well, what do you know? I guess you won't.

THE HEART OF THE MATTER

- Jesus invites you to leave your sins and your worries at the cross.
- When Jesus forgives the sin you confess, you need never bring it up again.
- God commands you to forgive others just as you have been forgiven.
- Even if you don't feel forgiven, it is a fact of your salvation.

MEMORY VERSES

This is it . . . one last review of your memory verses. Write out the words of Colossians 1:13–14 from memory in the space below. Reflect on what these words mean to you.

The Heart of Jesus

The disciples were gathered around the fire. The topic of conversation had turned to the importance of forgiveness. They were trying to pull together what they remembered from their Master's teaching over the last few months. It seemed to be a frequent topic of his teaching—forgiveness was important to Jesus. "We are to forgive one another, as well as our enemies," said one (see Matthew 5:43–44). "And if we don't forgive, God won't forgive us!" reminded another (see 6:15). "God won't even listen to our prayers if we are harboring a grudge against someone" (see Mark 11:25). "Our forgiveness must have no limits," said a wry Peter (Matthew 18:21). With a nod of approval, Jesus stated, "Forgive because you are forgiven."

WEEKLY BIBLE STUDY

READ: PSALM 55:16–23 AND MATTHEW 11:28–30

1. Jesus invites you to leave your bad moments, mad moments, and anxious moments at the cross. What type of "moment" was David experiencing in Psalm 55:16–17?

2. David was often pursued by enemies who wanted to take his life. What did David believe about God's hand of protection over him (see verses 18–19)?

3. David was able to cast his cares on the Lord. What does he say will happen when you do the same? What is the promise given to the righteous (see verses 22–23)?

4. Jesus offers to exchange the burdens you bear for his perfect peace. What invitation does he make to all who are weary and burdened (see Matthew 11:28)?

5. A *yoke* is a wooden crosspiece fastened over the necks of two animals that allows them to share a load. What invitation does Jesus extend regarding his yoke (see verse 29)?

6. The people in Jesus' day were often burdened by heavy yokes of rules and restrictions. What does Jesus say is different about his yoke (see verse 30)?

7. How have the passages you've studied this week helped you to understand the forgiveness that Jesus offers to you? What do you need to leave at the cross today?

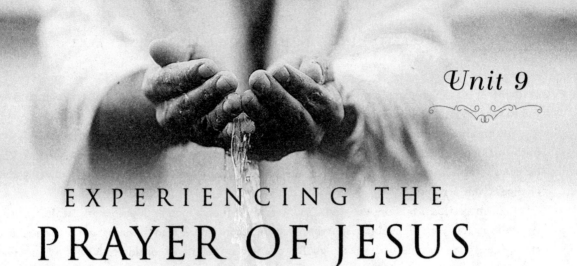

EXPERIENCING THE
PRAYER OF JESUS

I'd like to talk with you about your house. Let's step through the front door and walk around a bit. Every so often it's wise to do a home inspection, you know—check the roof for leaks and examine the walls for bows and the foundation for cracks. We'll see if your kitchen cupboards are full and glance at the books on the shelves in your study.

What's that? You think it odd that I want to look at your house? You thought this was a book on spiritual matters? It is. Forgive me, I should have been clearer. I'm not talking about your visible house of stone or sticks, wood or straw, but your invisible one of thoughts and truths and convictions and hopes. I'm talking about your spiritual house.

You have one, you know. And it's no typical house. Conjure up your fondest notions and this house exceeds them all. A grand castle has been built for your heart. Just as a physical house exists to care for the body, so the spiritual house exists to care for your soul.

You've never seen a house more solid: the roof never leaks, the walls never crack, and the foundation never trembles.

You've never seen a castle more splendid: the observatory will stretch you, the chapel will humble you, the study will direct you, and the kitchen will nourish you.

Ever lived in a house like this? Chances are you haven't. Chances are you've given little thought to housing your soul. We create elaborate houses for our bodies, but our souls are relegated to a hillside shanty where the night winds chill us and the rain soaks us. Is it any wonder the world is so full of cold hearts?

Doesn't have to be this way. You don't have to live outside. It's not God's plan for your heart to roam as a Bedouin. God wants you to move in out of the cold and live . . . with him. Under his roof there is space available. At his table a plate is set. In his living room a wingback chair is reserved just for you. And he'd like you to take up residence in his house.

You are always just one step away from the house of God. Wherever you are. Whatever time it is. Whether in the office or at soccer practice, you are only a decision away from the presence of your Father. You need never leave the house of God. You don't need to change your zip code or your neighborhood; all you need to change is your perception.

Remember, this is no house of stone. You won't find it on a map or described in a realtor journal. But you will find it in your Bible. You've seen the blueprint before. You've read the names of the rooms and recited the layout. You're familiar with the design. But chances are you never considered it to be a house plan. You viewed the verses as a prayer.

Indeed they are. The Lord's Prayer. It would be difficult to find someone who hasn't quoted the prayer or read the words:

> *Our Father in heaven, hallowed be Your name.*
> *Your kingdom come. Your will be done on earth as it is in heaven.*
> *Give us this day our daily bread.*
> *And forgive us our debts, as we forgive our debtors.*
> *And do not lead us into temptation, but deliver us from the evil one.*
> *For Yours is the kingdom and the power and the glory forever.*
> *Amen.* (Matthew 6:9–13 NKJV)

Children memorize it. Parishioners recite it. Students study it . . . but I want to challenge you to do something different throughout this week's lessons. I want you to live in it . . . to view it as the floor plan to your spiritual house. In these verses, Christ has provided more than a model for prayer; he has provided a model for living. These words do more than tell us what to say to God; they tell us how to exist with God. These words describe a grand house in which God's children were intended to live . . . with him, forever.[22]

— PRAYER —

Dear Father, thank you for providing a home for my heart through prayer and fellowship with you. I am struck with awe at your greatness and humbled that my words of praise are precious to you. I trust that you hear me, and I depend on you to answer. Amen.

— MEMORY VERSE —

Pray in the Spirit on all occasions with all kinds of prayers and requests. With this in mind, be alert and always keep on praying for all the Lord's people.

EPHESIANS 6:18

Week 41: A HEAVENLY AFFECTION

No telescope is needed in this room. The glass ceiling magnifies the universe until you feel the sky is falling around you. Elevated instantly through the atmosphere, you are encircled by the heavens. Stars cascade past until you are dizzy with their number. Had you the ability to spend a minute on each planet and star, one lifetime would scarcely be enough to begin.

Jesus waits until you are caught up in the splendor of it all, and then he reminds you softly, "Your Father is in heaven."

I can remember as a youngster knowing some kids whose fathers were quite successful. One was a judge. The other a prominent physician. I attended church with the son of the mayor. In Andrews, Texas, that's not much to boast about. Nevertheless, the kid had clout that most of us didn't. "My father has an office at the courthouse," he could claim.

Guess what you can claim? "My Father rules the universe."

"The heavens declare the glory of God; the skies proclaim the work of his hands" (Psalm 19:1). Nature is God's workshop. The sky is his résumé. The universe is his calling card. You want to know who God is? See what he has done. You want to know his power? Take a look at his creation. Want to know his size? Step out into the night, stare at starlight emitted one million years ago, and then read 2 Chronicles 2:6: "Who is able to build a temple for him, since the heavens, even the highest heavens, cannot contain him?"

God is untainted by the atmosphere of sin, unbridled by the timeline of history, unhindered by the weariness of the body. What controls you doesn't control him. What troubles you doesn't trouble him. What fatigues you doesn't fatigue him. Is an eagle disturbed by traffic? No, he rises above it. Is the whale perturbed by a hurricane? Of course not, he plunges beneath it. Is the lion flustered by a mouse in his way? No, he steps over it.

How much more is God able to soar above, plunge beneath, and step over the troubles of the earth! "With man this is impossible, but with God all things are possible" (Matthew 19:26). He can be everywhere at one time. (He is not bound by a body.) He can hear all the prayers that come to him. (Perhaps his ears are different from ours.) He can exist as the Father, the Son, and the Holy Spirit. (Heaven has a different set of physics from earth's.)

How vital that we pray armed with the knowledge that God is in heaven. Pray with any lesser conviction and our prayers are timid, shallow, and hollow. But spend time walking in the workshop of the heavens, seeing what God has done, and our prayers are energized.

God dwells in a different realm. "The foolishness of God is wiser than human wisdom, and the weakness of God is stronger than human strength" (1 Corinthians 1:25). He occupies another dimension. "My thoughts are not like your thoughts. Your ways are not like my ways" (Isaiah 55:8 NCV).

Make special note of the word *like*. God's thoughts are not our thoughts, nor are they even *like* ours. We aren't even in the same neighborhood.

We're thinking, *Preserve the body*; he's thinking, *Save the soul*. We dream of a pay raise. He dreams of raising the dead. We avoid pain and seek peace. God uses pain to bring peace. "I'm going to live before I die," we resolve. "Die, so you can live," he instructs. We love what rusts. He loves what endures. We rejoice at our successes. He rejoices at our confessions.

Our thoughts are not like God's thoughts. Our ways are not like his ways. He has a different agenda. He dwells in a different dimension. He lives on another plane. And that plane is named in the first phrase of the Lord's prayer, "Our Father, who is in heaven."

Now, let me pose a few questions to you as you consider all these truths.

If God has the universe as a workshop, and he is able to place the stars in their sockets and suspend the sky like a curtain, do you think it is remotely possible that he is able to guide your life?

If God is mighty enough to ignite the sun, could it be that he is mighty enough to light your path?

If God cares enough about the planet Saturn to give it rings or Venus to make it sparkle, is there an outside chance that he cares enough about you to meet your needs?

And is it possible that when God says he wants you to share his home, that he means it?

For you have been invited to live in your Father's house. Any place less than his is insufficient. Any place far from his is dangerous. Only the home built for your heart can protect your heart. And your Father wants you to dwell in him.

No, you didn't misread that last sentence, and I didn't miswrite it. Your Father doesn't just ask you to live *with* him; he also asks you to live *in* him.

As Paul said, "For in him we live and move and have our being" (Acts 17:28). Don't think you are separated from God, he at the top end of a great ladder, you at the other. Dismiss any thought that God is on Venus while you are on earth. Since God is Spirit (see John 4:24), he is next to you.

God himself is your roof.

God himself is your wall.

And God himself is your foundation.

God *wants* to be your dwelling place. He has no interest in being a weekend getaway or a Sunday bungalow or a summer cottage. Don't consider using God as a vacation cabin or an eventual retirement home. He wants you under his roof now and always. He wants to be your mailing address, your point of reference; he wants to be your home. Listen to the promise of his Son: "Anyone who loves me will obey my teaching. My Father will love them, and we will come to them and make our home with them" (John 14:23).

This might be a new thought for you. We think of God as a deity to discuss, not a place to dwell. We think of God as a mysterious miracle worker, not a house to live in. We think of God as a Creator to call on, not a home to reside in. But our Father wants to be much more. He wants to be the one in whom "we live and move and have our being" (Acts 17:28).

THE HEART OF THE MATTER

- You have a loving heavenly Father who controls the very universe.
- God can soar above, plunge beneath, and step over the troubles of earth.
- God has a different agenda and dwells in a different dimension.
- God wants to be your foundation, walls, roof . . . your dwelling place.

MEMORY VERSE

Take a few moments to review your Bible memory verse for this unit, and then write out the words of Ephesians 6:18 by heart in the space below.

The Heart of Jesus

They were always together. Walking, talking, eating, sleeping. They had watched him do the impossible. They had seen him change lives. They knew the sound of his step, the tone of his voice, the echo of his laughter. The twelve disciples of Jesus knew their Master like no one else could. But then there were times when Jesus would simply slip away by himself to be alone. Sometimes for a few hours at a time. Sometimes for the whole night. Where did he go? What was he doing? A couple of them were curious enough to follow Jesus cautiously. Even from a distance, they could see him—first sitting quietly, then pacing back and forth, with the sound of his voice drifting through the night. When they asked him about it in the morning, his answer astonished them. He was talking with his Father. They exchanged glances. They had watched him do the impossible. They had seen him change lives. They wanted to be like him. Their plea rose up from the longing in their hearts. "Please, Jesus, teach *us* to pray" (see Luke 11:1).

WEEKLY BIBLE STUDY

READ: DEUTERONOMY 10:12–17 AND JOHN 14:15–21

1. Moses desired for the Israelites to always fear God, obey him, and walk in his commands. What did he add about what belongs to the Lord (see Deuteronomy 10:12–14)?

2. God, who owns everything, had no obligation to show mercy to the Israelites. Yet what does Moses say that he had demonstrated to his people (see verse 15)?

3. Moses' call to his people was to turn from their rebellious ways. What reminder did he give to the Israelites about God's authority (see verses 16–17)?

4. God's desire is for you to dwell in him. He wants to guide you through life. What did Jesus promise his disciples that God would give them (see John 14:15–17)?

5. Jesus said the world would not accept the Holy Spirit because "it neither sees him nor knows him." How would the disciples know the Holy Spirit (see verse 17)?

6. What did Jesus say would happen in the disciples' hearts after he was no longer present with them? What would be the proof of their love for him (see verses 19–21)?

7. God wants to be your dwelling place. What do you need to release today to make him the center of your life? How do you sense he is inviting you to abide in him?

Week 42: TOUCHING THE KING'S HEART

Our family went desk hunting recently. I needed a new one, and we'd promised Andrea and Sara desks for their rooms. Sara was especially enthused.

So off to the furniture store we went. Andrea and Sara succeeded quickly in making their selections, and I set out to do the same. Somewhere in the process, Sara learned we weren't taking the desks home that day. The news disturbed her deeply. I explained that the piece had to be painted and they would deliver the desk in about four weeks.

I might as well have said four millennia. Her eyes filled with tears.

"But, Daddy, I wanted to take it home today."

Much to her credit, she didn't stomp her feet and demand her way. She did, however, set out on an urgent course to change her father's mind.

"Daddy, don't you think we could paint it ourselves?"

"Daddy, I just want to draw some pictures on my new desk."

"Guess what, Daddy? It'll fit in the back of the car!"

You and I know that a seven-year-old has no clue what will or won't fit in a vehicle, but the fact that she had measured the trunk with her arms softened my heart. The clincher, though, was the name she called me: "Daddy." The Lucado family took a desk home that day.

I heard Sara's request for the same reason God hears ours. Her desire was for her own good. What dad wouldn't want his child to spend more time writing and drawing? Sara wanted what I wanted for her, she only wanted it sooner. When we agree with what God wants, he hears us, as well (see 1 John 5:14). God, too, is moved by our sincerity. The "earnest prayer of a righteous man has great power" (James 5:16 TLB).

But most of all, God hears our requests because we are his children. The King of creation gives special heed to the voice of his family. He is not only *willing* to hear us but also *loves* to hear us. He even tells us what to ask him. "Your kingdom come."

We're often content to ask for less. We enter the throne room of God with a satchel full of requests—promotions desired, pay raises wanted, transmission repairs needed, and tuitions due. We say our prayers as casually as we would order a burger at the drive-through: "I'll have one solved problem and two blessings, cut the hassles, please."

Such complacency seems inappropriate. Here we are, before the King of kings. Do we just rush in with a list of all our requests? Not that our needs don't matter to him, mind you. The pay raise is still needed and the promotion is still desired. But is that where we start?

Jesus tells us how we *should* begin. "This, then, is how you should pray: 'Our Father in heaven, hallowed be your name, your kingdom come'" (Matthew 6:9–10). When you say "Your kingdom come," you are inviting the Messiah himself to walk into your world. "Come, my King! Take your throne in our land. Be present in my heart. Be present in my office. Come into my marriage. Be Lord of my family, my fears, and my doubts." This is no feeble request; it's a bold appeal for God to occupy every corner of your life.

Who are you to ask such a thing? You are God's child, for heaven's sake! And so you ask boldly. "So let us come boldly to the very throne of God and stay there to receive his mercy and to find grace to help us in our times of need" (Hebrews 4:16 TLB).

A wonderful illustration of this kind of boldness is in the story of Hadassah. Though her language and culture are an atlas apart from ours, she can tell you about the power of a prayer to a king. There are a couple of differences, though. Her request was not to her father but to her husband, the king. Her prayer was for the delivery of her people. And because she entered the throne room, because she opened her heart to the king, he changed his plans and millions of people in one-hundred-twenty-seven different countries were saved.

Oh, how I'd love for you to meet Hadassah. But since she lived in the fifth century BC, such an encounter is not likely. We'll have to be content with reading about her in the book which bears her name—her *other* name—the book of Esther.

Esther, Mordecai's adopted daughter, became queen by winning a Miss Persia contest. In one day she went from obscurity to royalty. In more ways than one, she should remind you of you. Both of you are residents of the palace: Esther, the bride of Xerxes, and you, the bride of Christ. Both of you have access to the throne of the king, and you both have a counselor to guide and teach you. Your counselor is the Holy Spirit. Esther's counselor was Mordecai.

It was Mordecai who urged Esther to keep her Jewish nationality a secret. It was also Mordecai who persuaded Esther to talk to Xerxes about the impending massacre. You may wonder why she would need any encouragement. Mordecai must have wondered the same thing. Listen to the message he got from Esther: "No man or woman may go to the king in the inner courtyard without being called. There is only one law about this: Anyone who enters must be put to death unless the king holds out his gold scepter. Then that person may live. And I have not been called to go to the king for thirty days" (Esther 4:11 NCV).

As strange as it may sound to us, not even the queen could approach the king without an invitation. To enter his throne room uninvited was to risk a visit to the gallows. But Mordecai convinced her to take the risk. Here is how she responded: "Esther put on her royal robes and stood in the inner court of the palace, in front of the king's hall" (Esther 5:1).

Here is how Xerxes responded: "When he saw Queen Esther standing in the court, he was pleased" (verse 2). Let me give you my translation of that verse: "When the king saw Queen Esther standing in the courtyard, he said, 'a-hubba-hubba-hubba.'" He held out the gold scepter that was in his hand, and Esther went forward and touched the end of it.

How does the story end? Haman got Mordecai's rope. Mordecai got Haman's job. Esther got a good night's sleep. The Jews lived to see another day. And we get a dramatic reminder of what happens when we approach our King.

Like Esther, we have been plucked out of obscurity and given a place in the palace. Like Esther, we have royal robes; she was dressed in cloth, we are dressed in righteousness. Like Esther, we have the privilege of making our request in the great throne room of the King.

THE HEART OF THE MATTER

- God is moved by the sincerity of your prayers.
- God hears your request because you are his child.
- Appeal for God to occupy every corner of your life.
- You have the privilege of making your requests to God.

MEMORY VERSE

Your memory verse for this unit is Ephesians 6:18. Take a few moments to review this verse, and then write it out from memory in the space below.

The Heart of Jesus

Jesus was a prayer warrior. He fasted and prayed for forty days. He found time for hours of solitude in the midst of a busy schedule. He sometimes prayed throughout the night. When Jesus prayed, people were healed, released, and made whole. When he spoke to his Father, God answered. Such an impressive prayer résumé is a little intimidating. How can we possibly emulate our Savior in this way? But Jesus didn't just pray about the big stuff in big ways. He prayed the same kinds of everyday prayers that we lift up today. Did you know that Jesus thanked the Father for his food and blessed it before eating (see Matthew 14:19)? Anytime we pause in our days to whisper a few words to our Father, we are being just like Jesus.

WEEKLY BIBLE STUDY

READ: LUKE 11:9–13 AND ESTHER 4:1–5:2

1. God is not only *willing* to hear from you but also *loves* to hear from you. What promise did Jesus give to those who seek God in prayer (see Luke 11:9–10)?

2. God is frequently described in Scripture as a heavenly *Father*. What does Jesus say about the ways that earthly fathers answer their children's requests (see verses 11–12)?

3. What point is Jesus making about the way God—who is your *heavenly* Father—will answer your requests? What does Jesus say God will give to you (see verse 13)?

4. The story of Esther reveals how you can approach God in prayer. What was the crisis that Mordecai, Esther, and all the Jewish people faced (see Esther 4:7–8)?

5. What reasons did Esther give to Mordecai for being reluctant to approach the king in his throne room? What reply did Mordecai give back to Esther (see verses 10–14)?

6. Esther resolved to make her request known to the king even if it resulted in her death. How did the king respond when he saw her (see Esther 5:1–2)?

7. What do the passages you've studied this week reveal about God's desire to hear from you and answer your requests? What do you need to take to him today?

Week 43: BECAUSE SOMEONE PRAYED

I'd like you to think about someone. His name is not important. His looks are immaterial. His gender is of no concern. His title is irrelevant. He is important not because of who he is but because of what he did.

He went to Jesus on behalf of a friend. His friend was sick, and Jesus could help, and someone needed to go to Jesus, so someone went. Others cared for the sick man in other ways. Some brought food, others provided treatment, still others comforted the family. Each role was crucial. Each person was helpful, but none was more vital than the one who went to Jesus.

He went because he was asked to go.

An earnest appeal came from the family of the afflicted. "We need someone who will tell Jesus that my brother is sick. We need someone to ask him to come back here. Will you go?"

The question came from two sisters. They would have gone themselves, but they couldn't leave their brother's bedside. They needed someone else to go for them. Not just anyone, mind you, for not just anyone could. Some were too busy, others didn't know the way. Some fatigued too quickly; others were inexperienced on the path. Not everyone could go.

And not everyone would go. This was no small request the sisters were making. They needed a diligent ambassador, someone who knew how to find Jesus. Someone who wouldn't quit mid-journey. Someone who would make sure the message was delivered. Someone who was as convinced as they were that Jesus *must* be told of what had happened.

They knew of a trustworthy person, and to that person they went. They entrusted their needs to someone, and that someone took those needs to Christ. "So Mary and Martha sent *someone* to tell Jesus, 'Lord, the one you love is sick'" (John 11:3 NCV, emphasis added).

Someone carried the request. Someone walked the trail. Someone went to Jesus on behalf of Lazarus. And because someone went, Jesus responded.

Let me ask you, how important was this person in the healing of Lazarus? How essential was his role? Some might regard it as secondary. After all, didn't Jesus know everything? Certainly he knew that Lazarus was sick. Granted, but he didn't respond to the need until someone came to him with the message. "When Jesus heard this, he said, 'This sickness will not end in death. It is for the glory of God, to bring glory to the Son of God'" (verse 4 NCV).

When was Lazarus healed? After *someone* made the request. Oh, the healing wouldn't unfold for several days, but the timer was set when the appeal was made. All that was needed was the passage of time.

Would Jesus have responded if the messenger had not spoken? Perhaps, but we have no guarantee. We do, however, have an example: the power of God was triggered by prayer. Jesus looked down the very throat of death's cavern and called Lazarus back to life . . . all because someone prayed.

The phrase the friend of Lazarus used is worth noting. When he told Jesus of the illness he said, "Lord, the one you love is sick." He didn't base his appeal on the imperfect love of the one in need but on the perfect love of the Savior. He didn't say, "The *one who loves you* is sick." He said, "The one *you love* is sick."

The power of the prayer, in other words, does not depend on the one who makes the prayer but on the one who hears the prayer.

Although we may love our friends and family more than anyone on earth, Jesus wants us to know that he loves them more than anyone in heaven and earth. If we are concerned for our loved ones, how much more is he! We can, and must, repeat the phrase in manifold ways. "The one you love is tired, sad, hungry, lonely, fearful, depressed."

The words of the prayer vary, but the response never changes. The Savior hears the prayer. He silences heaven so he won't miss a word. He hears the prayer. Remember the phrase from John's Gospel? "When Jesus *heard* this, he said, 'This sickness will not end in death'" (John 11:4 NCV, emphasis added).

The Master heard the request. Jesus stopped whatever he was doing and took note of the man's words. This anonymous courier was heard by God.

You and I live in a loud world. To get someone's attention is no easy task. The person must be willing to set everything aside to listen: turn away from the monitor, take off the headphones, turn the corner of the page and set down the book. When someone is willing to silence everything else to hear us clearly, it is a privilege. A rare privilege, indeed.

You can talk to God because God listens. Your voice matters in heaven. He takes you very seriously.

When you enter his presence, the attendants turn to you to hear your voice. No need to fear that you will be ignored. Even if you stammer or stumble, even if what you have to say impresses no one, it impresses God—and he listens.

He listens to the painful plea of the elderly in the rest home. He listens to the gruff confession of the death-row inmate. When the alcoholic begs for mercy, when the spouse seeks guidance, when the businessman steps off the street into the chapel, God listens.

Intently. Carefully. The prayers are honored as precious jewels. Purified and empowered, the words rise in a delightful fragrance to our Lord. As the apostle John would later describe in a vision he witnessed, "The smoke of the incense, together with the prayers of God's people, went up before God from the angel's hand" (Revelation 8:4).

Incredible. Your words do not stop until they reach the very throne of God.

John continues: "Then the angel took the censer, filled it with fire from the altar, and hurled it on the earth" (verse 5). One call and heaven's fleet appears. Your prayer on earth activates God's power in heaven, and God's will is done in earth as it is in heaven.

You are the someone of God's kingdom. You have access to God's furnace. Your prayers move God to change the world. You may not understand the mystery of prayer. You don't need to. But this much is clear: actions in heaven begin when someone prays on earth. What an amazing thought!

When you speak, Jesus hears.

And when Jesus hears, thunder falls.

And when thunder falls, the world is changed.

All because someone prayed.

THE HEART OF THE MATTER

- God responds when someone carries the request to him in prayer.
- Prayer has the power to trigger a response from God.
- The power of the prayer does not depend on the one who makes the prayer.
- Your prayer on earth activates God's power in heaven.

MEMORY VERSE

Your memory verse for this unit is Ephesians 6:18. Take a few moments to review this verse, and then write it out from memory in the space below.

The Heart of Jesus

Jesus didn't have to pray out loud. God knew his thoughts. The Son didn't have to share his private conversations with his Father. According to the Gospels, Jesus often slipped away from the disciples and the rest of humanity and spent most of his prayer time in solitude. No eavesdroppers allowed! His inner musings and urgent entreaties to God might never have reached the pages of our Bibles. But Jesus welcomed us into those intimate moments. He offered us a peek at his prayers. He guided his disciples through a primer of petition. He led the way to the throne of God. Jesus prayed out loud for our benefit.

WEEKLY BIBLE STUDY

READ: JOHN 11:1–16 AND JAMES 5:13–18

1. When the brother of Mary and Martha fell ill, the sisters sent "someone" to find Jesus. What ultimate impact did this have on Jesus' actions (see John 11:1–7)?

2. Jesus was taking no small risk in answering this messenger's call. What did the disciples—and Jesus—know could happen if they returned to Bethany (see verses 8–16)?

3. The power of prayer does not depend on the one who makes the prayer but on the one who hears the prayer. How was this true in this story?

4. Prayer has the power to trigger a response from God. What does James advise those "in trouble" to do? What does he advise the sick to do (see James 5:13–14)?

5. What does James say will happen when a prayer is offered up to the Lord in faith? What course of action doe he advise followers of Jesus to take (see verses 15–16)?

6. It is easy to fall into the trap of thinking that God answers prayers only from spiritual saints. What example does James use to counter this claim (see verses 17–18)?

7. What do the passages you've studied this week reveal about the importance of interceding for others? Who is someone you know who needs God's touch today?

Week 44: GOD'S ABUNDANT TABLE

Who is more concerned with your basic needs than your Father in heaven? God is not a mountain guru only involved in the spiritual. The same hand that guides your soul gives food for your body. The same one who clothes you in goodness also clothes you in cloth. In the school of life, God is both the teacher and the cook. He provides fire for the heart and food for the stomach. Your eternal salvation, and your evening meal, come from the same hand.

God doesn't leave you out in the cold. He sees your needs and longs to invite you inside to join him at his abundant table. And his table is long, with many chairs set around it. The food is ample. On the wall hangs a simple prayer: "Give us today our daily bread" (Matthew 6:11). Beneath this, I envision two statements. You might call them the "rules of the kitchen."

Rule #1: Don't be shy, ask. "Give us today our daily bread" seems abrupt and even demanding. Wouldn't an "if you don't mind" be more appropriate? Perhaps a "pardon me, but could I ask you to give . . . " would be better? Are we not being irreverent if we say, "Give us today our daily bread"? Well, we are if this is where we begin. But it isn't. Up to this point in Jesus' model for prayer, the preoccupation has been on God's wonder rather than on our stomachs. The first three petitions are God-centered, not self-centered. "Hallowed be your name . . . your kingdom come . . . your will be done" (verses 9–10).

Proper prayer follows such a path, revealing God to us before revealing our needs to God. (You might want to reread that one.) The purpose of prayer is not to change God but to change us, and by the time we reach God's kitchen table, we are changed people. Wasn't our heart warmed when we called him Father? Weren't our fears stilled when we contemplated his constancy? Weren't we amazed as we stared at the heavens?

Seeing his holiness caused us to confess our sin. Inviting his kingdom to come reminded us to stop building our own. Asking God for his will to be done placed our will in second place to his. And realizing that heaven pauses when we pray left us breathless in his presence.

By the time we step into the kitchen, we're renewed! We've been comforted by our Father, conformed by his nature, consumed by our creator, convicted by his character, constrained by his power, commissioned by our teacher, and compelled by his attention to our prayers.

The next three petitions in Jesus' prayer encompasses all the concerns of life.

First, our need for "bread." The term means all of a person's physical needs. Martin Luther defined bread as, "Everything necessary for the preservation of this life, including food, a healthy body, house, home, wife, and children." We are urged to talk with God about the necessities of life. He may also give us the luxuries of life, but he certainly will grant the necessities.

God is committed to caring for our needs. Paul tells us that a man who won't feed his own family is worse than an unbeliever (see 1 Timothy 5:8). So how much more will a holy God care for his children?

After all, how can we fulfill his mission unless our needs are met? How can we teach or minister or influence unless we have our basic needs satisfied? Will God enlist us in his army and not provide a commissary? Of course not.

We pray, only to find our prayer already answered! We are like the high-school senior who decides to go to college and then learns the cost of tuition. He runs to his father and pleads, "I'm sorry to ask so much, Dad, but I have nowhere else to go. I want to go to college and I don't have a penny."

The father puts his arms around the son and says, "Don't worry. The day you were born I began saving for your education. I've already provided for your tuition."

The boy made the request only to find the father had already met it. The same happens with you. At some point in your life, it occurs to you that someone is providing for your needs. You take a giant step in maturity when you agree with David's words in 1 Chronicles 29:14: "Everything we have has come from you, and we only give you what is yours already" (TLB).

You may be paying the grocery bill and stirring the soup, but there's more to putting food on the table than that. What about the ancient symbiosis of the seed and the soil and the sun and the rain? Who created animals for food and minerals for metal? Long before you knew you needed someone to provide for your needs, God already had done it. This bring us to . . .

Rule #2: Trust the cook. The kitchen in God's house is no restaurant. It's not owned by a stranger; it's run by your Father. It's not a place you visit and leave; it's a place to linger and chat. It's not open one hour and closed the next; the kitchen is ever available. You don't eat and then pay; you eat and say thanks. But perhaps the most important difference between a kitchen and a restaurant is the menu. A kitchen doesn't have one.

God's kitchen doesn't need one. Things may be different in your house, but in the house of God, the one who provides the food is the one who prepares the meal. We don't swagger into his presence and demand delicacies. Nor do we sit outside the door and hope for crumbs. We simply take our place at the table and gladly trust him to "Give us today our daily bread."

What a statement of trust! Whatever God wants us to have is all we want.

In his book *Victorious Praying*, Alan Redpath translates the phrase, "Give us this day bread suited to our need."[23] Some days the plate runs over. God keeps bringing out more food and we keep loosening our belt. A promotion. A privilege. A friendship. A gift. A lifetime of grace. An eternity of joy. And then there are those days when we have to eat our broccoli. Our daily bread could be tears or sorrow or discipline. Our portion may include adversity as well as opportunity.

"We know that in all things God works for the good of those who love him" (Romans 8:28). We, like Paul, must be able to say, "I have learned the secret of being happy at any time in everything that happens, when I have enough to eat and when I go hungry, when I have more than I need and when I do not have enough. I can do all things through Christ, because he gives me strength" (Philippians 4:12–13 NCV).

THE HEART OF THE MATTER

- Your heavenly Father is concerned with your basic needs.
- God invites you to not be shy in asking for your needs.
- The purpose of prayer is not to change God but to change *you*.
- You can trust that the Lord will provide your "daily bread."

MEMORY VERSE

Your memory verse for this unit is Ephesians 6:18. Take a few moments to review this verse, and then write it out by heart in the space below.

The Heart of Jesus

There had been urgency in his eyes. "Come with me tonight. Pray with me." The disciples were accustomed to Jesus slipping away into the night to pray. He often had such interludes with his Father. But he had never asked for company before. Tonight was different—there was tension in the air, a sense of imminence. Something was about to happen, and their Master had invited them to join him to pray. Peter, James, and John were delighted but drowsy. Their good intentions would have ended in a good night's sleep had Jesus not shaken their shoulders to rouse them. Seeing the sorrow in the Savior's eyes, they renewed their efforts to intercede. On a night when distress threatened to overwhelm Jesus, he asked his closest friends to do the one thing that could help. Jesus asked them to pray for him, for he knew he needed peace, encouragement, and strength from the Father for the day ahead (see Matthew 26:36–46).

WEEKLY BIBLE STUDY

READ: 1 KINGS 17:7–16 AND MATTHEW 6:25–34

1. God desires to meet even your most basic needs. What basic need did Elijah have? What more dire need did the widow in Zarephath have (see 1 Kings 17:7–12)?

2. What instruction did Elijah give to the widow to meet this need? What did he say would happen when she followed his instructions (see verses 13–14)?

3. What was the result when the widow obeyed (see verses 15–16)? What does this story reveal about God's willingness and ability to meet your daily needs?

4. Jesus also spoke about God's desire to care for his children's basic needs. What did Jesus say about the way God provides food for his children (see Matthew 6:25–27)?

5. What did Jesus say about the way God provides for other basic needs, such as clothing? What did Jesus say about the *abundant* way God provides (see verses 28–30)?

6. Jesus' instruction to his listeners was to not worry about what they would eat, drink, or wear, for God knew about their needs. What should they do instead (see verses 31–34)?

7. What do the passages you've studied this week reveal about the way God cares for your basic needs? What worries and anxieties do you need to take to him today?

Week 45: RELYING ON GOD'S POWER

I came across a story of a lady who went up a mountain that she should have avoided. At twelve below zero, even Frosty the Snowman would have opted for a warm fire. Hardly a day for snow skiing. But her husband insisted, and so she went.

While waiting in the lift line, she realized she was in need of a restroom—in *dire* need of a restroom. Assured there would be one at the top of the lift, she and her bladder endured the bouncy ride, only to find there was no facility there. She began to panic. Her husband had an idea: Why not go into the woods? Since she was wearing an all-white outfit, she'd blend in with the snow. And what better powder room than a piney grove?

What choice did she have? She skied past the tree line and arranged her ski suit at half-mast.

Unfortunately, her husband hadn't told her to remove her skis. Before you could say, "Shine on harvest moon," she was streaking backward across the slope, revealing more about herself than she ever intended. (After all, hindsight is 20/20.) With arms flailing and skis sailing, she sped under the very lift she'd just ridden and collided with a pylon.

As she scrambled to cover the essentials, she discovered her arm was broken. Her husband summoned the ski patrol, who transported her to the hospital.

While being treated, a man with a broken leg was carried in and placed next to her. By now she'd regained enough composure to make small talk. "So, how'd you break your leg?" she asked.

"It was the darndest thing," he said. "I was riding up the ski lift, and suddenly I couldn't believe my eyes. There was this crazy woman skiing backward, at top speed. I leaned over to get a better look and I guess I didn't realize how far I'd moved. I fell out of the lift."

Then he turned to her and asked, "So, how'd you break your arm?"

Don't we make the same mistake? We try to go up when we should have stayed down, and as a result, we take some nasty spills in full view of a watching world. The tale of the lady (sorry, I couldn't resist) echoes our own story. There are certain mountains we were never meant to ascend. Stay away from them, and we sidestep a lot of stress.

These mountains are described in the final phrase of the Lord's prayer: "For Yours is the kingdom and the power and the glory forever" (Matthew 6:13 NKJV). A trio of peaks mantled by the clouds. Admire them, applaud them, but don't climb them. Not that you aren't welcome to try; it's just that you aren't able. The pronoun is *yours* is the kingdom, not *mine* is the kingdom. If the word *Savior* is in your job description, it's because you put it there. Your role is to help the world, not save it. Mount Messiah is one mountain that you weren't made to climb.

If Jesus' prayer teaches us anything, it is to depend on God. You were not made to run a kingdom, nor are you expected to be all-powerful. And you certainly can't handle all the glory. Mount Applause is the most seductive of the three peaks. The higher you climb, the more people applaud, but the thinner the air becomes. More than one person has stood at the top and shouted "Mine is the glory!" only to lose their balance and fall.

"Yours is the kingdom and the power and the glory forever." What protection this final phrase affords! As you confess that God is in charge, you admit that you aren't. As you proclaim that God has power, you admit that you don't. And as you give God all the applause, there is none left to dizzy your brain. Jesus' prayer leads you to begin and end your prayers thinking of your heavenly Father.

Jesus is urging you to look at the peak more than you look at the trail. The more you focus "up there," the more inspired you will be "down here."

Some years ago, a sociologist accompanied a group of mountain climbers on an expedition. Among other things, he observed a distinct correlation between cloud cover and contentment. When there was no cloud cover and the peak was in view, the climbers were energetic and cooperative. When the gray clouds eclipsed the view of the mountaintop, though, the climbers were sullen and selfish.

The same thing happens to us. As long as our eyes are on God's majesty, there is a bounce in our step. But let our eyes focus on the dirt beneath us and we will grumble about every crevice we have to cross. As Paul urged, "Don't shuffle along, eyes to the ground, absorbed with the things right in front of you. Look up, and be alert to what is going on around Christ—that's where the action is. See things from *his* perspective" (Colossians 3:2 MSG).

Paul challenges us to "be alert to what is going on around Christ" (verse 2 MSG). The psalmist reminds us to do the same, only he uses a different phrase: "O magnify the LORD with me, and let us exalt his name together" (Psalm 34:3 NRSV).

Magnify. What a wonderful verb to describe what God wants us to do.

When we magnify an object, we enlarge it so that we can understand it. When we magnify God, we do the same. We enlarge our awareness of him so we can understand him more. This is exactly what happens when we worship—we take our mind off ourselves and set it on God. The emphasis is on him. "Yours is the kingdom and the power and the glory forever."

And this is exactly the purpose of this final phrase in the Lord's prayer. These words magnify the character of God. I love the way this phrase is translated in *The Message*: "You're in charge! You can do anything you want! You're ablaze in beauty! Yes. Yes. Yes" (Matthew 6:13 MSG).

Could it be any simpler? God is in charge! This concept is not foreign to us. When the restaurant waiter brings you a cold hamburger and a hot soda, you want to know who is in charge. When a young fellow wants to impress his girlfriend, he takes her down to the convenience store where he works and boasts, "Every night from five to ten o'clock, I'm in charge." We know what it means to be in charge of a restaurant or a store, but to be in charge of the universe? This is the claim of Jesus.

"God raised him from death and set him on a throne in deep heaven, in charge of running the universe, everything from galaxies to governments, no name and no power exempt from his rule. And not just for the time being, but *forever*. He is in charge of it all, has the final word on everything. At the center of all this, Christ rules the church" (Ephesians 1:22–23 MSG, emphasis added).

Doesn't he deserve to hear us proclaim his authority? Isn't it right for us to shout from the bottom of our hearts and at the top of our voice, "Yours is the kingdom and the power and the glory forever!" Isn't it right for us to stare at these mountain peaks of God and worship him? Of course it is. Not only does God deserve to hear our praise, but we need to give it!

THE HEART OF THE MATTER

- There are certain mountains that you were never meant to ascend.
- Jesus' model prayer teaches you to depend completely on God.
- Jesus urges you to look at the peak more than the trail.
- God deserves to hear your praise—and you need to give it!

MEMORY VERSE

This is it . . . one last review of your memory verse. Write out the words of Ephesians 6:18 from memory in the space below. Reflect on what these words mean to you.

The Heart of Jesus

It was as if Jesus knew how difficult the next days would be for the disciples. He would have to leave them soon. They would be plunged into fear, confusion, disbelief, pain, grief, desolation. They didn't really understand what lay ahead, even though he had tried to prepare them. So, Jesus prayed for them. He gathered his followers together and prayed aloud for each of them. "These men are mine. I have kept them safe. Protect them when I am gone. Give them my joy." He could not change what was coming, nor make things any easier for them, but he could pray for them. And his prayers would carry them through (see John 17:6-19).

WEEKLY BIBLE STUDY

READ: DANIEL 4:28–37 AND 1 PETER 5:5–9

1. The story of King Nebuchadnezzar is a lesson about the dangers of pride. What did Nebuchadnezzar say as he was walking on his roof (see Daniel 4:28–30)?

2. How did God respond to this bold claim from Nebuchadnezzar? What did the Lord say would happen to the king because of his pride (see verses 31–32)?

3. Nebuchadnezzar soon found himself out in the fields eating grass like an ox. What did he acknowledge when God returned him to his senses (see verses 34–37)?

4. Peter instructed the early followers of Jesus to also avoid the perils of pride. In what did he say the believers were to "clothe" themselves (see 1 Peter 5:5)?

5. What did Peter say would happen when the believers chose to humble themselves before God? What else did he instruct them to do (see verses 6–7)?

6. Satan likes to prey on the proud. What does Peter say about Satan's nature and schemes? What are believers to do when attacked (see verses 8–9)?

7. Are there any "mountains" you are climbing that God never intended you to climb? What do the passages you've studied this week reveal about the need for humility?

EXPERIENCING THE
HOPE OF JESUS

You are in your car driving home. Thoughts wander to the game you want to see or meal you want to eat, when suddenly a sound unlike any you've ever heard fills the air. The sound is high above you. A trumpet? A choir? A choir of trumpets? You don't know, but you want to know. So you pull over, get out of your car, and look up. As you do, you see you aren't the only curious one. The roadside has become a parking lot. Car doors are open, and people are staring at the sky. Shoppers are racing out of the grocery store. The Little League baseball game across the street has come to a halt. Players and parents are searching the clouds.

And what they see, and what you see, has never before been seen.

As if the sky were a curtain, the drapes of the atmosphere part. A brilliant light spills onto the earth. There are no shadows. None. From whence came the light begins to tumble a river of color—spiking crystals of every hue ever seen and a million more never seen. Riding on the flow is an endless fleet of angels. They pass through the curtains one myriad at a time, until they occupy every square inch of the sky. North. South. East. West. Thousands of silvery wings rise and fall in unison, and over the sound of the trumpets, you can hear the cherubim and seraphim chanting, "Holy, holy, holy."

The final flank of angels is followed by twenty-four silver-bearded elders and a multitude of souls who join the angels in worship. Presently the movement stops and the trumpets are silent, leaving only the triumphant triplet: "Holy, holy, holy." Between each word is a pause. With each word, a profound reverence. You hear your voice join in the chorus. You don't know why you say the words, but you know you must.

Suddenly, the heavens are quiet. All is quiet. The angels turn, you turn, the entire world turns—and there he is. Jesus. Through waves of light you see the silhouetted figure of Christ the King. He is atop a great stallion, and the stallion is atop a billowing cloud. He opens his mouth, and you are surrounded by his declaration: "I am the Alpha and the Omega."

The angels bow their heads. The elders remove their crowns. And before you is a figure so consuming that you know, instantly you know: nothing else matters.

Forget stock markets and school reports. Sales meetings and football games. Nothing is newsworthy. All that mattered matters no more, for Christ has come.

I wonder how those words make you feel. Wouldn't it be interesting to sit in a circle and listen to people's reactions? If a cluster of us summarized our emotions regarding the return of Christ in one word—what words would we hear? What word would you use?

Discomfort? You've been told your mistakes will be revealed. You've been told your secrets will be made known. Books will be opened, and names will be read. You know God is holy. You know you are not. How could the thought of his return bring anything but discomfort?

Denial? Ambiguity is not a pleasant roommate. We prefer answers and explanations, and the end of time seems short on both. Why consider what you can't explain? If he comes, fine. If not, fine. But I'm going to bed. I have to work tomorrow.

Disappointment? Who would feel disappointment at the thought of Christ's coming? A mother-to-be might—she wants to hold her baby. An engaged couple might—they want to be married. A soldier stationed overseas might—he wants to go home before he goes home.

I wonder what God would want us to feel. It's not hard to find the answer. Jesus said it plainly: "Do not let your hearts be troubled. You believe in God; believe also in me. . . . I will come back and take you to be with me" (John 14:1, 3).

It's a simple scenario. Jesus has gone away for a while. But he will return. And until then, he wants his children to be at peace.[24]

— PRAYER —

Dear Father, thank you for your promise that Jesus will return to this world. Stir up anticipation in my heart for that long-awaited moment. When I begin to feel hopeless in the midst of life's worries and burdens, please open my eyes to what really matters. Give me a glimpse of eternity this week and encourage me by ever increasing my hope in Jesus' return. Amen.

— MEMORY VERSE —

May the God of hope fill you with all joy and peace as you trust in him, so that you may overflow with hope by the power of the Holy Spirit.

ROMANS 15:13

Week 46: THE BEGINNING OF THE BEST

In a comprehensive survey conducted by Lucado and Friends (I interviewed a couple of people in the hallway), I determined the most dreaded question in parentdom. It's the one posed by the five-year-old on the trip: "How much farther?"

Give us the dilemmas of geometry and sexuality, just don't make a parent answer the question, "How much farther?" It's an impossible question. How do you speak of time and distance to someone who doesn't understand time and distance? The world of a youngster is delightfully free of mile markers and alarm clocks. So what do you do?

Most parents get creative. When our girls were toddlers, they loved to watch *The Little Mermaid*. So Denalyn and I used the movie as an economy of scale. "About as long as it takes you to watch *The Little Mermaid* three times." For a few minutes that helped. But sooner or later, they asked again. And sooner or later, we say what all parents eventually say, "Just trust me. You enjoy the trip and don't worry about the details. I'll make sure we get home."

Sound familiar? It might. Jesus has said the same to us. Just prior to his crucifixion, he told his disciples that he would be leaving them. "Where I am going, you cannot follow now, but you will follow later" (John 13:36). Such a statement was bound to stir some questions. Peter spoke for the others and asked, "Lord, why can't I follow you now?" (verse 37).

Jesus' reply reflects the tenderness of a parent to a child: "Don't let your hearts be troubled. Trust in God, and trust in me. There are many rooms in my Father's house; I would not tell you this if it were not true. I am going there to prepare a place for you . . . I will come back and take you to be with me so that you may be where I am" (John 14:1–3 NCV).

All of Jesus' words can be reduced to two: *trust me.* Don't be troubled by the return of Christ. Don't be anxious about the things we cannot comprehend. Issues like the millennium and the Antichrist are intended to challenge and stretch us, but not overwhelm us, and certainly not divide us. For the Christian, the return of Christ is not a riddle to be solved or a code to be broken but rather a day to be anticipated. In its purest form, hope comes from childlike trust—not from scratching our heads trying to figure out everything (as if we could!).

Jesus goes on to reassure us with three truths.

Truth #1: I have ample space for you. "There are many rooms in my Father's house" (verse 2 NCV). Why does Jesus make a point of mentioning the size of the house? You can answer that question as you think of the many times in life you've heard the opposite. Haven't there been occasions when you've been told, "We have no room for you here"?

Have you heard it in the workplace? "Sorry, I don't have room for you in my business."

From someone you love? "I don't have room for you in my heart."

Most sadly, have you heard it from a church? "You've made too many mistakes. We don't have room for you here."

Jesus knew the sound of those words. He was still in Mary's womb when the innkeeper said, "We don't have room for you." The residents of his hometown said the same when they tried to kill him: "We don't have room for prophets in this town." And when he hung on the cross, wasn't the message one of utter rejection? "We don't have room for you in this world."

Even today, Jesus is given the same treatment. He goes from heart to heart, asking if he might enter. But more often than not, he hears the words of the Bethlehem innkeeper: "Sorry, too crowded. I don't have room for you here." But every so often, he is welcomed. And to that person Jesus gives this great promise: "Do not let your heart be troubled. Trust in God. And trust in me. In my Father's house are many rooms."

Truth #2: I have a prepared place for you. Jesus said, "I am going there to prepare a place for you" (verse 2). Some years back, I spent a week speaking at a church in California. The members of the congregation were incredible hosts and hostesses. All my meals were lined up. But after a few meals, I noticed something strange. All we ate was salad.

At first I thought it was a California thing. But finally I had to ask. The answer confused me. "We were told that you eat nothing but salads." I quickly corrected them, but then wondered how the distortion had happened. As we traced the trail back, we determined a miscommunication had occurred between our office and theirs.

The hosts meant well, but their information was bad. I'm happy to say that we corrected the problem. I'm even happier to say that Jesus won't make the same mistake. He is preparing a place for you, but he knows *exactly* what you need. You needn't worry about getting bored or tired or weary with seeing the same people or singing the same songs. And you certainly needn't worry about sitting down to meal after meal of salad.

Truth #3: I'm not kidding. "I will come back and take you to be with me so that you may be where I am" (verse 3 NCV). Can you detect a slight shift of tone? The first sentences are couched in warmth. "Don't be troubled." "Trust God." "There are many rooms." But then the tone changes. The kindness continues but is now spiked with conviction. "I *will* come back."

George Tulloch displayed similar determination. In 1996, he led an expedition to the spot where the Titanic sank in 1912. In his search, Tulloch realized that a large piece of the hull had broken from the ship and was resting not far from the vessel. He immediately saw the opportunity at hand. Here was a chance to rescue part of the ship itself.

The team set out to raise the twenty-ton piece of iron, but a storm blew in, and the Atlantic reclaimed her treasure. Tulloch was forced to retreat. But before he left, he descended into the deep and, with the robotic arm of his submarine, attached a strip of metal to a section of the hull. On the metal he'd written these words: "I will come back. George Tulloch."

At first glance, his action is humorous. I mean, it's a piece of junk at the bottom of the ocean. We wonder why anyone would be so attracted to it. One might say the same about you and me. Why would God go to such efforts to reclaim us?

He must have his reasons, because two thousand years ago he entered the murky waters of our world in search of his children. And on all who will allow him to do so, he lays his claim and tags his name. "I will come back," he says. George Tulloch did. Two years later, he returned and rescued the piece of iron.

THE HEART OF THE MATTER

- The return of Christ is a day to be anticipated.
- Jesus has ample space for you in his Father's house.
- Jesus has prepared a place for you in his Father's house.
- Jesus has assured you that he *will* come back.

MEMORY VERSE

Take a few moments to review your Bible memory verse for this unit, and then write out the words of Romans 15:13 by heart in the space below.

The Heart of Jesus

He'd spent most of his life in dark corners and back alleys. He'd stolen from shops, from market vendors, from homes. He'd done shameful things, wicked things, things he'd never tell about. Now it was too late for him. As the soldier pinned his hands and feet to the beams of a cross, the thief writhed from both pain and regret. His eyes shifted to the two crosses nearby. A criminal on one cross was taunting a silent man on another. It was as if he wanted to rile the man. After a while, he told the mocker to shut his mouth. "We are getting what our deeds deserve," he said. "But this man has done nothing wrong." Then he said, "Jesus, remember me when you come into your kingdom." At that, Jesus' eyes turned to his. When he spoke, it was with words of forgiveness and hope. "You will be with me today in paradise." Even a dying man can experience the hope of Jesus for the first time (see Luke 23:39–43).

WEEKLY BIBLE STUDY

READ: JOHN 14:1–14 AND REVELATION 1:4–8

1. Jesus had just told his disciples that he would be leaving them. He now tells them not to be troubled. What promise does he give about where he is going (see John 14:1–4)?

2. Jesus' announcement of his departure prompted concern among the disciples. What question did Thomas ask him? How did Jesus respond (see verses 5–7)?

3. What question did Philip ask Jesus? What does Jesus' response reveal about what it means to believe in him and draw on his authority (see verses 8–14)?

4. John would later receive a vision of the events that would transpire upon Jesus' return. How does John describe Jesus in the opening of his letter (see Revelation 1:4–5)?

5. Jesus was not kidding when he told the disciples he would return. What does John write about Jesus' arrival? What will happen to the peoples on earth (see verses 6–7)?

6. Jesus states that he is "the Alpha and the Omega," which are the first and last letters of the Greek alphabet (see verse 8). What is the significance of this title?

7. How have the passages you've studied this week encouraged you to trust that Jesus is preparing a place for his followers? What hope does that bring to you today?

Week 47: WAITING FORWARDLY

Funny how Scripture remembers different people. Abraham is remembered trusting. Envision Moses, and you think of a person leading. Paul's place in Scripture was carved by his writing and John is known for his loving. But Simeon is remembered, interestingly enough, not for leading nor preaching nor loving, but rather for looking.

"Now in Jerusalem there was a man named Simeon. He was an upright and devout man; he *looked forward* to the restoration of Israel and the Holy Spirit rested on him" (Luke 2:25 NJB, emphasis added). Simeon . . . the man who knew how to wait for the arrival of Christ. The way he waited for the first coming is a model for how we should wait for the second coming.

Our brief encounter with Simeon occurs eight days after the birth of Jesus. Joseph and Mary have brought their son to the temple. It's the day of a sacrifice, the day of circumcision, the day of dedication. But for Simeon, it's the day of celebration.

Let's imagine a white-headed, wizened fellow working his way down the streets of Jerusalem. People in the market call his name and he waves but doesn't stop. Neighbors greet him and he returns the greeting but doesn't pause. Friends chat on the corner and he smiles but doesn't stop. He has a place to be and he hasn't time to lose.

"Prompted by the Spirit he came to the Temple" (Luke 2:27 NJB). Simeon apparently had no plans to go to the temple. God, however, instructed him otherwise. We don't know how the prompting came—a call from a neighbor, an invitation from his wife, a nudging within the heart—but somehow Simeon knew to clear his calendar and put away his golf clubs.

On this side of the event, we understand the prompting. This wasn't the first time God had tapped him on the shoulder. At least one other time in his life, he had received a message from the Lord. "The Holy Spirit had revealed to him that he would not die until he had seen him—God's anointed King" (verse 26 TLB).

You've got to wonder what a message like that would do to a person. We know what it did to Simeon. He was "constantly expecting the Messiah" (verse 25 TLB). He was "living in expectation of the 'salvation of Israel'" (verse 25 PHILLIPS). He "watched and waited for the restoration of Israel" (verse 25 NEB). Simeon was a man on tiptoes, wide-eyed and watching for the one who would come to save Israel.

Maybe you know what it's like to look for someone who has come for you. I do. When I travel to speak, I often don't know who will pick me up at the airport. Hence, I exit the plane searching for a face I've never seen. But though I've never seen the person, I know I'll find him. He may have my name on a sign or just a puzzled expression on his face. Were you to ask me how I will recognize the one who has come for me, I would say, "I don't know, I just know I will." I bet Simeon would have said the same. "How will you know the King, Simeon?" "I don't know. I just know I will." And so he searches.

The Greek language has a stable full of verbs that mean "to look." Of all the forms, the one that best captures what it means to "look for the coming" is the term used to describe the action of Simeon: *prosdechomai*. (*Dechomai*, meaning "to wait"; *pros*, meaning "forward.") Combine them and you have the graphic picture of one "waiting forwardly." The grammar is poor, but the image is great. Simeon was waiting—not demanding, not hurrying, but waiting.

At the same time, Simeon was waiting forwardly. Patiently vigilant. Calmly expectant. Searching the crowd for the right face, and hoping the face appeared that day. Such was the lifestyle of Simeon, and such can be ours. Haven't we, like Simeon, been told of the coming Christ? Aren't we, like Simeon, heirs of a promise? Are we not prompted by the same Spirit?

Absolutely. In fact, the same verb is used later in Luke to describe the posture of the waiting servant: "Be dressed ready for service and keep your lamps burning, like servants waiting [*prosdechomai*] for their master to return from a wedding banquet. . . . Truly I tell you, he will dress himself to serve, will have them recline at the table and will come and wait on them" (12:35–37). Note the posture of the servants: ready and waiting. Note the action of the master: so thrilled that his attendants are watching for him that he takes the form of a servant and serves them! They sit at the feast and are cared for by the master!

Why are they honored in such a way? The master loves to find people looking for his return. The master rewards those who "wait forwardly." Both words are crucial.

First, we must *wait*. Paul says, "We are hoping for something we do not have yet, and we are waiting for it patiently" (Romans 8:25 NCV).

Simeon is our model. He was not so consumed with the "not yet" that he ignored the "right now." Luke says Simeon was "righteous and devout" (Luke 2:25). Peter urges us to follow suit. "You ought to live holy and godly lives as you look forward to the day of God and speed its coming" (2 Peter 3:11–12).

Second, we wait *forwardly*. Most of us are so good at waiting that we don't wait forwardly. We forget to look. We are so patient that we become complacent. We are too content. We seldom search the skies. We rarely run to the temple. We seldom, if ever, allow the Holy Spirit to interrupt our plans and lead us to worship so that we might see Jesus.

It is to those of us who are strong in waiting and weak in watching that our Lord was speaking when he said, "But about that day or hour no one knows, not even the angels in heaven, nor the Son, but only the Father. . . . Therefore keep watch, because you do not know on what day your Lord will come. . . . So you also must be ready, because the Son of Man will come at an hour when you do not expect him" (Matthew 24:36, 42, 44).

Simeon reminds us to "wait forwardly." Patiently vigilant. But not so patient that we lose our vigilance. Nor so vigilant that we lose our patience.

In the end, the prayer of Simeon was answered. "Simeon took the baby in his arms and thanked God: 'Now, Lord, you can let me, your servant, die in peace as you said'" (Luke 2:28–29 NCV).

One look into the face of Jesus, and Simeon knew it was time to go home. And one look into the face of our Savior, and we will know the same.

THE HEART OF THE MATTER

- Followers of Jesus are to "wait forwardly" for his return.
- Jesus wants to find people vigilantly looking for his return.
- Lead a holy and God-honoring life as you wait.
- Don't become complacent as you wait for Jesus' return.

MEMORY VERSE

Your memory verse for this unit is Romans 15:13. Take a few moments to review this verse, and then write it out from memory in the space below.

The Heart of Jesus

Saul was an enthusiast. He had deep convictions, and he lived by them. Self-assured. Confident. Driven. When he did something, he gave it 100 percent. No holds barred. Full throttle. Relentless. Tireless. All very good qualities, of course. Unless you are hopelessly misguided. Saul was living his life for God and giving it his best shot, but he was out of the loop. He knew his Bible forward and backward. He knew all the rules for righteous living like the back of his hand. But he didn't know Jesus. Enthusiasm, sincerity, and effort don't count for much if you're on the wrong path. So Jesus dazzled Saul's eyes and grabbed his attention. He set him straight and channeled his go-getter attitude in the right direction. Saul, now called Paul, was introduced to the hope that only Jesus holds, and it changed his life forever (see Acts 9:1–19).

WEEKLY BIBLE STUDY

READ: LUKE 2:22–35 AND 2 PETER 3:8–14

1. Simeon was *waiting forwardly* for the arrival of the Messiah. What was the occasion that prompted Mary and Joseph to bring Jesus to the temple (see Luke 2:22–24)?

2. How is Simeon described when he is first introduced in the passage? What had been revealed to him by the Holy Spirit (see verses 25–26)?

3. How did Simeon react when he saw the child Jesus in the temple courts? What blessing and prophetic words did Simeon utter to Mary (see verses 27–35)?

4. Followers of Jesus are instructed not to just *wait* for his return—but to *wait forwardly* for his second coming. How would you define what it means for you to wait forwardly?

5. Jesus said that no one but the Father knows the day of his return (see Matthew 24:36). What does Peter say about your heavenly Father's timing (see 2 Peter 3:8–10)?

6. It is critical to not become complacent as you wait for Jesus' return. What does Peter say you should be doing as you wait forwardly for Christ (see verses 11–14)?

7. What do the passages you've studied this week reveal about living in expectation of Jesus' return? What do they reveal about what you should be doing as you wait?

Week 48: THE BRAND-NEW YOU

Suppose you were walking past my farm one day and saw me in the field crying. (Okay, I don't have a farm, nor am I prone to crying in fields, but play along with me.) There I sit, disconsolate at the head of a furrowed row. Concerned, you approach me and ask what is wrong.

I look up from beneath my John Deere tractor hat and extend a palm full of seeds in your direction. "My heart breaks for the seeds," I say. "My heart breaks for the seeds."

"What?" you ask.

Between sobs I explain, "The seeds will be placed in the ground and covered with dirt. They will decay, and we will never see them again."

As I weep, you are stunned. You look around for a turnip truck off which you are confident I tumbled.

Finally, you explain to me a basic principle of farming. Out of the decay of the seed comes the birth of a plant. You kindly remind me, "Do not bemoan the burial of the seed, for soon you witness a mighty miracle of God. Given time and tender care, this tiny kernel will break from its prison of soil and blossom into a plant far beyond its dreams."

Well, maybe you aren't that dramatic, but those are your thoughts. Any farmer who grieves over the burial of a seed needs a reminder: a time of planting is not a time of grief.

Any person who anguishes over the burial of a body needs the same. We need the reminder Paul gave the Corinthians: "There is an order to this resurrection: Christ was raised as the first of the harvest; then all who belong to Christ will be raised when he comes back" (1 Corinthians 15:23 NLT).

Upon death, our souls will journey immediately to the presence of God while we await the resurrection of our bodies. And when will this resurrection occur? You guessed it. When Christ comes. "When Christ comes again, those who belong to him will be raised to life, and then the end will come" (verses 23–24 NCV).

But what does Paul mean, "Those who belong to him will be raised to life"? What will be raised? Our bodies? If so, why *this* body? Why don't we start over on a new model?

Come with me back to the farm, and let's look for some answers.

If you were impressed with my seed allegory, I'd better be honest. I stole the idea from Paul. He writes, "But someone will ask, 'How are the dead raised? With what kind of body will they come?' How foolish! What you sow does not come to life unless it dies. When you sow, you do not plant the body that will be, but just a seed, perhaps of wheat or of something else. But God gives it a body as he has determined, and to each kind of seed he gives its own body" (verses 35–38).

In other words, you can't have a new body without the death of the old body. (Unless, of course, you are alive when Christ returns, and then you will also get a new body.) As Paul states, "What you sow does not come to life unless it dies" (verse 36).

A friend told me that Paul's parallel between seeds sown and bodies buried reminded her of a remark made by her youngest son. He was a first grader, and his class was studying plants about the same time the family attended a funeral of a loved one. One day, as they were driving past a cemetery, the two events came together in one statement. "Hey, Mom," he said, pointing toward the graveyard. "That's where they plant people."

Paul would have liked that. He wants us to change the way we think about the burial process. The graveside is not a burial, but a planting. The grave is not a hole in the ground but a fertile furrow. The cemetery is not the resting place but the transformation place.

Most assume that death has no purpose. It is to people what the black hole is to space—a mysterious, inexplicable, distasteful, all-consuming power. We do all we can to live and not die. God, however, says we must die in order to live. When you sow a seed, it must die in the ground before it can grow. What we see as the ultimate tragedy, he sees as the ultimate triumph. And when a Christian dies, it's not a time to despair, but a time to trust.

Out of curiosity, I made a list of the news I've heard in the last twenty-four hours concerning failing health. A professor was diagnosed with Parkinson's disease. A friend's father is scheduled for eye surgery. Another friend had a stroke. A minister died after four decades of preaching. If you can relate, I wonder if God wants to use the next few lines to speak directly to you. Your body is so tired, so worn. Joints ache and muscles fatigue. You understand why Paul described the body as a tent. "We groan in this tent," he wrote (2 Corinthians 5:2 NCV).

Your body will be changed. You will not receive a different body; you will receive a *renewed* body.

Just as God can make an oak out of a kernel or a tulip out of a bulb, he will make a "new" body out of the old one. A body without corruption. A body without weakness. A body without dishonor. A body identical to the body of Jesus.

My friend Joni Eareckson Tada made this same point. Rendered a quadriplegic by a teenage diving accident, she has spent the majority of her life in discomfort. She, more than most, knows the meaning of living in a lowly body. At the same time, she, more than most, knows the hope of a resurrected body.

Listen to her words: "Somewhere in my broken, paralyzed body is the seed of what I shall become. The paralysis makes what I am to become all the more grand when you contrast atrophied, useless legs against splendorous resurrected legs. I'm convinced that if there are mirrors in heaven (and why not?), the image I'll see will be unmistakably 'Joni,' although a much better, brighter Joni. So much so, that it's not worth comparing . . . I will bear the likeness of Jesus, the man from heaven."[25]

Your pain will *not* last forever. Believe it. Are your joints arthritic? They won't be in heaven. Is your heart weak? It will be strong in heaven. Has cancer corrupted your system? There is no cancer in heaven. Are your thoughts disjointed? Is your memory failing? Your new body in heaven will have a new mind.

Does the body you now have seem closer to death than ever before? It should. It is. And unless Christ comes first, your body will be buried. Like a seed is placed in the ground, so your body will be placed in a tomb. And for a season, your soul will be in heaven while your body is in the grave. But the seed buried in the earth will blossom in heaven.

Your soul and body will reunite, and you will be like Jesus.

THE HEART OF THE MATTER

- When Christ comes back, all his people will be raised.
- You can't have a new body without the death of the old body.
- When a Christian dies, it's not a time to despair but a time to trust.
- The seed (body) buried in the earth will blossom in heaven.

MEMORY VERSE

Your memory verse for this unit is Romans 15:13. Take a few moments to review this verse, and then write it out from memory in the space below.

The Heart of Jesus

Peter was stranded in a hopeless situation. The authorities had begun arresting some of those in the church. The disciple James had already been put to death, and it looked like the same would happen to Peter. He had been caught, locked in a jail cell, and threatened with his very life. Now, as he sat in the moldy straw of the jail cell and listened to scurrying mice, he turned his heart toward his Savior in prayer. Across the same town, his friends were doing the very same. The other disciples had quietly gathered together when they heard the news that Peter had been arrested. In the face of hopelessness, they, too, prayed. And God answered by doing the impossible. An angel appeared, shackles fell, doors opened, and the prisoner was set free. Nothing is too hard for God. With him, there is always hope (see Acts 12:1–11).

WEEKLY BIBLE STUDY

READ: 1 CORINTHIANS 15:12–28 AND 1 JOHN 3:1–6

1. The believers in Corinth had questions about their resurrected bodies when Jesus returns. What does Paul imply was one of their questions (see 1 Corinthians 15:12)?

2. What proof does Paul provide that the believers' bodies will one day be raised from the dead? What would it mean if they were *not* raised to life (see verses 13–19)?

3. Paul reminds the believers that there is an order to the resurrection. What comes first in this process? What will happen next (see verses 20–23)?

4. Paul adds one further detail about what will happen when Jesus returns. What will Christ do once and for all when he again appears in this world (see verses 24–28)?

5. When a Christian dies, it's not a time to despair but a time to trust. What does John say that you can trust will happen when Jesus returns (see 1 John 3:1–2)?

6. John also notes that anticipating Jesus' return should have an impact on how you live. What does he say those who live in Christ no longer do (see verses 3–6)?

7. How do the passages you've studied this week give you hope and reassurance that followers of Jesus will have a resurrected body? What are you most looking forward to about that day?

Week 49: AMAZED AT JESUS

Augustine once posed the following experiment. Imagine God saying to you, "I'll make a deal with you if you wish. I'll give you anything and everything you ask: pleasure, power, honor, wealth, freedom, even peace of mind, and a good conscience. Nothing will be a sin; nothing will be forbidden; and nothing will be impossible to you. You will never be bored and you will never die. Only . . . you will never see my face."[26]

The first part of the proposition is appealing. Isn't there a part of us—a pleasure-loving part of us—that perks up at the thought of guiltless, endless delight? But then, just as we are about to volunteer, we hear the final phrase: "You will never see my face."

Never know the image of God? Never behold the presence of Christ? At this point, for some of us the bargain begins to lose its appeal. But for others, it doesn't raise as much interest as it does a question. One you may be hesitant to ask for fear of sounding naive or irreverent.

Since you may feel that way, why don't I ask it for you? At the risk of putting words in your mouth, let me put words in your mouth. "Why the big deal?" you ask. "No disrespect intended. Of course I want to see Jesus. But to see him forever? Will he be that amazing?"

According to Paul, he will. "On the day when the Lord Jesus comes . . . all the people who have believed will be amazed at Jesus" (2 Thessalonians 1:10 NCV). Amazed at Jesus. Not amazed at angels, or mansions, or new bodies, or new creations. Paul doesn't measure the joy of encountering the apostles or embracing our loved ones. If we will be amazed at these, which certainly we will, he does not say. What he does say is that we will be amazed at Jesus.

What we have only seen in our thoughts, we will see with our eyes. What we've struggled to imagine, we will be free to behold. What we've seen in a glimpse, we will then see in full view. And, according to Paul, we will be amazed.

What will be so amazing? Of course, I have no way of answering that question from personal experience. But I can lead you to someone who can.

One Sunday morning many Sundays ago, a man named John saw Jesus. And what he saw, he recorded; and what he recorded has tantalized seekers of Christ for two thousand years.

This wasn't John's first time to see the Savior. We only read about the hands that fed the thousands. But John saw them—knuckled fingers, callused palms. We only read about the feet that found a path through the waves. But John saw them—sandaled, ten-toed, and dirty. We only read about his eyes—flashing eyes, fiery eyes, weeping eyes. John saw them. Gazing on the crowds, dancing with laughter, searching for souls. John had seen Jesus.

For three years, he had followed Christ. But this encounter was different from any in Galilee. The image was so vivid, the impression so powerful, that John was knocked out cold. "When I saw him I fell in a dead faint at his feet" (Revelation 1:17 NJB).

What does John reveal that we will see? We will see Christ as the perfect priest. "He was dressed in a long robe and had a gold band around his chest" (verse 13 NCV). The first readers of this message knew the significance of the robe and band. Jesus is wearing the clothing of a priest. A priest presented people to God and God to people.

You have known other priests. There have been others in your life, whether clergy or not, who sought to bring you to God. But they, too, needed a priest. Some needed a priest more than you did. They, like you, were sinful. Not so with Jesus. "Jesus is the kind of high priest we need. He is holy, sinless, pure, not influenced by sinners, and he is raised above the heavens" (Hebrews 7:26 NCV). Jesus is the perfect priest.

He is also pure and purifying: "His head and hair were white like wool, as white as snow, and his eyes were like flames of fire" (Revelation 1:14 NCV). What would a person look like if he had never sinned? If no worry wrinkled his brow and no anger shadowed his eyes? If no bitterness snarled his lips and no selfishness bowed his smile? We will know when we see Jesus. What John saw on that Sunday was absolutely spotless. He was reminded of the virgin wool of sheep and the untouched snow of winter.

John was also reminded of fire. Others saw the burning bush, the burning altar, the fiery furnace, or the fiery chariots, but John saw the fiery eyes. And in those eyes, he saw a purging blaze that will burn the bacteria of sin and purify the soul. When we see Jesus, we will see absolute strength. "His feet were like bronze that glows hot in a furnace" (verse 15 NCV).

John's audience knew the value of this metal. Eugene Peterson wrote, "Bronze is a combination of iron and copper. Iron is strong but it rusts. Copper won't rust but it's pliable. Combine the two in bronze and the best quality of each is preserved, the strength of the iron and the endurance of the copper. The rule of Christ is set on this base: the foundation of his power is tested by fire."[27]

Every power you have ever seen has decayed. The muscle men in the magazines, the automobiles on the racetrack, the armies in the history books. They had their strength and they had their day, but their day passed. But the strength of Jesus will never be surpassed. Never. When you see him, you will—for the first time—see true strength.

Ever wonder how you would feel if Jesus spoke to you? John felt like he was near a waterfall: "His voice was like the noise of flooding water" (verse 15 NCV). The sound of a river rushing through a forest is not a timid one. It is the backdrop against all other sounds. Even when nature sleeps, the river speaks. The same is true of Christ. In heaven, his voice is always heard—a steady, soothing, commanding presence.

What are we to do with such a picture? How are we to assimilate these images? Are we to combine them on a canvas and consider it a portrait of Jesus? I don't think so. I don't think the goal of this vision is to tell us what Jesus looks like but rather to tell us who Jesus is.

The perfect priest. The only pure one. The source of strength. The sound of love. The everlasting light. When you see Jesus, you will see unblemished purity and unbending strength. You will feel his unending presence and know his unbridled protection. And all that he is, you will be, for you will be like Jesus. Wasn't that the promise of John? "We know that when Christ comes again, we will be like him, because we will see him as he really is" (1 John 3:2 NCV).

THE HEART OF THE MATTER

- You will be amazed at Jesus when you see him at his return.
- When you see Christ, you will see the perfect priest.
- When you see Christ, you will see sinless perfection.
- When you see Christ, you will see absolute strength.

MEMORY VERSE

Your memory verse for this unit is Romans 15:13. Take a few moments to review this verse, and then write it out by heart in the space below.

The Heart of Jesus

When someone that we love is suddenly gone, it hurts. We miss them. We miss the way things were. We want them back. When Mary and Martha were faced with the death of their brother, they reacted differently. Mary hid herself away, not wanting to leave her room. Martha went on the warpath, looking for someone to blame. Jesus confronted Martha. With a sigh, she admitted that she knew, really knew, that she would see her brother again someday. Clinging to that hope, she returned home to comfort her sister. Jesus offers that same hope to every Christian—we will see our brothers and sisters in Christ again someday, at the resurrection. Though we all grieve differently, we all can cling to the same hope (see John 11:20–24).

WEEKLY BIBLE STUDY

READ: REVELATION 1:9–18 AND 2 THESSALONIANS 1:6–10

1. John had followed Jesus for three years, but what he saw of Christ in his vision was vastly different. What happened to John on the Lord's Day in Revelation 1:9–11?

2. What did John see when he turned around to look at who was speaking to him? How does this image represent the *perfect priest* (see verses 12–13)?

3. What John saw on that Sunday was absolutely spotless. How does he describe Jesus as *pure* and *purifying*? As one of *absolute strength* (see verses 14–16)?

4. How did John respond when he beheld Jesus in this way? What did Jesus say to his faithful disciple to calm him and encourage him (see verses 17–18)?

5. God promises to care for those who have accepted his offer of salvation. What will happen on the day of Jesus' return to those who have not (see 1 Thessalonians 2:6–8)?

6. Those who want nothing to do with Jesus will get their wish—they will be shut out of God's presence. What does Paul say God's people will do on that day (see verses 9–10)?

7. What do the passages you've studied this week tell you about the way Jesus will return to this world? What are some ways that Jesus has amazed you so far in your life?

Week 50: CROSSING THE THRESHOLD

The story of the prince and his peasant bride. A more intriguing romance never occurred. His attraction to her is baffling. He, the stately prince. She, the common peasant. He, peerless. She, plain. Not ugly, but she can be. Not the kind of soul you'd want to live with.

But, according to the prince, she is the soul he can't live without. So he proposed to her. "I'll return for you soon," he promised. "I will be waiting," she pledged.

No one thought it odd for the prince to leave. He was, after all, the son of the king. Surely he had some kingdom work to do. What's odd was not his departure, but her behavior during his absence. She forgot that she was engaged!

You would think the wedding would ever be on her mind. But it's not. Some of her friends have never even heard her speak of the event. Days pass—even weeks—and his return isn't mentioned. Why, there have been times when she has been seen cavorting with the village men. Flirting in the bright of day. Dare we wonder about her activities in the dark of night?

Is she rebellious? Maybe. But mostly, she is just forgetful. She keeps forgetting that she is engaged. "That's no excuse," you say. "His return should be her every thought! How could a peasant forget her prince? How could a bride forget her groom?"

It's a good question. How could we?

You see, the story of the prince and his peasant bride is not an ancient fable. Rather, it is a portrayal of us. Are we not the bride of Christ? Have we not been set apart "as a pure bride to one husband" (2 Corinthians 11:2 NLT)? Did God not say to us, "I will betroth you to me forever" (Hosea 2:19)?

I first witnessed the power of a marriage proposal in college. I shared a class with a girl who got engaged. She was shy and unsure of herself. She didn't stand out in the crowd—and seemed to like it that way. No makeup. No dress-up. But one day, that all began to change. Her hair changed. Her dress changed. Even her voice changed. She spoke with confidence.

What made the difference? Simple. She was chosen. A young man she loved said, "Come and spend forever with me." And she was changed. Empowered by his proposal. Validated by his love. His love for her convinced her that she was worth loving.

God's love can do the same for us. We, like the girl, feel so common. Insecurities stalk us. Self-doubt plagues us. But the marriage proposal of the prince can change all that.

Want a cure for insecurity? Meditate on these words intended for you: "You have stolen my heart . . . with one glance of your eyes, with one jewel of your necklace. How delightful is your love, my sister, my bride! How much more pleasing is your love than wine, and the fragrance of your perfume more than any spice!" (Song of Songs 4:9–10).

Do you find it odd to think of God as an enthralled lover? Do you feel awkward thinking of Jesus as a suitor intoxicated on love? If so, how else do you explain his actions? Did logic put God in a manger? Did common sense nail him to a cross? Did Jesus come to earth guided by a natural law of science?

No, he came as a prince with his eye on the maiden, ready to battle even the dragon itself if that's what it took to win her hand.

And that is exactly what it took. It took a battle with the dragon of hell. He has "loved you with an everlasting love; [he has] drawn you with unfailing kindness" (Jeremiah 31:3).

Have you ever noticed the way a groom looks at his bride during the wedding? I have. Perhaps it's my vantage point. As the minister of the wedding, I'm the one to give him the signal when it's our turn to step out of the wings up to the altar. I've been with him backstage as he tugged his collar and mopped his brow. He follows me into the chapel like a criminal walking to the gallows.

But all that changes when she appears.

Most miss it because they are looking at her. But when other eyes are on the bride, I sneak a peek at the groom. When he sees her, it's written all over his face. "Who could bear to live without this bride?" And such are precisely the feelings of Jesus.

Look long enough into the eyes of our Savior and, there, too, you will see a bride. Dressed in fine linen. Clothed in pure grace. From the wreath in her hair to the clouds at her feet, she is royal. She is the princess. She is the bride. His bride. Walking toward him, she is not yet with him. But he sees her, he awaits her, he longs for her.

Ever feel like you have nothing? Just look at the gifts that he has given you. He has sent his angels to care for you, his Holy Spirit to dwell in you, his church to encourage you, and his Word to guide you. You have privileges only a fiancée could have. Anytime you speak, he listens. Make a request, and he responds. He will never let you be tempted too much or stumble too far. As much as you want to see him, he wants to see you more.

He is building a house for you. And with every swing of the hammer and cut of the saw, he's dreaming of the day he carries you over the threshold (see John 14:2–3). You have been chosen by Christ. You are released from your old life in your old house, and he has claimed you as his beloved. "Then where is he?" you might ask. "Why hasn't he come?"

There is only one answer. His bride is not ready. She is still being prepared. Engaged people are obsessed with preparation. The right dress. The right hair. The right tux. They want to look their best because their fiancée is marrying them. The same is true for us. We want to look our best for Christ. We want our hearts to be pure and our thoughts to be clean. We want our faces to shine with grace and our eyes to sparkle with love. We want to be prepared.

Why do we want to be prepared? In hopes that he will love us? No. Just the opposite. Because he already does. You are engaged, set apart, a holy bride. You have been chosen for his castle. So don't settle for one-night stands in the arms of a stranger.

Be obsessed with your wedding date. Guard against forgetfulness. Be intolerant of memory lapses. Memorize verses. Do whatever you need to do to remember. "Aim at what is in heaven. . . . Think only about the things in heaven" (Colossians 3:1–2 NCV).

You are engaged to royalty, and your Prince is coming to take you home.

THE HEART OF THE MATTER

- Jesus has chosen you and promised to return for you.
- Jesus came ready to battle the dragon itself to win you.
- Jesus battled the enemy and loves you with an everlasting love.
- Be obsessed with remembering that Jesus is coming back.

MEMORY VERSE

This is it . . . one last review of your memory verse. Write out the words of Romans 15:13 from memory in the space below. Reflect on what these words mean to you.

The Heart of Jesus

Jesus faced hunger, discomfort, tiredness, and pain. He reached out to thousands of individuals. He traveled with faithless disciples. He spent sleepless nights in prayer. He endured the testing and word traps of religious rulers. He was forced to turn away people who thought he was some kind of circus act. He was driven out of synagogues and towns. His own family questioned his sanity. You'd think he would just throw up his hands in frustration and say, "What next?" What kept Jesus focused? *Hope.* He had the hope of returning to his Father one day, his task complete. He cherished the hope of returning for his followers and carrying them back to heaven with him. He knew that eternity was waiting just beyond their sight, and he wanted to enter it triumphantly. For the sake of what was ahead of him, for the hope of what he knew was coming, Jesus endured everything that life could throw at him (see Hebrews 12:2).

WEEKLY BIBLE STUDY

READ: MATTHEW 25:1–13 AND 1 THESSALONIANS 5:1–8

1. Jesus told a parable to his followers about what it meant to wait expectantly for his return. Who were the primary characters in his story (see Matthew 25:1–4)?

2. The bridegroom in the story was a long time in returning. What did the foolish virgins have to do when they learned the bridegroom had arrived (see verses 5–9)?

3. What happened while the foolish virgins were out trying to secure oil for their lamps? What did the bridegroom say to them when they returned (see verses 10–13)?

4. No bride-to-be would forget that she is engaged—but Christians often forget about their "engagement" to Jesus. What is the lesson of Jesus' parable of the ten virgins?

5. Paul described the return of Jesus like a thief coming in the night. What will happen when Jesus suddenly makes his appearance to the world (see 1 Thessalonians 5:1–3)?

6. Paul states that followers of Jesus do not live in darkness and thus have their eyes open to these coming events. How should this influence how they live (see verses 4–8)?

7. How have the passages you've studied in this unit changed the way you think about Jesus' return? What have you discovered about *waiting forwardly* for his coming?

EXPERIENCING THE
CALLING OF JESUS

WEEK 51: FISHERS OF MEN

WEEK 52: COME AND SEE

What if, for one day, Jesus were to become you? What if, for twenty-four hours, Jesus woke up in your bed, walked in your shoes, lived in your house, assumed your schedule? Your boss became his boss, your mother became his mother, your pains became his pains? With one exception, nothing about your life changed. Your health didn't change. Your circumstances didn't change. Your schedule wasn't altered. Your problems weren't solved. Only one change occured.

What if, for one day and one night, Jesus lived your life with his heart? Your heart got the day off, and your life was led by the heart of Christ. His priorities governed your actions. His passions drove your decisions. His love directed your behavior.

What would you be like? Would your family see something new? Would your coworkers sense a difference? What about the less fortunate? Would you treat them the same? And your friends? Would they detect more joy? How about your enemies? Would they receive more mercy from Christ's heart than from yours?

And you? How would you feel? What alterations would this transplant have on your stress level? Your mood swings? Your temper? Would you see sunsets differently? Death differently? Taxes differently? Any chance you'd need fewer aspirin or sedatives? How about your reaction to traffic delays? (Ouch, that touched a nerve.) Would you still dread what you are dreading? Better yet, would you still do what you are doing?

Keep working on this for a moment. Adjust the lens of your imagination until you have a clear picture of Jesus leading your life, then snap the shutter and frame the image. What you see is what God wants. He wants you to "have the same mindset as Christ" (Philippians 2:5).

God's plan for you is nothing short of a new heart. If you were a car, God would want control of your engine. If you were a computer, God would claim the software and the hard drive. If you were an airplane, he would take his seat in the flight deck. But you are a person, so God wants to change your heart. He is *calling you* to change your heart.

It's dangerous to sum up grand truths in one statement, but I'm going to try. If a sentence or two could capture God's desire for each of us, it might read like this: "God loves us just the way we are, but he refuses to leave us that way. He wants us to be just like Jesus."

When my daughter Jenna was a toddler, I used to take her to a park near our apartment. One day as she was playing in a sandbox, an ice cream salesman approached us. I purchased her a treat, and when I turned to give it to her, I saw her mouth was full of sand. Where I intended to put a delicacy, she had put dirt.

Did I love her with dirt in her mouth? Absolutely. Was she any less my daughter with dirt in her mouth? Of course not. Was I going to allow her to keep the dirt in her mouth? No way. I loved her right where she was, but I refused to leave her there. I carried her over to the water fountain and washed out her mouth. Why? Because I love her.

God does the same for us. He holds us over the fountain. "Spit out the dirt," he urges. "I've got something better for you." And so he cleanses us of filth: immorality, dishonesty, prejudice, bitterness, greed. We don't enjoy the cleansing; sometimes we even opt for the dirt over the ice cream. "I can eat dirt if I want to!" we pout and proclaim.

But if we do, the loss is ours. God has a better offer. He is calling us to something better. You aren't stuck with today's personality. You aren't condemned to "grumpydom." You are tweakable. Even if you've worried each day of your life, you needn't worry the rest of your life.

Where did we get the idea we can't change? From whence come statements such as, "It's just my nature to worry," or, "I'll always be pessimistic," or, "I can't help the way I react"? Would we make similar statements about our bodies? "It's just my nature to have a broken leg." Of course not. If our bodies malfunction, we seek help. Shouldn't we do the same with our hearts? Shouldn't we seek aid for our sour attitudes? Can't we request treatment for our selfish tirades? Of course we can. Jesus can change our hearts. He wants us to have a heart like his. Can you imagine a better offer?[28]

— PRAYER —

Heavenly Father, I want to heed your calling to be like Jesus. Help me this week to tune out the voices of the world and focus on hearing you. Thank you for speaking your words of wisdom, mercy, and love into my life. Draw me closer to you each day and guide me with your gentle voice.

— MEMORY VERSE —

Nevertheless, each person should live as a believer in whatever situation the Lord has assigned to them, just as God has called them.

1 CORINTHIANS 7:17

Week 51: FISHERS OF MEN

When I was in high school, our family used to fish every year during spring break. One year my brother and my mom couldn't go, so my dad let me invite a friend. I asked Mark. He was a good pal and a great sport. He got permission from his parents, and we began planning our trip.

Days before leaving, we could already anticipate the vacation. We could feel the sun warming our bodies as we floated in the boat. We could feel the yank of the rod and hear the spin of the reel as we wrestled the white bass into the boat. And we could smell the fish frying in an open skillet over an open fire.

We could hardly wait. Days passed like cold molasses. Finally, spring break arrived. We loaded our camper and set out for the lake.

We arrived late at night, unfolded the camper, and went to bed—dreaming of tomorrow's day in the sun. But during the night, an unseasonably strong norther blew in. It got cold fast! The wind was so strong that we could barely open the camper door the next morning. The sky was gray. The lake was a mountain range of white-topped waves. There was no way we could fish in that weather.

"No problem," we said. "We'll spend the day in the camper. After all, we have Monopoly. We have some magazines to read. We all know a few jokes. It's not what we came to do, but we'll make the best of it and fish tomorrow."

So, huddled in the camper with a Coleman stove and a Monopoly board, we three fishermen passed the day—indoors. The hours passed slowly, but they did pass. Night finally came, and we crawled into the sleeping bags, dreaming of angling. Were we in for a surprise. The next morning it wasn't the wind that made the door hard to open; it was the ice!

We tried to be cheerful. "No problem," we mumbled. "We can play Monopoly . . . again. We can reread the magazines. And surely we know another joke or two." But as courageous as we tried to be, it was obvious that some of the gray had left the sky and entered our camper.

I began to notice a few things I hadn't seen before. Like the fact my friend Mark had a few personality flaws. He was a bit cocky about his opinions. He was easily irritated and constantly edgy. He couldn't take any constructive criticism. Even though his socks did stink, he didn't think it was my business to tell him.

"Just looking out for the best interest of my dad's camper," I said, expecting Dad to come to my aid. But Dad just sat over in the corner, reading. *Humph,* I thought, *where is he when I need him?* And then I began to see Dad in a different light. When I mentioned to him that the eggs were soggy and the toast was burnt, he invited me to try my hand at the portable stove. *Touchy, touchy,* I said to myself. *Nothing like being cooped up in a camper with someone to help you see his real nature.*

It was a long day. It was a long, cold night. When we awoke the next morning to the sound of sleet slapping the canvas, we didn't even pretend to be cheerful. We were flat-out grumpy. Mark became more of a jerk with each passing moment. I wondered what spell of ignorance I must have been in when I invited him. Dad couldn't do anything right. I wondered how someone so irritable could have such an even-tempered son. We sat in misery the whole day, our fishing equipment still unpacked.

The next day was even colder. "We're going home," my father said. No one objected.

I learned a hard lesson that week. Not about fishing, but about people. When those who are called to fish don't fish, they fight.

When energy intended to be used outside is used inside, the result is explosive. Instead of casting nets, we cast stones. Instead of extending helping hands, we point accusing fingers. Instead of being fishers of the lost, we become critics of the saved. Rather than helping the hurting, we hurt the helpers.

The result? Church Scrooges. "Bah humbug" spirituality. Beady eyes searching for warts on others while ignoring the warts on the nose below. Crooked fingers that bypass strengths and point out weaknesses. Split churches. Poor testimonies. Broken hearts. Legalistic wars. And, sadly, poor go unfed, confused go uncounseled, and lost go unreached. When those who are called to fish don't fish, they fight.

But note the other side of this fish tale. When those who are called to fish, fish—they flourish! Nothing handles a case of the gripes like an afternoon service project. Nothing restores perspective better than a visit to a hospital ward. Nothing unites soldiers better than a common task.

Leave soldiers inside the barracks with no time on the front line and see what happens to their attitude. The soldiers will invent things to complain about. Bunks will be too hard. Food will be too cold. Leadership will be too tough. The company will be too stale. Yet place those same soldiers in the trench and let them duck a few bullets, and what was a boring barracks will seem like a haven. The beds will feel great. The food will be almost ideal. The leadership will be courageous. The company will be exciting.

When those who are called to fish, fish—they flourish!

Jesus understood this truth. On the day that he performed the miracle of feeding the five thousand, he had just learned of the death of John the Baptist. When he arrived at Bethsaida, he was sorrowful, tired, and anxious to be alone with the disciples. No one would have blamed him had he dismissed the crowds who followed him on foot from the towns. No one would have criticized him had he waved away the people.

But he didn't.

Instead, "when Jesus landed and saw a large crowd, he had compassion on them and healed their sick" (Matthew 14:14). The Greek word used for *compassion* in this verse is *splanchnizomai*, which won't mean much to you unless you are in the health professions and studied splanchnology in school. If so, you remember that splanchnology is a study of the visceral parts. Or, in contemporary jargon, a study of the gut.

When Matthew writes that Jesus had compassion on the people, he is not saying that Jesus felt casual pity for them. No, the term is far more graphic. Matthew is saying that Jesus felt their hurt in his gut. He felt the limp of the crippled. He felt the hurt of the diseased. He felt the loneliness of the leper. He felt the embarrassment of the sinful.

And once he felt their hurts, he couldn't help but heal their hurts. He was moved in the stomach by their needs. He was so touched by their needs that he forgot his own needs. He was so moved by the people's hurts that he put his hurts on the back burner.

Self was forgotten . . . others were served . . . and stress was relieved. Make a note of that. The next time the challenges "outside" tempt you to shut the door and stay inside, stay long enough to get warm. Then get out. When those who are called to fish don't fish, they fight.

THE HEART OF THE MATTER

- When those who are called to fish don't fish . . . they fight.
- When those who are called to fish do fish . . . they flourish!
- Jesus felt the hurt of people deep inside—in his gut.
- Jesus was so touched by others' needs that he forgot his own needs.

MEMORY VERSE

Your memory verse for this final unit is 1 Corinthians 7:17. Take a few moments to review this verse, and then write it out from memory in the space below.

The Heart of Jesus

They had received the call and responded. Going out in pairs of two, they went to every town and place where Jesus was planning to visit. They were like the workers in a field who prepared the soil for the seed that the farmer would then sow. And they couldn't believe the results. "Lord," they exclaimed when they returned, "even the demons obeyed us when we used your name!" (Luke 10:17 NCV). Jesus couldn't contain his excitement. "I saw Satan fall like lightning from heaven," he said to them (verse 18). God's workers flourish when they heed his call and take on his authority to "trample on snakes and scorpions" (verse 19). And the enemy falls.

WEEKLY BIBLE STUDY

READ: LUKE 5:1–11 AND JAMES 1:22–27

1. Several of the disciples that Jesus called to follow him were fishermen. How did Jesus encounter Peter in this story? What request did Jesus make to him (see Luke 5:1–4)?

2. Peter wasn't eager to throw out the nets again . . . but he followed Jesus' direction. What happened when he did? What did he then say to Jesus (see verses 5–10)?

3. Jesus told Peter that he would now fish for people. What did Peter do immediately afterward (see verses 10–11)? How do you think this calling forever changed his life?

4. Jesus actively met the needs of others—and he calls his followers to do the same. What does James say about the importance of acting on God's Word (see James 1:22)?

5. What illustration does James use to demonstrate what a person is like who doesn't act on God's Word? What does a person receive who does act on it (see verses 23–25)?

6. What does James state about the importance of showing love to others not only through the words you speak but also through your acts of kindness (see verses 26–27)?

7. How have the passages you've studied this week helped you to recognize what it means to "fish for people"? Who do you know who needs your acts of compassion today?

Week 52: COME AND SEE

There are times when we see. And there are times when we *see*. Let me show you what I mean.

Imagine one morning you see a "For Sale" sign on your neighbor's boat. The boat you've been coveting for the past three summers. All of a sudden, nothing else matters. A gravitational tug pulls you over to your neighbor's yard. You sigh as you behold your dream glistening in the sun. You run your fingers along the edge, pausing to wipe the drool from your shirt. As you gaze, you are transported to Lake Tamapwantee. It's just you, the glassy waters, and your boat.

Or maybe the following scenario explains it better. You are sitting in your English Lit class when suddenly you see *him* enter the room. Just enough swagger to be cool. Just enough smarts to be classy. You've seen him before, but only in your dreams. Now he's here, and you can't take your eyes off him. By the time class is over, you've memorized every curl and lash. By the time the day is over, you've resolved he's going to be yours.

There are times when we see. And then there are times when we *see*. There are times when we observe, and there are times when we memorize. There are times when we notice, and there are times when we study. Most of us know what it means to fix our eyes on a new boat or a new boy. But do we know what it is like to fix our eyes on Jesus (see Hebrews 12:2)?

We've been taking an in-depth look at what it means to experience the heart of Jesus. The world has never known a heart so pure or a character so flawless. His spiritual hearing was so keen he never missed a heavenly whisper. His mercy so abundant he never missed a chance to forgive. No lie left his lips; no distraction marred his vision. He touched when others recoiled. He endured when others quit. Jesus is the ultimate model for every person.

And what we have done in these pages is precisely what God invites you to do with the rest of your life. He urges you to fix your eyes on Jesus. Heaven invites you to set the lens of your heart on the heart of the Savior and make him the object of your life. For that reason, I want us to close our time together with this question: *What does it mean to see Jesus?*

The shepherds can tell us. For them, it wasn't enough to see the angels. You'd think it would have been. Night sky shattered with light. Stillness erupting with song. Simple shepherds roused from their sleep and raised to their feet by a choir of angels: "Glory to God in the highest heaven" (Luke 2:14). Never had these men seen such splendor.

But it wasn't enough to see the angels. The shepherds wanted to see the one who sent the angels. Since they wouldn't be satisfied until they saw him, you can trace the long line of these Jesus-seekers to a person of the pasture who said, "Let's go to Bethlehem and *see* this thing that has happened, which the Lord has told us about" (Luke 2:15, emphasis added).

The examples continue. Consider John and Andrew. They were rewarded for seeking out Jesus. For them, it wasn't enough to listen to John the Baptist. Most would have been content to serve in the shadow of the world's most famous evangelist. Could there be a better teacher? Only one. And when John and Andrew saw him, they left John the Baptist and followed Jesus.

Note the request they made. "Rabbi . . . where are you staying?" (John 1:38). It's a pretty bold request.

They didn't ask Jesus to give them a minute, or an opinion, or a message, or a miracle. They asked for his address. They wanted to hang out with him. They wanted to know him. They wanted to know what caused his head to turn and his heart to burn and his soul to yearn. They wanted to study his eyes and follow his steps.

Jesus' answer to the two men? "Come and see" (verse 39 NCV). Bring your bifocals and binoculars! This is no time for side-glances or occasional peeks. And so "the two men went with Jesus and saw where he was staying and stayed there with him that day" (verse 39 NCV).

The fisherman fixes his eyes on the boat. The girl fixes her eyes on the boy. The disciple fixes his eyes on the Savior. That's what Zacchaeus did.

He was far from a big guy. In fact, he was so small that he couldn't see over the crowd that lined the street the day Jesus came into Jericho. Of course, the crowd might have let him elbow up to the front, except that he was a despised tax collector. But he had a hunger in his heart to see Jesus.

It wasn't enough for Zacchaeus to stand at the back of the crowd. It wasn't enough for him to peer through a cardboard telescope. It wasn't enough for him to listen to someone else describe the parade of the Messiah. Zacchaeus wanted to see Jesus with his own eyes. So he went out on a limb. Clad in a three-piece Armani suit and brand-new Italian loafers, he shimmied up a sycamore tree in hopes of seeing Christ.

Would you go out on a limb to see Jesus? Not everyone would. In the same Bible where we read about Zacchaeus crawling across the limb, we read about a young ruler. Unlike the way they treated Zacchaeus, the crowd parted to make room for him. He was the . . . ahem . . . *rich* young ruler. Upon learning that Jesus was in the area, he called for his limo, cruised across town, and approached the Carpenter. Note the question he had for Jesus: "Teacher, what good thing must I do to have life forever?" (Matthew 19:16 NCV).

Bottom line sort of fellow. No time for formalities. "Let's get right to the issue. Your schedule is busy; so is mine. So just tell me how I can get saved." There was nothing wrong with his question, but there was a problem with his heart. Contrast his desire with that of Zacchaeus: "Can I make it up that tree?" Or John and Andrew: "Where are you staying?"

See the difference? The rich young ruler wanted medicine. The others wanted the Physician. The ruler wanted an answer to the quiz. They wanted the Teacher. He was in a hurry. They had all the time in the world. He settled for a cup of coffee at the drive-through window. They wouldn't settle for anything less than a full-course meal at the banquet table. They wanted more than salvation. They wanted the Savior. They wanted to see Jesus.

"He is a rewarder of those who diligently seek Him" (Hebrews 11:6 NKJV). *Diligently*—what a great word. Be diligent in your search. Be hungry in your quest, relentless in your pilgrimage. Step away from the puny pursuits of possessions and positions and seek your King. Do as the shepherds did and seek him. Do as John and Andrew did and ask for his address. Imitate Zacchaeus and climb out on a limb.

Risk whatever it takes to truly see Christ.

THE HEART OF THE MATTER

- Heaven invites you to set the lens of your heart on the Savior.
- Don't be content with anything less than intimately knowing Jesus.
- God is a rewarder of those who diligently seek him.
- Risk whatever it takes for you to truly see Christ.

MEMORY VERSE

This is it . . . one last review of your memory verse for the entire study! Write out the words of 1 Corinthians 7:17 from memory in the space below. Reflect on what these words mean to you.

The Heart of Jesus

She spent her days and nights in the temple. Fasting and praying. Waiting in expectant hope. Looking forward to the day the promised Messiah would arrive and the redemption of God's people would begin. By this point, she had been waiting a very long time. "A prophet, Anna . . . was very old; she had lived with her husband seven years after her marriage, and then was a widow until she was eighty-four" (Luke 2:36–37). But everything changed when she saw Jesus with her own eyes. Mary and Joseph had taken him to the temple to present him to the Lord. When she saw Jesus, "she gave thanks to God and spoke about the child to all" (verse 38).

WEEKLY BIBLE STUDY

READ: JOHN 1:35–46 AND LUKE 19:1–9

1. There are times when we see. And there are times when we *see*. What did John the Baptist "see" clearly about Jesus when he passed by (see John 1:35–36)?

2. When John and Andrew—the disciples of John the Baptist—heard this, they followed after Jesus. What did Jesus say to them? How did they respond (see verses 37–38)?

3. John and Andrew were not asking to just hang out with Jesus but to get to *know* him. What did Jesus say to their request? What did Andrew do next (see verses 39–42)?

4. Jesus also called Philip to follow him—and he found Nathanael. What did Philip say when Nathanael asked if anything good could come from Nazareth (see verses 43–46)?

5. Zacchaeus was so small that he couldn't see over the crowd that lined the street when Jesus came to Jericho. What did he do to see Jesus (see Luke 19:1–4)?

6. What invitation did Jesus extend to Zacchaeus when he saw him in the sycamore tree? How did the encounter change Zacchaeus's life (see verses 5–9)?

7. What has this study taught you about experiencing the heart of Jesus each day of your life? What especially stands out to you about what you have learned?